Reborn into Tragedy

Book two

JD Grace

Reborn into Tragedy

Printed in the United States of America
First Printing, 2019
ISBN 978-0-578-50532-9

www.jdgrace.org

Cover design by: Bethany Faye Photography

Editor: Brittney Anderson

For all of the incredible people I've had the
pleasure of knowing and working with in EMS.
This one's for you.

Prologue

Two years later in Auburn, Washington...

"THIS IS DETECTIVE Natalie Stone. It's March seventh at zero-five-forty hours. I'm currently on scene of a homicide that appears to be related to our ongoing investigation of the four other girls we've found this year. The victim is a young girl, possibly fifteen-sixteen years old. She appears to have been assaulted multiple times over a significant period of time, due to the multiple bruises in different stages of healing. There's also evidence of possible sexual assault, which stays in line with the other bodies we've found. We'll have to wait for the coroner's report to be sure but, I think it's safe to say that we're looking at the same person for all of these victims."

She shut off the power to the voice recorder with her latex gloved hand. Standing over the victim, she stared at the lifeless body of a young girl, and thought of how she had her whole life a head of her—full of promise—just ripped away. The opportunity to experience the good side of what life has to offer would never come to fruition for this girl. The bruising on her hands indicated that she put up quite the fight. *I hope you gave him a few good ones. Give that Son of a Bitch something to remember you by.* Natalie internally made the same promise she always made with every victim she encountered. *I'm so sorry for what you've endured resulting in your death but, I promise that I'll do everything I can to bring you justice.*

The crisp air enveloped Natalie's lungs as she took a deep breath in and heavily exhaled, forcing her to shake off the break in her heart and the cold creeping in around her. Ribbons of fog lingered in the dim light of dawn, hovering above the field like the sadness that now clouded her mind. Officers searched the surrounding fields for clues to catch the perpetrator but, the burden of caring for this dead woman, until justice could be served, rested on Natalie's shoulders—and hers alone. She knew as soon as they were able to identify the victim, she would have to tell this girl's parents of the death of their daughter in horrific detail. Grimly she thought of the tears and contorted faces of anger and loss inevitably in her near future. Natalie knew what a tragic death this girl had, just by looking at her body and again, forced down the emotions surrounded by this girl's ill fate.

"Detective Stone?" one officer called.

"Yes?"

"We found something."

Natalie briskly walked over to where the rookie cop was standing. *He looks young enough to be my nephew.* The thought briefly crossed her mind. Natalie certainly wasn't new to the cop gig. It wasn't long after her seventh birthday when she'd made up her mind that she was going to be a detective, no matter what. All she wanted to do was help people and solve mysteries. The first four years on the force as a beat cop, she learned everything that she could about police work, and how to be the best. During those years, she took classes to work toward becoming a detective. After acing the detective's exam on her very first try she immediately got assigned to the Gun's and Gang's unit in Auburn. After spending a year dealing with the bleed over from the gangs in the Seattle area, she was finally transferred to her dream job as a homicide detective. She was now coming up on five years in homicide and still loves her job just as much now as she did back then. She enjoyed finding justice for those who have been wronged.

She was actually assigned this case when the first body was discovered eight months ago.

Her Captain told her, "Stone, this one's yours. Looks like a rape and homicide, and I feel that you're the right detective for the job."

Natalie couldn't help but feel she was only assigned the case because she still wasn't being taken seriously enough as the only female detective in the unit. Had Natalie known how big this case would blow up she probably wouldn't have sneered at the thought of being low balled because she was a woman. She wanted something bigger, and had no idea of how close she was to getting just that.

"What'd ya find?" she asked while peering into the tall grass where the rookie was pointing.

"Looks like a piece of metal that broke off something, like maybe a keychain or from the vehicle used to dump the body."

"Good work, bag it and put it in with evidence." Natalie started to walk away, just before she turned her back, she glanced over just in time to see the rookie bending down without gloved hands. "Stop, for Christ's sake! Put some damn gloves on first!" She snapped, remembering her first homicide as a rookie and swearing she never made mistakes that stupid.

"Oh! Uh, right," his eyes wide with panic fumbling over himself, searching his pockets before finally finding a pair of latex gloves.

Natalie rolled her eyes before turning around and walking away.

The sun had finally begun to rise over the mountains, mixing colors of pink and orange with the clouds that hung at the top of the high peaks. The crisp air gradually warmed up, and rays of sunlight popped out, shooting up, one by one, into the blue sky above. Natalie recorded a few more notes on her voice recorder before gathering her things.

"Chad?" she called out into the sea of officers at the scene.

Chad Platt popped his head up, "Yea?"

"Time to go," she motioned to the car. Chad trotted over to Natalie. "I know that you have quite the experience as a cop and all but, sifting through the grass is for the beat cops. You're a detective now, and you need to act like it, got it?"

"Yes ma'am."

"And don't call me ma'am. It's Natalie, or Stone, or even Detective Stone, but never ma'am, understand?"

"Yes, Detective Stone, my apologies.

All rookie detectives are damn near the same, aren't they? Natalie thought mindlessly staring out the windshield with one hand at the top of the steering wheel, and the other hand holding her now cold coffee.

"Chad, I really think that you're going to be a fantastic detective one day. The hardest part over the next few months will be breaking your old routine as a cop in uniform, and creating your new routine as a detective. You get to be a part of the 'D Squad', man." Chad's head snapped up toward her, with one brow raised, and his mouth twisted up with confused amusement. Natalie chuckled at herself, "That sounded better in my head. Whatever, anyway, my point is that you have some serious potential Platt, don't piss it away."

"I got it," he tried to remain serious but a grin took up his entire face.

When they arrived back at the station there was a small package lying on Natalie's desk. It was placed neatly in the middle of her disorganized mess of paperwork and files, memos, and notepads.

"How do you ever find anything on this desk?" Chad laughed.

"I have a system," she moved files around to the sound of Chad's concealed laughter. "Oh, shut your mouth, rook! I know where everything is, okay... usually."

"Who's the package from?" Chad asked with the joking aside and curiosity in full effect.

"Looks like it was sent to me from an address here in Auburn, but there's no name on it." She picked up the small bag feeling her way around. "It feels like its small... and solid... hmm." She felt the bag some more trying to figure out what it was. Feeling the predominant edges and thin width, "Maybe it's a flash drive or something like that?" She opened up the top with a pair of scissors and dumped out a flash drive on her desk. "Man I'm good."

"What do you think it is?"

"Honestly, it could be a number of things." She popped the end into the USB of the computer. "Let's find out, shall we?"

The flash drive opened and on the computer screen were countless files all marked with women's names. Natalie swallowed hard, fearful for what she was going to find. She and Chad looked at each other, a tinge of hesitation in both of their eyes. The first file was marked 'Brittney', so she hovered the mouse and clicked play.

They both sat in horror, watching as a girl who appeared to be no older than fourteen years old was physically assaulted. As soon as she was able to process what it was she was actually seeing, Natalie quickly shut it off.

"Holy shit!" she breathed, staring at the numerous files on the flash drive. Her hands trembled. "It's her," Natalie's voice trailed off.

"It's who?" Chad asked.

"Shush," Natalie motioned here hand, waving it in his face telling him to be quiet while her wheels spun out of control. "Cap!" the words suddenly burst from her mouth, before ejecting the flash drive and heading into her captain's office. "Cap, I need you to come with me to a screening room, right now, sir." She didn't bother knocking, not with this.

"Stone, what's wrong?" Captain Ward scoffed, obviously displeased with her interruption

"Just come, please, I need another set of eyes on this." She waved at him to follow her.

Captain Bart Ward stared at her for a good thirty seconds before lifting his bushy eyebrows in surrender of the request. He pushed his tall lanky body up out of his undersized chair and followed behind Natalie.

"Come on, kid," Captain Ward motioned to Chad. "Are you gonna tell me what this is all about, Stone, or are you gonna keep me in the dark?"

"I'll explain, but first, just watch." She plugged the flash drive into the large screen, and within seconds the rows of files popped up. "Okay, see all of these files?" Bart nodded his head. "I'm thinking each of these files contain a video with a different girl in them. These files are all named after girls I'm assuming are victims, showing a whole other world of disgusting, which we'll get to in a second. But, this first file named 'Brittney,' I'm pretty sure is Brittney Waters, the young girl we found in the lake a few months back."

"Okay," Barry seemed to know where this was going, his body language was tense.

"I have a terrible gut feeling, Sir... all four of the girls we've found are going to all be on this drive."

"What makes you say that?"

"The names, Sir," Natalie pointed at the screen to a different file. "This file is labeled 'Penelope', and it just might be Penelope Stevenson, our first victim. This file is labeled, 'Sara', which could be Sara Higgins. And over here is, 'Claire', which is probably Claire Clemmons." Natalie turned to face Captain Ward. "I don't have a name on the fifth victim yet, but I would be willing to bet my badge that her name will have a file in here too."

"Well, there's only one way to find out if your theory is right, and that's to watch each file and see if the girls are our victim's."

"Sir, I don't know if that's such a good idea. We started watching Brittney's file, and these videos are probably the most horrific thing that I've ever seen. I can tell you that just in the minute we watched the video, my stomach turned."

"I've been doing this for almost forty years now, I've seen my share of disturbing things Stone, play the damn video." Arrogance and irritation spilled out as he sat up straight, staring with cold eyes at Natalie.

Natalie clicked Penelope's file, and when it popped up, she recognized Penelope Stevenson right away with her distinct birth mark on her left shoulder. She lost her breath as she watched this faceless man defile the young girl. She pushed fast forward, only to discover there were multiple videos in her file alone. After running it through seven different videos at high speed, Natalie moved on to Sara's file.

Sara had red hair and freckles saturating the bridge of her nose. Her small and tiny body visibly trembled, even in the dim lights. *That's Sara Higgins alright, no doubt about it.* Natalie's fears were confirmed.

She clicked on the last file, "Claire," she was the youngest of all the victims, only twelve years old. Her long dirty blonde hair in a French braid was unmistakable—her mother said that was how she had her hair the day she vanished. Claire was laying in the morgue now, a cold lifeless body with the French braid still in her hair.

Captain Ward squirmed in his chair as discreetly as he could and Chad looked as green as the Washington mountain range. Natalie forgot to stop the video of Claire when she turned to address Captain Ward.

"Like I've been saying all along, it's one person doing this, and this proves that my theory is right." Natalie looked into the grief stricken eyes of her Captain. "All we need to do is identify this man." She pointed her finger toward the screen, but refused to turn to look at it.

"There's a woman in this one!" Chad chimed in, concentrating hard on the screen wishing he could will the camera to give a better angle, hoping he could figure out who the cold-blooded couple were.

"What the hell?" Natalie whipped around, puzzled. "A woman helped him?" as Natalie forced herself to look at the screen once again, she could distinctly see a woman's hands curled around the young girl's wrists to aid in holding her down as she was being brutally assaulted.

Chad's eyes widened and shock visibly rippled through his body when the man's face came into focus. It was only for a split second, but that was long enough to know exactly who he was looking at.

"Holy shit, I know who that is." He breathed out past his horror.

Chapter 1

THE ROAD BACK home to Texas was long and desolate. Auburn was finally so far out of her rearview Reese could no longer see the peaks of the mountains she so loved no matter how hard she tried. Her heart broke thinking about how she left her Fire Station 23 family behind to embark on this new and uncharted adventure. Walking away from Auburn was one of the hardest things she's ever had to do. It wasn't easy coming to terms with the reality that she wouldn't be coming back, and that was going to take a while for her to digest.

She hadn't passed another car for hours, the isolation allowed for a flood of memories to play in her mind like a movie while driving down the straight two-lane road. Alex Cunningham was now, and would always be, a vivid part of her past. She would never forget the sting on her skin as he slapped her repeatedly during a fit of rage. He had controlled her every move, like she was his puppet stuck on strings that only he could compose. He demanded perfection from an imperfect woman and he never let her forget it. Alex schemed his way under her skin, attaching his puppeteer strings unbeknownst to Reese. Blinded by his intellect and strength, she allowed him to slowly control her. *How could I have been so blind? Why didn't I leave after the first time he hit me?*

Flashes of the abuse she endured during her two-and-a-half year relationship with Alex jammed her memories, playing out on a continuous and terrifying loop. She recalled every bruise she was forced to hide, and every shift she had to miss because he had hurt her so bad she wasn't able to cover it up. She strived for the perfection he demanded, and bled for it when she failed. Alex Cunningham shattered her soul and the woman she once was seemed to no longer exist.

Alex was not just controlling, he was also untrusting and jealousy poured out of every fiber of his being. Reese paid the price at home when Alex found out about her misgivings, like the time he found out she tried to secretly maintain her friendships with the men at work. It was just another beating she was forced to endure, and another morning of revealing the true extent to which Alex was willing to punish. Reese would dread looking in the mirror the next day and seeing the damage he did to her. In the past she would occasionally wonder to herself, *what could I have possibly done to deserve this,* usually followed by justifications and excuses—*I just need to do better.* Alex would graciously remind Reese that she deserved every bit of the punishment he gave her. She'd heard the words, "you're worthless," so many times that she actually believed them. Soon, she became very familiar with the ground, afraid to look up and see the world in front of her, to see Alex for who he really was.

A slight smirk swept across her face as she thought of how she finally got the courage to leave, after finally putting her foot down and standing up to him by saying, "enough!". She relished in this memory, remembering how Alex lost all his power over her.

She decided to give Alex the chance to love her for the woman she was but, once she found out he had been cheating on her, it was the final straw. Reese finally mustered up enough strength and ended the relationship. Unfortunately for her, with a lapse in judgment on a drunken night, she realized her life would forever be changed once again by Alex—the night that began this new adventure.

Four weeks later, Reese held up multiple pregnancy tests baring the same positive results of her careless night with Alex. She knew, given the opportunity, Alex would destroy this child the way he destroyed her. Reese struggled with her decision whether to tell him about the baby or not but, as her memories of his abuse graphically echoed within her, she made up her mind, and chose to not tell Alex. Instead, she decided to raise the baby on her own without any help from him. Reese wholeheartedly believed this was the only way to ensure her unborn child's safety, and the only way she could protect this child from his destructive behavior.

Unfortunately, word traveled faster in small towns and it wasn't long before Alex caught wind that Reese was pregnant. She held her ground when he confronted her, reassuring him that this baby wasn't his. It was after her encounter with him that Reese knew she was making the right decision by not including Alex in the baby's life and ultimately, leaving Auburn. She packed up her life and left it all behind. She left Alex and his temper but not without sacrifice, she also had to leave the people who became her family at Station 23.

Now on the open road, Reese's heart ached thinking of how much she already missed them, cursing her choice to move back home, despite it being the best choice for her and her unborn child. She kept driving. Further and further away from what once was while her mind continued to race. Visions of her Gran's slender weathered face popped into her mind, leaving Reese yearning for the opportunity to have just one last conversation with the only woman she could truly relate to in all of this.

Although Esther Landon lived to be ninety-seven years old and enjoyed a full and meaningful life, she slipped through their fingers before Reese could simply ask her how she dealt with raising four kids as a single mother. She wanted to ask her how to deal with all of this anger she now harbored within her. Anger with Alex, with God, and even with her parents for asking her to come home and offering their help and guidance but, more importantly, she needed to know how to deal with the anger she felt towards herself.

And then there was Officer Chad Platt, the wonderful man she left behind in Auburn. She continued to drive, all the while questioning if she had made the right decision by leaving him. He was everything she wanted from a significant other, and he certainly didn't seem to mind that she was pregnant. She believed with all of her heart, that he could have been something special in her life, and blamed Alex for her losing the opportunity to find out. Even after they ended, Alex still seemed to have control over her life. She knew, undoubtedly, leaving was her only chance at truly freeing herself from him, she just wished she could've wrapped Chad up and brought him with her. That's the hardest part about what-if's, the imagination tends to show them filled with wonderful and shiny possibilities, before leaving us drowning in a sea of regret.

Nevertheless, despite the anger and despite the brokenness, she knew saying good-bye to her life in Auburn was the right choice. She aimlessly drove down the road, trying to imagine the new life that awaited her roughly seven months from now. A faint smile parted her lips at the thought of holding her sweet baby in her arms, not knowing how much this sweet child would save her from her own worst enemy; herself.

After several days on the road with uncomfortable hotel beds and boredom, she finally arrived at her parents' house. It was the house she grew up in and the house that was once again her home. She smiled pulling into the driveway, thinking of how much she loved growing up on this ranch, and with a light pat of her stomach, she knew that her child would love it too.

Reese's parents lived in an old fashioned farmhouse. It was a two story home that had been freshly painted white with dark green trim, and had five steps leading up from the drive way to a beautiful wrap around porch. Reese remembered as a kid sitting on the front porch swing that sat just off the side of the door, with Sophie and her mom. They would swing and enjoy the nice weather during the spring before the almost unbearable heat would lay over them like a suffocating blanket of humidity. She stared at the swing, imagining her with her own child swinging on the same porch and building similar memories. Despite the feeling of regret that consumed her mind during her drive, she felt at ease pulling up to the house. This was home, and although she was forced to leave a piece of her heart in Auburn, she knew this was where she was meant to be. The life she left behind would always be a part of who she was and no amount of time or distance would ever change that for her.

Denton, Texas was a smaller town, northeast of Dallas, and it sat just under the Oklahoma border. Her parents owned a relatively large ranch not too far out of town. It was sixty-five acres filled with cows that her father raised for meat. Rusty Landon was always up with the first light of dawn and he was off tending to the livestock by five in the morning. He was a hard worker, and when he wasn't outside fixing fences and checking the health of the herd, he was in the office that sat just off of the side of the house, working on the business side of being a rancher. Growing up, Reese and her sister Sophie knew that when the door to his office was closed, Rusty was not to be disturbed.

Reese got out of her car and looked over at her Dad's office, smiling as she took a moment to remember the first job that her dad had given her. She was around four years old when he taught her how to shred papers. She remembered the excitement she felt feeding the machine small stacks of paper, and watching them come out the other side in pieces. The loud roar of the machine made her feel important and powerful. The room would be filled with her laughter and wonderment with each stack shredded. Her favorite part was that Rusty would pay her in hugs and kisses. Those were some of her most fond memories with her father.

Once Reese turned thirteen, she moved on to answering phones and taking messages for her dad. The best part of this new job was that Rusty actually paid her for her time with real money. It was nothing significant because she was only thirteen but, it was still a small sense of freedom, and Reese felt that made the job well worth it. She saved her money and went out with her friends to the movies and shopping at the mall. She saved for two months just to buy the pair of cowgirl boots she wanted and once they were hers she wore them everywhere she went.

"Reese!" Maggie interrupted her thoughts, "You're finally here! How was the drive?"

Reese met her mom with a drawn out embrace. "Long!" she said before releasing Maggie. "I'm so happy to finally be here!"

"How's our little nugget doin'?" Maggie placed her hand firmly on Reese's stomach.

"This baby hates me already, I swear." Reese chuckled. "I got car sick while driving on a straight road, no bumps or turns!"

"Oh no, that's awful! Well, sis, hold on for a long pregnancy. I was sick with both you and your sister for the full nine months."

"Seriously, you're joking, right!? Ugh, that sucks!" Reese grunted.

"Are you hungry at all, sweetheart?"

Reese made a few moans and groans as she shook her head no. "No thanks, Ma." She rubbed her stomach in hopes the motion would calm the raging storm within her causing her nausea to flare up relentlessly.

"Come on, sis, let's get you inside. Daddy should be done with work soon, he's so happy you decided to move back home."

"I'm happy I decided to move home too, Mama." Reese suppressed all of the sadness she felt and put on a happy face.

Telling her mom she was happy to be home wasn't a complete lie. She was, in fact, very happy to be home but, she greatly missed the life she left behind. She wished she had been able to pack everyone she loved up and move them with her. In a perfect world, maybe that would have worked but, Reese didn't live in a perfect world, far from it actually. Anger flared up within her as she secretly, once again, blamed Alex.

Reese turned and walked back to her car to grab the suitcase that she'd packed with her essentials for the drive home. When she and Maggie walked into the house, Reese took in the alluring aroma of fresh fruit, flowers, and laundry soap. That combination always brought back wonderful memories of her childhood.

Looking into the living room she recalled the dozens of sleepless nights her and Rusty had playing video games. At the time Reese was fifteen, the whole family loved getting together in front of the TV and playing Mario Kart on the Super Nintendo they still had. Their Super Nintendo was outdated and most would have upgraded several times by then but, not the Landon family. Their family game nights consisted of competitive Mario Kart races and lots of trash-talking.

"Hey, Mom, remember when we used to play Mario Kart?"

Maggie's eyes danced over to the TV with delight. "Oh, my goodness, I do! Oh that was so much fun! Did you know I still have that Super Nintendo?"

"Wait, what?!" Reese felt like a child all over again. "Please tell me it still works!"

"Um, well, that I'm not sure of." Maggie motioned to Reese's travel bag she still held in her hand. "Let's go put your stuff down before we get side tracked."

"Good idea," Reese walked passed the living room and to the hallway.

She and the baby had their rooms down the hallway right next to each other and the bathroom was in the middle across the hall. Maggie and Rusty had their master suite upstairs. When Reese turned the corner into her room, she saw that Maggie had made up the bed and the entire room was in pristine condition. Her old dresser had been dusted and it shined like it was brand new. The walk in closet on the other hand, was half-filled with her mother's clothes, not leaving very much room for her own clothes and shoes. *What the hell, Mom?* Her eyes scanned the room, calculating very quickly that all of her things were simply not going to fit. *Maybe I can move this stuff to the baby's room or somethin'.* She dropped her bag next to the closet, vowing to deal with it later.

"Reese, I found all the pieces to the Super Nintendo. Get in here and help me see if this thing still works." Maggie yelled from the living room.

Reese came down the hallway to see her mom untangling wires and cables. She had untangled them from around each other and subsequently wrapped herself up in the process. Reese tried to conceal a chuckle under her breath. When Maggie heard her, she snapped her head around giving Reese a sharp look.

"Same team, Maggie, I'm on the same team!" Reese laughed with her hands held out in front of her in surrender.

"Oh stop that laughin' and get over here and help me!" Maggie pleaded.

Reese continued to laugh, her faint chuckle quickly turned into a roar of laughter. It was the kind of laughter that was contagious, and it wasn't long before Maggie had joined in. Both ladies were lost in the hilarity of the moment, so much so they didn't notice Rusty had come through the door.

"What'd I miss?" He asked while skeptically looking at them both trying to figure out answers to the array of questions he must've had.

"Mom—" Reese couldn't catch her breath she was laughing so hard. "She's all— She's tangled up!"

Rusty looked back at Maggie and saw that she had cables wrapped around her, and was unable to get up. A mischievous grin came across his face as he approached Maggie.

"Oh she's not tangled up." Rusty said before lunging forward toward Maggie, grabbing the cables he wrapped them around her tighter.

With each loop that wrapped around her, the three of them laughed harder and harder. Reese, for the first time in a very long time, was wiping tears of joy from her face. Those were the kind of tears she didn't mind shedding, no matter who was around.

"Rusty! Stop it!" Maggie pleaded amidst her laughter.

Once she was hog-tied to perfection he knocked her over and showered her with kisses, breaking only to tickle her. Reese leaned up against the couch laughing at her mother's despair. *They're so cute. That right there, that's what I want.* She smiled knowing that she was exactly right where she was meant to be. She was home and in the midst of the laughter and the happiness, she made her peace with that.

Eventually, Rusty decided to let Maggie free, unwrapping her, taking sporadic cheap shots poking at her or tickling her. Maggie playfully refused to kiss him back until he had completely untangled her from the cables. Basking in his upper hand he took his time giving Maggie what she wanted. Reese came over and helped unravel her, sort out all the cables, and find the ones they needed for the Super Nintendo.

19

Rusty and Reese sat on the floor figuring out how to hook up the game to the new flat screen TV her parents just bought. Maggie walked into the bathroom to fix her hair that inevitably got destroyed in the struggle. She reemerged from the hallway with a neatly done French braid in her hair. She made it back just in time to see the television screen flash with the Super Nintendo logo.

"Oh, yay, y'all did it!" Maggie celebrated, clapping her hands vigorously together.

"I'm gonna order a pizza." Rusty said with satisfaction as he got up and left the room.

Grabbing her phone from her back pocket, Reese realized she hadn't sent the crew a text to let them know she had made it safely back home. She sent a group text to Louie, Stump, Kyra, and Jess.

REESE: *Hey guys, just wanted to shoot y'all a quick text and let y'all know I made it home safely. Love y'all so much! 7:43PM*

It wasn't long before she received a reply.

LOUIE: *Back in Texas for 1 day and she's already using y'all like a comma! Ha ha! Glad you're safe Reese! 7:44PM*

She smiled watching her phone light up with various smiley faces and hearts. Louie's response made her laugh. *I guess I did use y'all quite a bit in that text,* she chuckled. After about a minute she locked her phone and set it down on the dining room table.

With genuine happiness twinkling in her eyes and a soft smile on her lips she sat down on the floor next to her dad. "You ready to get crumpled, old man?" she teased.

"I'm sorry did you just say old!? Who are you callin' old, young lady?"

"I'm callin' you old, obviously dad, duh! Maybe you need to turn your hearing-aids up, Grandpa." Reese giggled.

The characters where strategically picked and the carts adjusted to each one's liking. The countdown began on the screen and Reese felt her heart pick up its pace. Excitement rushed through her body and pulsated through her veins. In bold letters the word, "GO!" flashed across the screen and both cars took off.

Rusty was never the one to play fair. Reese sat focused on her player, intently turning the entire remote with every curve on the track. She bit her bottom lip, her breathing increased as she bobbed and weaved her way into first place.

"Ha, ha, eat my dust, Gramps!" she boasted. Rusty followed closely behind her in second place. As they rounded the last corner and were in the final stretch before the finish line. Rusty threw his arm over the front of Reese, ultimately knocking the remote out of her hand and causing her to fall behind. "You are such a cheater!" Reese yelled.

"Cheater, who me, I would never?" Rusty dramatically opposed. "I can't help it if you can't hold on to your controller!" He snickered.

The words "WINNER!" lit up on Rusty's screen, and Reese's character was left to throw a tantrum in her kart.

"Well played old man but, know this, I'm comin' for ya!" Reese narrowed her eyes in his direction.

After a few races had passed the doorbell rang and Rusty excused himself to get the pizza. Maggie and Reese were left to battle out the next lap. This race started out more civilized than the ones between Reese and her father, that was until Reese knocked Maggie out of bounds to win at the last second.

"I swear, you and your Father are two peas in a pod."
Maggie scoffed.

"Mama, don't be mad because I'm better than you are!"
Reese laughed, poking her finger at Maggie's side.

"Who's hungry?" Rusty announced.

Maggie and Reese both got up, headed into the dining
room and gathered around the table. They grabbed their
desired slices and sat down to eat. Reese felt hungry for the
first time in days and the pizza tasted so good, she scarfed
down two slices. She sat across from Maggie, making small
talk, when all of a sudden the pizza no longer felt like a good
idea.

Reese quickly got up and took off running down the
hallway to the bathroom. The seat of the porcelain toilet was
cold against her arm as she laid it across the back of the seat.
Her throat burned from the marinara sauce and pepperoni.
Both slices made their way out of her stomach and into the
toilet. When she flushed the toilet she also flushed any further
desire she had for pizza. After rinsing out her mouth she
returned to the dining room, but the smell of the pizza was
enough to send her stomach flopping again, and she took off
for the bathroom once more.

"Let's try this again, shall we?" Reese said when she
returned for the second time.

"Are you alright, sis?" Maggie asked.

"Yeah, I think I'm okay now." Reese turned her attention to
Rusty. "Dad, are we gonna unload my stuff tomorrow?"

"Well Uncle T and his friend Robert are gonna come over
tomorrow to help me unload it, you just gotta tell us where it
goes darlin'."

Reese was visibly irritated. "Dad, I'm not useless!"

"No one's sayin' you're useless but, you've got my grand baby growin' in there and I ain't gonna let you over do it. Neither is Uncle T or Robert. We'll be doin' the majority of the unloading young lady, and that's final." Rusty played it off in a joking manner but there was a stern undertone and Reese knew better than to keep pushing.

"Fine," she rolled her eyes and instantly felt like she was sixteen all over again.

The three of them returned to their game that patiently waited on pause. They played well into the night, enjoying every moment of laughter and trash talk that filled the Landon household. They all faced their losses with anger and more trash talk but, that night they were all winners, for the memories they made could never be taken from them.

Chapter 2

THE NEXT MORNING Reese woke up feeling rested and thoughts of Alex had finally subsided to distant memories. She was gradually becoming less broken, less damaged, and even less afraid. Part of her drive home from Auburn had made her feel incredibly alone, lost in her thoughts about Alex and his abuse, afraid his words, *who's going to love you, Reese,* would somehow ring true.

Inside the cheap hotels she stayed at after driving long hours, she got in the habit of casually talking to the life growing inside her. She really loved the fact she would always have her baby and felt talking to him or her was creating a special bound. When she woke up, before getting out of bed, she took a few moments to talk to her unborn child, and gradually, her loneliness subsided.

"Hey there little one," she lightly caressed her stomach. "We're finally home, now it's just you and I against the world. Mee-maw and Pee-paw are gonna be here to help us along the way. I can't wait for you to meet them. You're already so

24

incredibly loved." With a light pat on her stomach Reese got out of bed.

She came out of her bedroom, wearing yoga pants and a tank top with a slightly protruding belly, and headed down the hallway with determination to help unload, no matter what Rusty told her. The smell of pancakes filled the air around her. In the kitchen Maggie was busy at work, whisking eggs as a perfectly made circle of batter began to bubble on a hot skillet, a stack of fresh hot pancakes stood tall next to the stove. Maggie stood in front of the window that glowed golden as rays of the morning sun crept in, her blonde hair was in a side braid with just enough loose strands of hair to frame her round face, and despite new lines of age around Maggie's eyes, she looked as she always had when Reese came down for breakfast as a child.

"Mornin,' sleepy head, are ya hungry?" Maggie smiled revealing her perfectly straight smile lightly stained from many years of coffee drinking.

"Yes! Those pancakes smell amazing." Reese grabbed out a plate and fork before snagging two that were hot off the griddle.

Reese sat at the bar in the kitchen slowly eating her breakfast and realized there was a smell from her childhood missing, every morning the house would smell of a delicious breakfast and, of course, coffee. Her eyes casually scanned the white tile counter tops searching for the coffee pot. Both of her parents religiously drank it every morning. Rusty even took a large thermos filled with it in the wee hours of the morning to work. Yet, there was no coffee pot. Bewildered Reese got up and checked around the kitchen and dining room for any sign of it.

"Mom, where's the coffee pot?"

"Well, sweetheart, Kyra texted me right before you left to let me know that the smell of coffee has been making you vomit. So, Dad and I decided to make some adjustments."

"Mom, you didn't have to give up coffee for me!"

"Oh, sis, we didn't! Your dad and I love you, but we don't love you that much!" Maggie laughed. "We moved the coffee pot to our bathroom. We leave the door closed to the bathroom and to the bedroom. It keeps the coffee smell from finding its way downstairs."

"Well, that's kinda genius!" Reese smiled. "And it's also good to know where I stand." She laughed.

"It's about time you learned your place around here." Maggie sarcastically scoffed.

The words that were meant to be light-hearted and a joke had sparked a memory. Though she was sitting there laughing and rolling her eyes at her mom, Reese was allowing Alex's voice back into her head. *Know your place, Reese.* Internally, she relived the times Alex emotionally broke her down. For the briefest moment, had she not known any better, she could swear she felt the droplets of his spit fling onto her face. Her hands slightly trembled under the counter.

"Reese!" A familiar voice penetrated her fear. "It's about time you got here!"

She turned in her seat to see Uncle T walking toward her. His cowboy hat was tipped back on his head revealing his eyes that looked like sapphires against his tan skin. His face was scruffy with a stubble beard he had grown out. The wranglers he wore had always been a staple in his wardrobe. The only time Reese could recall seeing her uncle in anything other than wranglers was when he wore swim trunks at the lake on his boat.

"I'm sorry, do I know you?" Reese joked pulling herself out of her internal struggle. She got up out of her chair and practically ran over to Trevor and held him in a long overdue embrace. "Hey, Uncle T."

"Hey there, kiddo," his strong arms wrapped around her and held her tightly.

Trevor's best friend since childhood, Robert Garcia, stood behind Trevor smiling at Reese. Robert had become a part of the Landon family at a very young age. Rusty would always joke that Trevor and Robert found each other in pre-school and they decided right then they had found their soulmate, they never cared to make friends with anyone else, and the rest was history. They grew up together, they got into trouble together, they tried to impress the same girls, and even now to this day they worked together at one of the largest ranches in northeast Texas, Dunn's Cattle Ranch.

"Hey Ree," Robert smiled and went to give her a hug once Trevor released his grasp.

Reese felt a sense of panic come over her and without thinking she automatically took a few steps back. "Hey Rob," she muttered, before turning around and hastily making her way back to her pancakes.

Her heart was racing as she silently battled the brokenness within her. She didn't say another word as she stared down at her plate and the half eaten pancake that remained. She maintained a blank stare on her face as the hard-wire of fear took over. She heard Maggie reassuring whispers to Robert to just give Reese some time because she has been through a lot. Trevor walked over and kissed Reese on the top of the head but, she remained frozen with her eyes locked on her unfinished breakfast. Robert and Trevor walked out the back door to go find Rusty whose truck just pulled in.

"Reese?" Maggie softly tried to gain her attention. "Are you okay, sis?" Reese remained silent. "Reese," Maggie put her arm around her and squeezed her tightly. "You're okay, it's gonna be okay, just relax."

Reese felt like for the first time in what felt like an eternity, she exhaled, trying to catch her breath. Alex had snuck up on her out of nowhere. He bulldozed her down within seconds. She was not prepared for any of it and struggled to find solid ground. Maggie stood next to her, holding her tightly.

"I'm sorry, Mom, I don't know what happened. I heard his voice in my head and it was like I was launched back in time."

"He's not here, baby, and he can't find you here. It's gonna be okay, sis."

"You're right," Reese took a final deep breath before getting up and clearing her plate.

The sink water ran hot as Reese swirled the soapy sponge around the sticky plate. She knew her mom was right, but somehow she struggled to feel safe. She felt trapped in her mind, the same mind that Alex formed and compressed into what he wanted it to be. She was a prisoner in her own skin, stuck in the web of fear, deceit, and wounds Alex had created. As much as Reese thought there had been healing that morning, in an instant she was shown just how broken she still was. Reese needed much more repair than anyone initially understood. However, her pride would remain her biggest obstacle to overcome. She placed the now clean dishes in the drain before heading out the backdoor to find the guys to help them unload.

"Hey, so what's the plan?" she asked as she walked up to where the three of them stood. She turned to Robert, "Sorry about earlier. It's really good to see you Rob." Forcing past her struggle she gave him a quick hug.

"It's all good, Ree. It's good to see you too." He said with a soft smile and worry behind his eyes.

"Reese, just what do you think you're doin' out here?" Trevor asked with his southern twang.

"I'm helping! I'm not useless, Uncle T, and I'm most certainly not made of glass!"

Rusty placed his hands out in front of him to stop any further argument between the two of them. "She's right, Trev," he turned to Reese, "but, if you over-do it, I'm gonna whoop your butt."

"Dad," Reese rolled her eyes. "I'll be fine; I lift people for a livin', for Christ sake! My body can handle carrying in a few bags and boxes."

Trevor kept his eyes on Reese and motioned two fingers to his eyes and then at Reese. "I got my eye on you!"

Reese just rolled her eyes and let out a loud grunt. "Ugh."

She walked off in the direction of her car and opened the back door. The four of them worked for two solid hours, unloading all of her belongings. Sweat ran down all of their faces stacking the majority of her belongings into the garage. The rest was dropped in her room for her to sort out later. *So many clothes, such little closet space,* Reese chuckled to herself, *it is a major upgrade from the closet at Kyra's... once I get all Mama's clothes out of here.* She shook her head before walking out of the room.

She grabbed her keys off the dresser and headed back out to her car.

"I'll be back, I gotta go return this U-Haul trailer before they charge me for another day." She yelled to her mom who stood in the kitchen with Trevor, Robert, and Rusty.

"Hold up Ree, I'm gonna roll with you if that's alright." Trevor called out as he took off in her direction.

"Sure," Reese shrugged her shoulders. "What about Rob?"

"He's gonna hang back and help your dad with a few things."

"Is that the real reason you wanna come with me? So you don't have to help my dad?" sarcasm filled her voice.

"Well, of course! I don't wanna help that old geezer!" Trevor stuck out his tongue and they both laughed as they got into the 4Runner.

"You know that he is only ten years older than you. I mean, us youngsters already refer to you as an old man."

"Don't worry, Grandma, in another five years you'll turn thirty, and all the kids will call you old too."

Reese frowned at the thought. "Shut up!" She let out a fake cry.

They both laughed turning out of the driveway and heading down the road to return the U-Haul. They sang Garth Brooks at the top of their lungs and danced around to the latest Luke Bryan songs. The drive lasted about twenty-five minutes and every moment was filled with fun. Reese hadn't realized how much she really missed Trevor until today. She loved the way he made her laugh and how she always felt safe with him around. He had successfully made her forget all about her morning of the terror that haunted her memories.

Chapter 3

THE WIND RIPPED through Reese's hair as her and Trevor sped down the empty back country road. Reese wore her black framed Ray-Ban sunglasses and Trevor's cowboy hat was removed and replaced with precision on his head. His jugular veins popped out through the stubble on his neck as he belted out the words along with Garth. Of course there were sporadic air guitar solos by both of them, and Trevor even played the non-existent drums with utter conviction. They laughed, they smiled, and Reese enjoyed the simplicity of Trevor's company.

When they arrived at the U-Haul rental center she pulled in the driveway and parked her 4Runner off to the side and out of the way. The parking lot was almost empty with the exception of a white Mercedes. The back lot was filled with trucks in various sizes, and each one was labeled with the infamous U-Haul logo plastered all over them. Trevor and Reese walked up to the entrance, and he chivalrously opened the door for Reese. The bell at the top of the door rang out to announce their arrival.

Reese looked around the empty waiting area, her feet made their way across the threshold and onto the red carpeted door mat. There was a counter that ran the length of the office, dividing the waiting room and the offices of the workers. A deafening silence made their light footsteps ripple through the entire office.

"Where is everyone?" Reese turned to ask Trevor.

"I don't know."

"Hello?" Reese yelled toward the back offices behind the counter. "Is anyone here?"

"I'm gonna go check out back." Trevor said on his way out the door, once again the bell mounted above rang out and fell to a deafening silence.

Reese paced back and forth at the counter, walking the length of the office multiple times trying to see as much into the back as she could, looking for any signs of life. There was no one was to be found. A few moments later Reese whipped her body around as the bell rang out, Trevor was back.

"Found him! He was out back with a customer." He reported before a wide and unwavering smile emerged on his face. "You'll never guess who the customer is!" He looked as if he was trying to not laugh.

"Who is it T?" Reese begged. "Well... tell me!"

"What's it worth to ya?" he snickered.

"Uncle Trevor!"

Reese hastily walked over to her uncle with a plan to sock him in the arm, but she stopped dead in her tracks as she saw a sea of golden blonde hair flowing in the light breeze. *Oh God.* Reese would know that blonde hair and snooty walk anywhere. It was Mary Jane Wells. Or, MJ as everyone called her. She and Reese used to be friends in high school, but MJ's need for attention and her backstabbing tendencies became the ultimate demise of their friendship.

In high school the gossip and rumor mill ran at super speed, and as proven by MJ, the juicier the rumor, the faster it spread. When Reese came back junior year with curves and flawless skin, MJ became exceedingly jealous of Reese and the attention that she received from the boys around campus. By the second week of school Reese had several people ask if she was a lesbian or bi-sexual. Curious, Reese did some recon and found out MJ was behind the rumor that suggested Reese had fallen in love with a butch biker lesbian over the summer. Once Reese found out the details of the rumor, she laughed and handled the matter in typical Reese fashion, with hilarity and commitment.

After school she went to the second-hand store and purchased an oversized fake leather jacket and biker boots. The next day she came to school looking as if she belonged to some overzealous biker gang. She talked about this amazing "friend" she met over the summer and how Reese would ride on the back of her Harley while the hot summer air ripped across her face. She talked of how free she felt to truly be herself. Of course, when everyone asked if she was serious, that's when she abruptly said no and set them straight, group by group.

By the end of the day, Reese had convinced the majority of the school that she was, in fact, straight before terminating her friendship with MJ. After that, MJ tried to tear Reese down for about six months before realizing she wouldn't win. Reese handled every rumor with as much dignity as she could muster up, and luckily MJ gave up as Reese's patience began to wear thin.

The bell rang out when the door opened. Reese looked up to see MJ who was wearing white heels with an overly pink floral print dress. She clutched her prestigious Louis Vuitton purse close to her thin body. With her impeccably manicured hand she lifted her bug-eyed glasses off her face before her pale pink mouth fell open.

"Ree Ree, Is that you?"

Reese shook off her horror, "Hey, MJ."

"Ahhhh!" MJ shrieked before daintily running toward Reese. "I can't believe it's really you!" She announced before throwing her hands around Reese.

"Uh, yeah, it's good to see you too." Reese stood frozen with her arms down at her side before lightly patting MJ on the back with only one hand.

She looked to Trevor and mouthed the words 'help me' to him, but Trevor just concealed a chuckle before he chimed in.

"What are you doin' here, MJ?"

She immediately let Reese go and eagerly jumped at the opportunity to talk about herself.

"Well, Mr. Landon, Thomas and I are movin' to Dallas next month, so I'm over here pricin' out movers." A cheesy smiled beamed on her face.

"Is Thomas your husband?" Reese asked trying to make the small talk bearable.

"Why yes he is," she boasted before shoving her oversized ring in Reese's face. "Six and a half carats, thank you very much! In November we'll be married for three years! Can you believe it?"

"Wow," Reese said with false conviction as she bobbed and weaved her head trying to get the ring out of her face. "What does this Thomas of yours do to afford a ring like that?"

"You remember Thomas Carter, right?"

"Oh yeah, I remember Tommy! He led our team to the championship. I heard he got a full ride to UT Austin."

"Well, he started out at the University of Texas in Austin, finished his bachelors there. Then he went on to medical school, and he is now the best plastic surgeon in all of Texas." MJ flipped her hair with arrogance. "That's why we have to move, so he can be closer to his practice."

"Wow, what an accomplishment! Good for Tommy! Could you tell him I said hi?"

"Sure," MJ muttered, seemingly displeased with Reese's reaction. "So, Reese, I heard a rumor about you."

"I guess some things never change!" Reese rolled her eyes.

"Whatever," MJ huffed. "I was told that you are knocked up and that's why you moved back home."

Reese stood horrified at the snarky tone in her voice. "Well, MJ, not that it's any of your business, but yes, I am in fact pregnant." Reese took a step toward MJ. "Care to explain the tone in your voice?" Reese's voice was direct and unwavering.

"I-It's just—Well, I heard that this baby was an accident. You're not married and you let yourself go and get knocked up, and then came running home to Mommy and Daddy." Reese's blood boiled. Clenched her fist, she tightened her jaw at MJ and her cynical tone. "What I can't seem to understand, Ree Ree, is why come running home? Why not just take care of it? They have clinics for that sort of thing you know."

No matter how hard Reese fought back her anger, as soon as the words left MJ's mouth Reese's hands began to quiver with fury. She felt her face get hot within seconds.

"First of all, no one asked for your opinion. Second, you have no idea what happened, or why I'm really here. So maybe, before you go spreadin' bullshit rumors you should try keeping your fucking mouth shut for a change."

Trevor quickly pulled Reese back away from MJ and placed himself in between the two women. Reese's face and body language mimicked her primal instincts to defend herself and her unborn child. She was clearly ready to rip MJ's hair extensions from her head.

"I think everyone just needs to take a deep breath." Trevor looked at MJ. "That was a low blow, even for you. Just go, MJ."

A look of horror and dissatisfaction appeared on MJ's face. "I was outta line?"

"Yes, you were." He cut her off.

"Ugh, whatever," MJ flung her twelve-hundred dollar purse over her shoulder before turning her attention to the U-Haul attendant. "I'll be in touch, Henry." She announced before whirling around on her Jimmy Choo heels and abruptly leaving.

The door rang loud as MJ exited the office, alerting Reese that she could finally simmer down. She forcefully let out the air that was trapped in her lungs and tried to take a few deep breaths. Her fists were still clenched so tightly that she lost feeling in her fingers. She tried desperately to internally talk down her anger. *Breathe, just breathe, she's gone, you're fine.* She told herself over and over.

"You okay, Ree?" Trevor asked as he lightly placed his hand around her shoulder.

"I'm fine." She forced the words through her firmly clinched jaw before rolling her shoulder, knocking off Trevor's hand. "It's Henry, right?" Reese demanded more than she asked.

"Ye—yes ma—yes ma'am." Henry stumbled over his words.

"I need to return this." She slammed her papers down on the counter.

Henry fumbled with her papers and Reese noticed the beads of sweat that had accumulated on his forehead. His hands trembled with obvious fear as he clumsily shuffled through his routine. With a deep breathe, Reese felt terrible for her behavior, this wasn't her. Usually, she was able to let comments like MJ's roll off her back, but not today. Today she was ready to rip her to shreds with her bare hands. *What has gotten into me?*

"Henry?" With another deep breath, she calmly asked for his attention.

"Y–Yes–s, Miss L–L–Landon?"

"I'm so sorry for taking my anger out on you just now. MJ just makes me a little crazy." She placed her hands on each side of her head before dropping them back down on the counter, and leaned over. "Good luck with all of that if she rents moving trucks from you, by the way." Henry nervously laughed and struggled to get her receipt and papers together. They vigorously shook in his hands as he held them out for Reese to grab. "Thank you, Henry. Have a great day." Reese smiled in one last attempt to win Henry over.

"Y–You too," Henry called out shoving his wire rimmed glasses up on his sweaty face.

The bell rang one final time when Reese opened the door and headed out to her car. Trevor had gone outside before her to unhook the trailer while Henry took care of the paperwork. She looked up to see Trevor leaned up against the 4Runner, the rim of his golden raffia cowboy hat glowed in the sunlight.

"You ready to go, Uncle T?"

"Ready when you are, Mike Tyson."

Reese rolled her eyes. "Shut up! Get in the car so we can go get face tattoos and bite off peoples ears!" She laughed.

They both got into the car. The hot air blasted out of the vents at full speed when Reese started the engine. Trevor sat there and watched Reese situating herself in her OCD way. *Air vents, perfect; purse, in the back on the floor; seat belt, good,* she went about her routine when she noticed Trevor staring at her.

"What?" She asked.

"Are you sure you're okay, Reese?" He rubbed the front of his hat up and down on his forehead before tilting it back and exposing his palpable concern.

"I honestly don't know what happened back there. She called my baby a mistake and then said I should 'take care of it' like it doesn't matter." The thought of losing her baby made her nauseous. "This baby may have been a surprise, but it's most certainly not a mistake." She lightly caressed her stomach. "An unplanned blessing is more accurate." She softly smiled as she thought of Jess and how much she missed her.

"Them Mama Bear instincts are strong with this one." He teased.

"Shut up." Reese scoffed, rolled her eyes, and then smiled at Trevor because she knew he was right.

They pulled out of the driveway and took off for home, once again singing at the top of their lungs. Reese even got Trevor to listen to Jay-Z and Ice Cube as she effortlessly rapped along with her favorite songs. Trevor watched astonished that she could keep up.

"Impressive, little tike," He tipped his hat.

"You ain't seen nothin' yet, old man." She chuckled.

For the next twenty-five minutes, they performed their hearts out leaving a whirl of dust behind them, but the worry of the anger she displayed with MJ stayed just below the surface.

Chapter 4

REESE PULLED IN the driveway and steadily drove down the dirt road leading to the little white farmhouse, that felt more and more like home every time she saw it. They saw Robert and Rusty sitting on the porch engulfed in laughter.

"Looks like they're workin' real hard," Trevor snickered.

As he reached for the handle to get out of the car Reese stopped him. "Uncle T, can I talk to you for a sec?"

"Sure, kiddo, what's up?"

"It's just... Can we keep the MJ stuff between us? Mom's already watching me like a hawk and this'll just add to her already annoying and overwhelming concern. I'll be alright, I just don't wanna add to their worry, you know? It's already hard enough on them with this baby comin'."

"Sure thing, it'll be our little secret. Just like your first beer was, and the first time you smoked." He flashed a wicked smile and a wink before he opened his door to get out.

Reese let out a sigh of relief and also got out of the car.

She slowly walked up the stairs to the porch, watching some of the most important men in her life sitting around the wicker table outside, drinking sweet tea. Reese didn't have to taste it to know it was sweet tea, because her Mama didn't serve any other kind. Their glasses were half empty and Reese counted the seconds until Maggie came out the front door with a pitcher for refills. *Twenty-seven, twenty-eight, twent–,* Maggie suddenly swung open the front door, and sure enough she was carrying a large pitcher of sweet iced tea.

"Reesey Piecey, come over here and pull up a chair." Her dad called out.

Reese smiled before walking over and taking a seat in between Rusty and Trevor, leaving the open seat next to Robert for Maggie. Her father's old blood hound dog Hank lay at Rusty's feet snoring away. She looked over her shoulder and found the two Queensland's her dad had got about three years ago to help round up the cattle. Reese always found it amusing to watch Mae and Gracie torment Hank.

"How was the U-Haul place?" Robert asked drawing her attention back to the table.

Reese and Trevor shot each other a quick glance, confirming in their own way, that they were on the same page.

"Um, it was good. Got'er all returned." Reese said as casually as she could. Lying was not exactly her strong suit. "What did y'all do while we were gone?"

"Besides miss us, of course." Trevor grinned from ear to ear before making some barbaric noises, rounded out with deep laughter.

"Well, Robert helped me stack what was left of the hay in the barn and we also got the pig pen cleaned out."

Trevor scrunched up his nose. "So sad we missed it." Sarcasm ran from his mouth like a river.

"You could always help me with the horse stalls," Rusty devilishly smiled.

Trevor sat so still he looked like a piece of petrified wood while his wheels were obviously turning. They turned so loud that Reese swore she could hear them. No doubt that he was working overtime trying to come up with an excuse.

"Ugh, damn it, fine!" he threw his hands up in defeat.

Rusty laughed as the three of them got up and headed for the barn. Reese gathered up the glasses off the table and brought them all inside, setting them next to the sink in the kitchen. She found Maggie hard at work prepping for dinner.

"Need some help, Ma?"

"Sure, grab a knife and help me cut potatoes. Dad wants homemade fried chicken, mashed potatoes, and country gravy. Plus I'm pretty sure the two stragglers will be stayin' for dinner." She motioned outside with the tip of her knife.

Reese grabbed out another knife from the block that sat on the island next to where Maggie chopped and prepped the food. The two of them worked to the sound of Maggie humming church songs; Reese loved the sound of her mama's voice. She remembered how Maggie would sing to her before bed as a kid. She would sit on the edge of the bed, pulled the covers up and tucked Reese in as she sang one of Reese's favorite songs.

"As the deer panteth for the water, so my soul longeth after, Thee. You alone are my heart's desire, and I long to worship, Thee."

Maggie softly sang, gently caressing the bridge of Reese's nose. She would sing it a few times before quietly trying to leave the room. Most times Reese begged her to stay and sing it just a few more times before leaving, and Maggie graciously obliged more times than not. The thought of that memory made Reese smile as she joined her mom, by softly humming along to her childhood favorite.

The stove was hot as the potatoes boiled away. Reese quickly cleaned up the mess from chopping.

"What's next Mama?" She eagerly asked.

"Well, sis, do you wanna do the gravy? That way I can get the first batch of chicken goin'."

"Sure, I've mastered the art of gravy by the way." Reese boasted to her Mom while she pulled out the skillet from under the counter. "The guys at the station would always beg me to make it, so I would make the gravy and Louie would make the biscuit's." Reese felt a bolt of pain cross her heart at the memory.

"Perfect," Maggie said as she pointed her tongs at the refrigerator. "Bacon grease is in the fridge."

Reese pulled out a large mason jar that was filled with solidified bacon grease from the door shelf of the refrigerator. She scooped the solid white bacon fat into the warming skillet, the grease quickly dissipated across the pan and Reese went to work adding flour and milk, whisking continuously to avoid lumps. She taste tested, adding various spices until it tasted just right.

"You remind me so much of Gran when you cook. You use your taste versus a measurement."

Reese's face lit up at the compliment. "Thanks, Ma."

"I just wish I could do that." Maggie smiled before flipping the chicken in the hot oil.

"Gran always told me to slowly add spices in, 'you can always add more, sweetie, but you can't undo an over salting mishap.'" Reese said, mimicking her Gran.

The thought of Gran cooking on holidays brought happiness to Reese. As kids Sophie and Reese thought that the aprons Gran wore were just a part of her outfit. She loved wearing aprons and she had an array of colors that filled an entire drawer in her kitchen. Reese's favorite was the one she bought her for her eightieth birthday. It was a full length apron that had a bikini body on it with voluptuous curves, and Gran would wear it while cooking throughout the summer months. Reese mindlessly surfaced a crooked smile, whisking away at the gravy one last time before shutting off the flame to the burner.

"Gravy's all done. Are we doing a vegetable?" Reese asked.

"I believe there's a few cans of corn in the pantry. Can you double check for me, sweetie?"

"Sure." Reese rummaged through the pantry and stacked the cans in her arms. "Found 'em, but these are your last two cans."

"Perfect, thank you, sis!" Maggie took the cans from her hands and fluttered off to the can opener.

Reese set the table with plates and silverware, while Maggie finished up the final touches with dinner. The guys came in through the screen door that screeched every time it opened. Trevor and Robert were poking fun at each other and Rusty would occasionally join in.

"Don't you even think about it," Reese said with her back facing them.

"Don't even think about what?" Trevor inquired. "You can't even see us."

Reese smirked. "I don't have to see you to know that y'all think you're gonna sit down on the couch without washin' up first. We all know that sends Maggie into a tailspin, and after she just slaved away in the kitchen makin' fried chicken. I suggest all y'all go wash up right now." She turned her head just enough so she could see the three of them standing in the living room, dumbfounded. "Now go!" Reese sternly ordered them.

"How—How did she—Um...well okay then." Robert fumbled over his words.

"Com'on guys." Rusty laughed leading the way to the laundry room where they washed off the day.

Everyone sat quietly at the table waiting for Rusty to say grace. Trevor and Rusty removed their cowboy hats and Robert removed his ball cap and placed it on his knee. Rusty sat up straight in his chair and folded his hands.

"Let's pray, Dear Heavenly Father, we thank You for this wonderful day that You've given us, and for this amazin' food before us. May it nourish our bodies; thank You, Lord for all of the blessings that You've bestowed upon this family. We praise Your holy name, in Jesus' name, Amen."

A faint whisper rolled through the dining room like distant thunder, "Amen."

"Let's eat!" Trevor exclaimed.

"Dig in!" Maggie happily blurted out.

Reese's eyes danced with delight at the sound of the guys spewing compliments about how amazing everything smelled. She looked up in time to see her father look directly at her mother and blow her a kiss. Maggie returned his gesture with a slight purse of her lips and a wink.

"Thank you, Maggie!" Robert said after swallowing a huge bite.

"You're welcome, but y'all should be thankin' Reese, she made the gravy."

They all three stopped and looked at Reese completely surprised.

"You made the gravy?" Trevor muttered through his mouth full of food.

"Yes I did, now quit your gawkin' you three and finish the food in your mouth before y'all choke!"

Trevor chuckled as he chewed. "You're gonna make a great mom, Reese."

"I kinda got that 'mom voice' down, right?" Reese's face lit up with excitement and everyone laughed.

The night was filled with more moments of laughter. Each one of the guys ate every ounce of the food on their plates, practically licking them clean. As dinner came to an end, the boys got up and cleared the table. Trevor and Robert insisted on doing the dishes. Maggie was happy to give up dish-duty, but she couldn't help supervising them. They didn't bother protesting, Maggie's type-A personality wouldn't take no for an answer anyway. The three of them walked off into the kitchen, and Reese went down the hall to her room to organize it.

She opened all of the boxes, unloading one box at a time. She found a picture collage that was framed in the last box she opened. It was a large frame with multiple photographs pasted together of her time at AFD. *They must've snuck it in here when I wasn't looking.* Her hand covered her mouth and tears stung her eyes. She immediately got up, removed another picture that hung on the wall, and replaced it with the gift her crew left for her. She then pulled out her phone and sent a group text to all of them.

REESE: I just found the picture y'all left for me!!! I freaking love it! I miss y'all so damn much! Thank you!!! XOXO! 7:40PM

The next hour was spent catching up with everyone as each text came through telling Reese how much she was missed. Jess was the one who eased her nerves by telling her that as far as she knows Alex has no idea where she was. Reese exhaled a sigh of relief. They were safe, for now.

Chapter 5

REESE WAS SLEEPING soundly in her bed with her eyes peacefully closed. In the midst of the blackness behind her eyelids she felt a breeze come across her face, causing her to stir. *Did I leave my window open?* She popped one eye open in a fog of sleep. Her moonlit room gave just enough light to see that her window was in fact open. She moaned and grumbled as she rolled over, *I'm sure it's fine, I'll close it in the morning,* convincing herself it wasn't anything to worry about.

Admits the silence, Reese heard the faint screech of the screen door open and close. Her eyes automatically opened and checked the time on her phone. It was one in the morning, *there's no way Dad is leaving this early.* Reese jolted up in bed at the slow realization that someone might be in their house. She could hear the light steps of someone walking around in the living room. Reese sat there, frozen with fear. *Why the hell did I pack my shotgun away in the barn? And all of dad's guns are locked away in his safe, now what!?* She heavily sighed, irritated by her lapse in judgement, panic steadily creeping in.

Her heart pounded against her chest when the footsteps approached the hallway. Reese scanned the room for anything that could be used as some kind of weapon. *My old baseball bat!* She quietly got out of bed, tip-toed across the room and reached for her bat leaning against the corner wall. Her door creaked open before she could even turn around. Slowly standing upright she clutched her only weapon. She held her breath as if her breathing alone would give her away, praying the darkness of her room would conceal her. Despite being terrified, she had to confront the intruder, with a sharp exhale she pushed down her fear long enough to whip her body around, coming face to face with, Alex. Before she could even blink he towered over her. The bat fell out of her hands with a thud as it hit the floor, *what the*—her entire body felt numb and paralyzed, betraying her as she struggled to make a move.

He leaned over inches from her face, "Hi, sweetheart." His crazed eyes almost glowed like a beast in the moonlight.

Before she could scream out to her parents, or even utter a single word, he picked her up by the throat and with inhuman like strength, heaved her across the room, letting the wall break her flight. Reese crumbled to the floor, her body engulfed in pain. She tried with everything she had to scream— no sound came from her mouth. She tried to get up off the floor but, Alex was once again on her. Her head was forced back as he dragged her by the hair, she could feel rug burns forming on her back as she tried to dig her heels into the carpet desperate to get away. Blinding pain and sheer terror consumed her.

Please, don't, she begged internally, trying fiercely to make her words audible.

"I missed you, sweetheart." He forced her head back and jammed his tongue into her mouth.

He thrashed his tongue intrusively in her mouth, muffling her pleading cries, making it harder for her to breathe. Hot tears soaked her shirt as they cascaded down. He tightly grabbed under her exposed chin digging his fingers into her jaw, in one swift motion he raised her up, her toes barely touching the floor, and tossed her onto her bed.

He was on top of her in less than a second. The weight of his body crushed her ribs as his hands clasped tightly around her neck. She fought to breathe but, she felt as if her punches were weightless. With one last ditch effort she managed to punch him in the side of the head, knocking him off of her and rolling to the foot of the bed.

Reese couldn't replenish the lack of oxygen fast enough, her eyes were puffed up and throbbing, and her head was spinning. Her throat burned with every labored cough, holding her neck.

She finally belted out a loud scream, "Daddy, help me!"

She shoved her body across the bed and off the opposite side from where Alex laid on the floor. She continued to scream out for Rusty as she picked up the baseball bat, tightly gripping it in her sweaty hands. Her body trembled as she slowly made her way to where she believed Alex was. Her breath shook past her lips as she tip-toed closer. She rounded the end of the bed but, Alex was gone. She forced herself to turn around realizing Alex had slipped passed her and was once again looking down at her.

"That wasn't very nice, Reese."

She screamed and tried to run. She took two steps toward her freedom before he grabbed her from behind, her arms outstretched toward her closed door. She screamed as loud as she could, frantically kicking her legs trying to break free from his tightening grasp.

Reese popped upright in her bed gasping for air, adrenaline pumping as her eyes scoured the room as it came into focus in the darkness. She fell back into her pillow as realization overwhelmed her. She laid there momentarily breathless and drenched in sweat. She heard loud footsteps thundering down the hallway. Reese immediately pulled her quivering body upright, dreading her night terror had come to fruition.

"Please, no–" tears brimmed her eyes.

Her door flung open and light filled every nook and cranny of her room. Reese could see her dad standing in the doorway, tears steadily rolling down her cheeks. He held a shotgun, visibly distraught and out of breath.

"Reese, what's going on?" with one giant step Rusty was by her side.

"Dad...?" Reese's voice was small and quivering, she was confused and scared. "Where'd he go? He was right here... He was going to kill me!" She hysterically sobbed.

"Who, Ree, who was here, where is he?" Rusty firmly gripped the shot gun that lay on the bed next to him as he surveyed the room.

"Alex!" she cried out. Her dad looked into her eyes, pain surfaced as he assessed the situation.

"Alex isn't here, sweetheart. You must've had a nightmare." Rusty released his grasp on his gun and wrapped his arms around Reese. "Maggie!" he called out.

Maggie appeared within seconds on the other side of Reese, wrapping her arms around the shivering body of her daughter. Reese felt her mother's arms wrap tightly around her, the sudden sense of protection enveloped her, and she cried uncontrollably.

"It's okay, sweetheart, we got you." Maggie rocked her body, forcing Reese back and forth. "Shhhh, baby it's going to be okay ...shh, honey, you're safe."

After a long moment of frenzied sobs, Reese finally started to calm down.

"I'm sorry," Reese whimpered gulping in deep breaths. "It felt so real."

"It's okay, sweetheart," Maggie reassured her.

Rusty and Maggie slowly released her from their embrace. Reese leaned her body forward and dropped her head into her hands feeling defeated. Her hair was drenched in sweat as it hung lazily in her face, doing her best to calculate her breathing.

"Are you going to be okay? I can lay with you if you want." Maggie offered.

"I'll be alright, Mom." Reese lied. "Thank you though." She looked up and slightly smiled at Maggie.

"Are you sure, Reesey?" Rusty furrowed his brow with concern, scrutinizing the still present fear in his daughter's eyes.

"I'm fine, Daddy, I promise." she tried to say convincingly.

Rusty kissed Reese on the forehead and reluctantly stood up. "I'm gonna leave this here." He held up the shotgun that he came to her rescue with and leaned it up against her nightstand, next to her bed.

"Thank you, Daddy." She tried her best to keep her voice even.

Rusty smiled and slightly dipped his head down and grabbed Maggie's hand. "Com'on, darlin', let's give her some space."

Maggie looked at her daughter and wiped some of the hair back that clung to her face. "Are you sure?" Maggie intensely stared at Reese with warranted concern.

"I promise, Mom, I'm fine." She faintly smiled. "I'm sorry for scaring y'all half to death."

Rusty and Maggie reluctantly left the room hand in hand, and closed the door softly behind them. Reese took a final deep breath. She got up and quickly double checked her room for signs of Alex. She looked under the bed, in the closet, behind the dresser, and in every other open space her room had to offer.

Her heart banged against her chest as she reached her hand up and turned off the light switch and hastily made her way back to her bed. Reese stayed upright and pulled the covers over her lap, her eyes wide like a cat on high alert. She scanned the room, carefully watching the silhouettes of the furniture for signs of movement. Reese felt as if she was a small child again, terrified of the dark and of monsters under her bed. Alex was her reality though, her very real, grown version of a boogie monster. She pulled the chain switch of the lamp that sat on the nightstand, letting the dim glow ward off the boogie man that surely lurked in the shadows.

Grabbing her phone off the nightstand, she decided to play Candy Crush to ease her mind. After finally passing the level she had been stuck on for about a week she stifled her victory celebration. The next level came up and with each swipe of the candies on the screen her eyes burned from exhaustion. Reese fought her eyelids that grew heavier with each blink. When she didn't beat the next level she decided to put her phone down. She stopped, glanced at the lamp that burned brightly before her eyes, then rested on the shotgun that was propped up next to her bed. *You're safe, Reese, close your eyes.* That night she decided to sleep with the light on.

Chapter 6

A FEW HOURS later, the sun shone brightly in Reese's eyes from the open curtains, disturbing her slumber. She loudly huffed in defiance, feeling like she had finally just fallen asleep after her night terror. Just before she could dose off again there was a light knock at the door.

"Sis?" Maggie softly said. "Are you awake?"

Reese grunted and groaned, "Yes, Mom, I'm up."

Maggie slightly opened the door, poking her head in the room before sticking her arm through the opening. She was holding a large coffee mug up that had steam pouring off the top of it.

"I figured you could use some caffeine so its regular black tea with lemon and honey." She smiled sympathetically at Reese who looked as if she had taken a few spins in the dryer.

"Thank you," her voice was hoarse and made her sound like she smoked two packs a day.

She cleared her throat before sitting up and hanging her legs off the side of the bed. After catching a glimpse of herself in the mirror that hung on the closet door, she quickly tried to tame her wild and mangled hair. Her sheets felt damp when she placed her hands at her sides before standing up. She smiled at Maggie and took the hot mug from her.

One sip of the tea and she already felt better. The heat of the cup stung her hands, a sting she enjoyed. She took another sip.

"Com'on, sis, I made French toast."

"Mmm, I'll be right there." Reese gently made her way past Maggie and headed to the bathroom.

There were deep purple bags under Reese's eyes. *God, I look like a zombie!* She rubbed her hands across each side of her face before splashing water on herself, trying to wake up. *Well, now you look like a wet zombie. Perfect.* Groaning at herself in the mirror, she grabbed her tea and left the bathroom.

"What time is it, Mama?"

"Nine-eighteen," she said, sliding a plate with French toast in front of Reese. "How ya feelin' this mornin'?" Maggie earnestly examined Reese's undead face.

Reese slouched forward, her elbow on the counter and her face smashed against her hand, contorting it and causing it to look like something Picasso would paint. "Tired," she picked up the syrup and methodically poured it all over the plate. "I need to start putting in applications today."

"Oh... you think, already? I thought you had some time before you had to worry about all that." Maggie seemed concerned.

"Well, I wanna get a jump on it. Getting hired can be a long process, plus if I get hired and start working before my vacation runs out I can save the extra money for baby stuff. I priced cribs before I left Auburn, and let me just say, holy crap!" Reese talked with a continuous mouth full of food.

"Don't talk with your mouth full, Reese." Maggie scolded with a half-smile.

"Sorry, I'm starving!" Reese said covering her mouth that was still full.

"Hopefully this means you are coming out of the morning sickness stage! I wasn't so lucky with you or your sister."

"God I hope so, because your pregnancies sound terrible!"

"Yes, but I got two pretty great kids out of it." Maggie tucked Reese's hair behind her ear. "So it was worth it."

Reese looked up and smiled chewing the last remaining bites of her breakfast. She stood up to wash her dishes when Maggie took her plate and coffee mug from her hands.

"I'll take care of this, why don't you go 'n get a shower."

"Okay, thanks, Ma." Reese lightly kissed her on the cheek and headed off to the shower.

The hot water felt wondrous as it ran down her tired body. Reese stood there allowing the water to engulf her. She placed her head under the water and just stood there as it fell from the top of her, down her face all the way to her toes. She hoped that the water would wash away the fear she still harbored from her nightmare. *It felt so real.* She immediately shook off the thought.

"He's not here, he doesn't know where you are... you're safe." She whispered amidst the water before turning it off.

Wrapped in a towel she ran her hand across the condensation on the mirror and stared at herself through the water build up. Her hair still dripped with water as she just stood there—her mind blank staring at her tired face. The water slowly ran down the mirror. The world continued to move forward around her, but she felt stuck. She tried to move her body, but she just continued to stand—like a statue, staring at the terrified woman in the mirror. Suddenly she broke free from her trance and threw herself over the toilet as her entire breakfast came up. *Damn it.*

The porcelain was cold against her hot body. She slowly pulled herself from the floor and brushed her teeth, causing her once again to dry heave for the next several minutes.

"I was beginning to think you were finally going to let me eat, silly me." Reese spoke to the baby. Getting back up she used mouthwash to rinse before she continued. Placing her hand over her unborn child she smiled. "Hey there, nugget, I'm sorry if I scared you last night. The man in my dream is the reason why we're here. But, I promise I'll forever keep you safe, my love. I hope that you'll always know how much I love you."

She came down the hallway dressed in a clean pair of yoga pants and an over-sized shirt with her laptop in hand. She sat down on the couch and searched for jobs. She was hoping to find a job with one of the fire departments like she had with Auburn. She first pulled up the website for Dallas Fire Department and proceeded to fill out the application for a position on the ambulance. Once that was done she pulled up several other private ambulance companies and one by one filled out applications. Although she was apprehensive about working for the private sector she thought, *when one door closes the right door will open.* She closed her computer content for now with her choices.

Maggie came into the living room and sat down in the recliner, visibly tense, next to Reese on the couch. She folded her long skinny fingers in her lap and sheepishly glanced at

Reese. She vigorously moved her leg up and down, looking away every time Reese turned her focus to her mom.

"Mom, is there somethin' you wanted to say?" Reese knew where this was going. It was time to tackle the elephant in the room.

"Well, honey, I just think maybe if you saw a counselor... or even the pastor at church... it would help you. Last night was scary. I knew Alex wasn't a good person... I had no idea how terrified you are of him."

"Mom, I'm fine." Reese could feel a rush of opposition take over her. She refused to open up to anyone about all of this. The more people who knew the truth, the easier it would be for him to find her. She had to figure out how to deal with all of this and do it all by herself. "I don't need to talk to anyone. I'm not even really scared of him, I don't know why I thought he was gonna kill me." She strung an all too familiar web of lies. "I know he wouldn't cross that line. Before I fell asleep last night I was reading a magazine article about a woman who was seriously abused by her husband and I guess it seeped into my subconscious. I promise, Mom, I'm okay."

Maggie narrowed her eyes; she always knew when her daughter was lying. Reese braced herself for the lecture. "Just promise me that you'll think about it. Even though you think you're fine, you just might not be. Talking to someone about everything wouldn't hurt." Maggie had a look on her face Reese had never seen before, a look of anguish and almost desperation. She placed her hand on Reese's thigh and leaned over, kissing her on the forehead. "I love you, sissy."

"I love you too, Mama." Reese smiled up at Maggie, relieved that her lie wouldn't be further scrutinized.

She made the choice to put the thought of her anxiety and fear out of her mind and move on with her life as if she was fine. She figured if she told herself the words, "I'm fine," long enough, it would eventually be true.

Over the next several weeks, Reese got her room completely organized and even started working on the baby's room. She would, of course, have to wait until she knew the sex of the baby before she did anything drastic but, she could at least attempt to organize the mess her mom had going on in the soon-to-be nursery.

Reese had received call backs from almost every company she had applied for and had interviews set up throughout the following week. She decided to prep for her interviews by first deciding what to wear. What better way for her to shake her nerves than to see what interview-worthy outfit she owned would look best?

The first outfit was a pair of black slacks. They were her go-to pair of nice pants. She tugged them up over her hips, *these are a little snug.* She grabbed each side of the pants and tried to pull them together to button them. She strained pulling with all her might but, no luck. Instantly frustrated, she took off the pants and threw them across the room. Next she grabbed her deep red slacks. They are supposed to fit loose with a wide-leg. Unfortunately, the legs were not the problem, it was her waist. She tried on every pair of slacks she owned and she could only get one pair buttoned, but it hurt too much to leave it. She quickly undid the last pair of slacks and fell onto her bed.

She laid there, out of breath, and fighting back the urge to cry. She softly placed her hand on her small protruding belly, that seemed to develop overnight, and grunted. *Well, there goes my wardrobe.* She rolled her eyes before standing up. Putting back on her yoga pants she emerged down the hall.

"Mom?" Reese called out.

"I'm outside!" Maggie yelled.

Reese followed her mom's voice to the backyard letting the screen door screech open and slam behind her. She found Maggie coming out of the chicken coop with a basket half-filled with eggs. Maggie wiped the sweat from her forehead with the towel she took with her to work outside. Reese walked down the steps and toward Maggie.

"Hey, any chance these yoga pants will look good for an interview?" Maggie looked at her confused. "They're the only pants I have that fit." Reese pushed her bottom lip forward.

"Oh, honey," Maggie grabbed Reese and hugged her tightly. "Welcome to pregnancy!"

"Yeah," Reese tried to laugh off her devastation. "Well, I gotta go shopping for clothes that fit, wanna come with me?"

"Of course I do! Let me go put these eggs away and I'll jump in the shower. Give me...mmm... thirty minutes?"

"Sure, sounds good, but, let me take care of the eggs. You go shower." Reese insisted as she took the egg basket from her hands.

"Okay, sweetie, thank you."

Reese took the eggs to the table and filled up the empty carton Maggie had pulled out, and stored them on the back porch in their extra refrigerator. She returned the basket to the hook in the laundry room where it hung before washing her hands at the sink her dad frequently used. She finished getting ready, and decided that in an attempt to make herself feel better she quickly did her hair and makeup. It didn't really help, but at least she no longer resembled her former ragged self.

61

With her flip flops on she sluggishly came down the hallway to find Maggie descending off the final step to the stairs.

"You ready to go, sweetheart?" Maggie asked with a smile.

"Yes but, can you please stop enjoying this so much? This is it...my body is starting its demise." Reese whined.

"Oh no, it's not! Your body is changing so that it can carry the most precious thing you'll ever have."

"You can try to make it sound as magical as you want, Maggs, but reality is that I'm about to get seriously fat and have endless stretchmarks that cover my stomach." Reese grabbed her keys off the hook by the door. When she turned around Maggie was standing face to face with her.

She placed her hands on Reese's shoulders, "Oh sweetie, bless your heart, those are simply battle scars from growin' another human being. Women have been earning those scars for centuries, welcome to the club!" Maggie giggled and then walked out the door.

"Gee, thanks Mom! Good pep talk." Reese took a deep breath locking the front door behind her.

They pulled up to the maternity boutique down town, in hopes to find something without having to make a trip all the way into Dallas. She sat staring at the glass display windows where the mannequins looked like they were due with their own babies any day now. Fortunately, Reese happened to think the displayed mannequins were dressed fairly cute for the summer weather. Maggie nodded towards the store with a smile, Reese responded with a submissive shrug of her shoulders before they both hurriedly got out of the car.

The wooden front door to the boutique was deep purple and nothing like the standard metal and glass doors in the rest of the shopping areas of downtown. There were elegantly intricate flowers painted on the wood surrounding a stain glass window held in the center of the door. As Reese walked through the opening, she was met by a pleasantly faint clean smell, almost as if someone was doing laundry in the back room somewhere. The store had an open floor plan but, still managed to feel warm and inviting. Immediately, Reese spotted a pair of slacks she wanted to try on, black and straight legged, ideal for interviews, and walked straight for them.

She pulled her size from the rack and held them up to her. The length was perfect, and in her excitement she pulled all three colors the pants came in: black, navy, and deep purple.

"These just might work!" Reese smiled at her mom, "now to find a shirt."

"We should probably try on some jeans and maybe some summer dresses for you too, sweetie."

"You're right but, let me figure out an interview outfit first."

Maggie nodded her head in agreement and browsed shirts. They both pulled several shirts they thought were cute and would conceal the small baby bump that she now had.

"Can I start a room for you ladies?" A soft voice asked from behind them.

Reese turned her eyes to the woman standing in front of her. Mousey brown hair, thick rimmed glasses, and the slightest gap in her front teeth, she couldn't believe it.

"Penny Olsen? Is that you?" Reese's face lit up with joy.

"Ree Ree? Oh my God, it's been ages!"

The girls squealed and embraced each other as old friends do.

"I can't believe it's you! I haven't seen you since..." Reese's voice trailed off.

"...Since you left for Washington. I heard that you might be back."

Reese looked down, feeling embarrassed. "Yeah... I'm sorry that we lost touch."

"Don't be silly, Reese! You moved a few thousand miles away, it was sure to happen. I'm just glad that you're back! We should do dinner sometime!"

"I would love that!" Reese smiled. "How long have you worked here for?"

"I actually own this store." Penny boasted.

"Oh my God, that's awesome!"

"Good for you, Penny." Maggie said from the behind Reese.

"Mrs. Landon, I didn't even see you there! How are you?" Penny reached her arms out in front of her and wrapped them around Maggie.

"I'm good, dear. It looks like you're doing quite well for yourself."

"I am actually, thank you." Penny gently shoved her glasses up on her narrow nose. "I decided to open this store about two years ago when I was pregnant with my son. I thought it was tragic that the closest place I could buy cute maternity clothes was all the way in Dallas. Let's just face it, that's too far away."

"Amen, sister, preach it!" Reese joked. "Well, I have to say, I was seriously dreading this whole buying maternity clothes thing but, your store has definitely changed my mind."

"Yay!" Penny clapped her hands together. "So, how far along are you?"

"Almost fifteen weeks. I went to put on regular pants today and couldn't get any of them buttoned!"

"Oh no, I was around thirteen weeks when I couldn't button any of my pants either. Well, hopefully you can find a few items you like here. Are you looking for anything in particular?"

"Well, the most important thing is to find an outfit for the interviews I have this week. And then, maybe a maxi dress and a pair of shorts?"

"Perfect. Well, I'll go and get a dressing room started for you ladies really quick, we have great stuff in this section and one over by the counter there, and don't forget to check out the clearance. Also, you can get an additional thirty percent off your purchases with our Baby-Bumps store card, if you're interested!"

"Awesome, thanks, Pen," Reese said delighted.

Thumbing through the clothes, Reese remembered how she and Penny had been inseparable since they were four years old. They would play Barbie's and cowgirls out in her parent's barn. They occasionally expanded their duo throughout the years, but as others came and went, Penny and Reese remained. Sure they had their drama, as most adolescent girls do but, nothing ever broke their bond. *Nothing broke us, until I moved away and lost touch with everyone.* Reese cleared her throat as she continued to thumb through the clothes. She hoped that maybe with some time and effort, Penny would forgive her absence and they could build back the friendship they once had.

In no time at all Reese had both arms filled with various items to try on. When she scanned the store to find her mom, Reese noticed that Maggie had ventured across the store and found a heaping mound of clothes, twice the size of Reese's in her arms.

With a faint sigh she walked over to her mom. "I think it's safe to say that we are gonna be here awhile." Reese softly laughed.

"I know I'm sorry! Everything in here is just so darn cute, I couldn't help myself."

"Hey, Pen?" Reese called out.

"Yes?" Penny came out from the back room.

"Is that dressing room of yours big enough for all of this?"

All three of them burst out with laughter.

"I think so, well, shoot, I hope so!" Penny chuckled as she took the clothes from Maggie, and led them back to the dressing room. It looked like Penny had hung up as many clothes as she could. "The rest of these I'm going to hang out here and we can bring in more clothes when you're ready."

"Sounds good," Reese walked into the dressing room.

With the first couple of outfits she came out and discreetly modeled for Maggie but, by the time she got to her fourth outfit she had found her stride and turned the hallway into her own personal runway. Channeling her inner Tyra Banks, she performed the catwalk of her life. Reese even got her Mom and Penny to join in the fun.

The laughter enveloped the entire store and it was as if the whole world had faded away. Reese felt a sense of happiness she didn't think her life would ever possess again. She smiled watching Penny strut her catwalk down the hall wrapped up in an oversized coat. Happiness was a simple emotion in that moment. Reese forgot all about Alex and her struggle in making it passed her fears of him. She was able to let go of her terrified thoughts of becoming a mom and how to care for a child because right now, none of that mattered.

That day Reese walked out of the store with a smile, a lunch date planned for the following week, and a bag full of maternity clothes. She felt at peace, if only that peace could stay around longer.

Chapter 7

THE NEXT MORNING Reese was up before her alarm sounded, excited for her interview with Dallas Fire Department that afternoon. She happily bounced out of her room, down the hall, and into the shower. After her shower she stood in a towel, dripping wet, and stared at herself in the moisture filled mirror and practiced her smile and initial greeting.

"Hello, sir," her mouth twisted into a giant and almost clown like smile. "Oh, geez, yikes," she shook her head and started over. "Hello, sir," this time her smile seemed lifeless and un-genuine. She shook her whole body this time in hopes to make a difference. "Hello, sir," she extended her arm out in front of her with a genuine and non-creeper smile on her face. "Perfect."

She went about her morning routine while randomly answering questions that she anticipated them asking.

"Well, sir, my ten year plan would be to work here as I go to school to obtain my degree and pre-requisites for nursing. My ultimate goal is to be a flight nurse. If y'all offer flight medic jobs I wouldn't mind after putting in some time here to lateral over." *Is that really what I wanna say? I mean, don't they want someone who will stay there forever? Ugh, I don't even really know what I want for my future.* She placed her hand on her stomach. *I don't even know what my future will be like.* She slowly exhaled running her straightener through her long brown hair.

Wiping the sweat that accumulated on her forehead she continued, "Well, sir, the reason I got into this business is because I truly enjoy helping people, and frankly, I am very good at it." She paused and chuckled. "It would be a huge mistake to not hire me, I'm pretty awesome!" She dramatically flipped her hair back before giggling at herself. Reese really wanted this job to pan out. She enjoyed so much working for the fire department in Auburn, and all she wanted was to replace her old job with the familiar.

The time seemed to creep along at snail speed, dragging to the time Reese needed to leave. With every minute that passed she could feel another knot form in her stomach, and when it was finally time for her to leave, she nervously gathered up her things trying not to second guess herself.

"Good luck, sweetie, I know you'll do great." Maggie stopped Reese at the front door, wrapped her arms around her, squeezing her tight. "So, take a deep breath, and knock 'em dead." She smiled when she released Reese, and kissed her on the cheek. Despite the comfort offered by her mom, Reese still felt a little uneasy.

The drive took her about an hour but, she left early, giving her plenty of time to get to the interview and not feel rushed. When she pulled into the parking lot of the Dallas Headquarters she had forty-five minutes to spare. She sat in her car and went over her greeting and her mock answers again, slightly tweaking some of her answers and changing a few of her responses entirely.

"My ten year plan is to further my career within the fire department." *Short, sweet, and to the point.* She paused, *but what if it's too short?* She huffed, noticing that it was finally time to head inside.

Straightening the papers that were organized in a folder, she grabbed her purse from the passenger seat. After stepping out of her car, she adjusted her crisp white button down shirt and the deep purple slacks she bought from Penny's boutique. She tugged at her shirt once more, trying to conceal her baby bump before pulling the door of the headquarters open and walking inside. She ventured down the long and characterless hallway and found the room where she was instructed to check-in at.

The woman who sat behind the counter exuded the definition of a southern bell. Her shinny blonde hair was curled with an up-due teased as high as it could go and clipped in the back. Her ear lobes sagged from the weight of the large hoop earrings that dangled down, grazing her shoulders.

"Good afternoon, my name is Reese Landon. I have an interview today at one-fifteen." She pleasantly smiled at the woman.

"Hey, sweetie, go ahead 'n have yourself a seat, the chief will be with you shortly." She popped her gum when she spoke with a heavy twang in her voice.

"Thank you." Reese said before finding a chair in the small waiting room area.

Her leg mindlessly bounced up and down, trying to calm her nerves. Ultimately she decided to just be herself in the interview, stop over-thinking, and if it was truly the right fit then the door would be opened for her. A loud creak broke through the silence in the room, as the wooden door gently pushed open to reveal a large man who was as broad as a full-grown oak tree. His hair was white with hints of brown, and his face leathered with age.

"Reese Landon?' he asked, gesturing his large hand in her direction.

With a hard swallow she got up out of her seat, and nausea took over her. She couldn't tell if the nausea was from her nerves or from the baby.

"Yes, sir, hi, I'm Reese Lan–" She stuck her hand out for a shake, but he cut her off.

"Right this way." His monotone voice made her suddenly feel insecure.

He reminded her of Frankenstein with his lack of emotion. He did not seem the least bit lively or pleasant.

Reese followed behind the man, trying to keep up with his long strides and wondered if his demeanor was possibly because she was a woman or if he was, in general, a crass person. Either way, she was thankful that for whatever reason her stomach had eased and was no longer doing flips.

When they made it into the interview room, she found two other men sitting at a table. The large man gestured for her to take a seat in the empty chair across from them, and Reese did as instructed. She placed her purse at her feet on the floor and the folder that was filled with her accomplishments down on the table.

"Good afternoon, Ms. Landon," the large man started off. "I am Chief Reed, this," he pointed to the short plump man to the left, "is Chief Cain, and this," he pointed to the lean white haired man to his right, "is Chief Hudson."

"Good afternoon," she said, "it's nice to meet you all." She casually interlaced her fingers on the table and clasped her hands together.

Chief Cain started off the interview questions. "What drew you to apply for our department?"

"Well, sir, I live just north of here in Denton, and it has always been a dream of mine working for such a well-established department such as this. I actually applied about seven years ago but, unfortunately, you guys weren't hiring at that time. Before y'all opened up for hiring, I had accepted a job with Auburn Fire Department, out of Washington. Now that I'm back, I couldn't imagine working for any other department." She smiled. *Should I have said all of that?*

The three men were writing down notes, assumingly critiquing her answer. Their pens sounded like scratching on the wood table they sat at, and when they were finally done, Chief Reed asked the next question.

"Where do you see yourself in ten years?" The forlorn in his voice slowly spread through the small room.

"I've considered several options, to be honest, sir. I've recently registered for classes at the college so I can start on my general education requirements. I've considered the possibility of going into nursing school down the road, and working toward being a flight nurse. I've also considered working toward teaching emergency medicine. Whether or not I can accomplish any of those things in ten years, I'm honestly not sure, but I intend on giving everything I can to this department and doing the best I can to further and better myself within this department." Reese smiled, pleased with the answer that seemed to fall from her mouth.

Once again their pens scratched at the paper. Reese cleared her throat feeling nervous at the prolonged silence. She shifted her weight in the chair and mindlessly straightened the papers in the folder waiting for them to be done.

Chief Hudson looked up and said, "We have one last question for you. Why do you think we should hire you?" his voice was like silk.

"Well, sir, I'm a hard worker. I feel that in order to be successful in this business you must constantly push yourself to be better. Plus, I can make a mean biscuits and gravy that would definitely win over all of you." Reese joked with nervous laughter. *Why the hell did you say that?* Reese stood up, and the three chiefs followed suit. She stuck her hand out and shook each of their hands firmly. "Thank you so much for your time, I look forward to hearing from you." She held up the folder, "they told me to bring a resume, where should I leave this?"

"I'll take it," Chief Reed stuck out his large hand and gently took the folder from her.

"Thank you, have a wonderful day!" Reese said before grabbing her purse and walking out of the room.

Well that didn't go as well as I hoped. Reese dropped her head and shoulders as she exhaled.

She came through the door and into the waiting room, coming face to face with the next interviewer. He was young, tall, and well defined. The arms of his button down shirt fit snug around his bulging muscles. *Oh my,* Reese thought.

"Have a good day, Ms. Landon," a twangy voice interrupted her gawking.

"Thanks, you too!" she mindlessly answered before walking out of the room.

When she finally made it outside the warm air hit her face like heat from an oven. *Was it this hot when I went inside?* Sweat immediately gathered on her body. *Ah, Texas, I didn't miss your heat.* The sweat then slowly fell down her neck. She rolled the sleeves of her shirt up, pulled out her phone, and sent off a text to Kyra and Jess.

REESE: Hey girls, so I'm pretty sure I just bombed my interview! One of the chiefs looked like Lurch from the Adams family, NO JOKE! It kinda freaked me out. Oh well, if it's meant to be, it'll be, right? 1:55PM

JESS: OMG! That's crazy! I'm sure you did better than you think you did! They would be stupid not to hire you! 1:56PM

REESE: Thanks girl! I just want this so bad, maybe I want it too bad. 1:56PM

KYRA: Lurch!!! HA HA HA HA! That just made my freakin' day! Jess is right though, if they don't hire you, it's their loss! When is your next interview? 1:58PM

REESE: Thanks girls! Tomorrow morning at 10:30, it's with one of the ambulance companies in Denton. We'll see what happens. 2:00PM

JESS: You got this girl! 2:01PM

KYRA: You're gonna do awesome! Stop over thinking it! Oh, I almost forgot, Chad was asking about you the other day! 2:02 PM

The worry from her interview quickly faded and was replaced by a smile. Reese thought about Chad rather often, but never let herself think about him for too long. He was perfect and Reese only became more frustrated every time she allowed her thoughts to drift.

REESE: Oh yea? 2:03PM
JESS: Yup! He really misses you Reese! 2:03PM
REESE: I really miss him too... 2:04PM

The three of them caught up on life during Reese's drive home. They talked about Chad and how awful it was that Reese had to leave before they had a real chance to start anything good. Reese found out that Kyra has the hots for her new partner and how Jess thinks that Nate might propose soon. Reese smiled, she was beyond happy that her friend's lives were going on so well, even in her absence. Reese's smile slowly faded away, she couldn't help but think of the road ahead of her and worried, soon enough they'd all keep moving on with their lives and she would become a distant memory. Everyone's lives were moving forward but, Reese continued to feel stuck. *How am I supposed to move forward?*

That was the question that had haunted her for the last three and a half months. It was the question that refused to go away, instead it stayed right in her face, taunting her. The truth was that Reese had no idea what was next. *Woah, what was that?* She gasped when it felt like butterflies in her stomach. It was the same feeling she had the day she left Auburn, she hadn't felt it again since that day, but this time, it wasn't going away. Feeling uneasy, she quickly grabbed her phone and called her mom.

"Hey, Ree, how did your interview go!?"

"Mom, I feel something weird."

"What do you mean weird?" Maggie's voice quickly became concerned.

"I feel like there are butterflies literally flying around in my stomach, or like bubbles popping. Does that make sense?"

"Oh gosh, sis, you scared me! That's your baby sweetheart. Our little nugget is moving around in there!"

"Are you serious? That's amazing!"

She placed her hand on her stomach gently caressing it in a circular motion. Water filled her vision before a single tear of joy fell from her eye and down her face like molasses. Reese couldn't believe she could finally feel her baby moving around. The worry and stress of her interview melted away along with the rest of the world. The only thing that remained was her and her child, together now and for always.

After telling her mom all about her interview they hung up the phone and Reese decided to call Sophie and tell her about being able to feel the baby move. The phone rang several times before going to voicemail.

"Soph! It's your favorite sister! I was callin' to tell you that I felt the baby move today for the first time! It feels so weird, like bubbles or something! Anyway, I wanted to call and tell you that. I'm also pretty sure I bombed my Dallas interview today. Well, call me back, loser, love you!"

Reese hung up the phone as she pulled up to her parents' house. With a large sigh of disappointment in how her interview went she sat in her car staring off into space. Her mind wandered over analyzing every answer she gave. *Why the hell did I bring up biscuits and gravy? Ugh, I'm sure every woman that fought for female equality is turning over in their graves right now.* Reese shook her head in disappointment but, there was nothing she could do about it now. The damage had been done and all she could do now was move on and pray that her other few interviews would be better.

Chapter 8

THE NEXT DAY she woke up feeling more confident than she had the day before. She got dressed and tried not to over think her interview answers. *Just speak from the heart,* she told herself. Reese knew she was a damn good paramedic, and if all else fails, hopefully that alone would shine through the nerves. She took one last look at herself in the mirror and headed out the door.

Today she was interviewing at a local ambulance company in Denton called MedStar. It wasn't exactly what she wanted, but it was close to home and it definitely would be nice once the baby was born to be close, just in case. During her drive to the MedStar headquarters she once again told herself; *just let the right door open, wherever that might be.* Her mom had always told her, "God has a plan for all of us," Reese just wished she believed the way her mom did.

Pulling up to the building she noticed a few crew members dressed in all dark blue uniforms. Everyone outside seemed to be relatively happy as they carried on joking with each other. It vaguely reminded Reese of Auburn, a faint smile easily spread on her face. She knew that Station 23, with Auburn Fire Department, was a one in a million gig, a once in a lifetime opportunity that she had to leave, and she would never be able to replace those special memories. There was no way she would ever be able to replicate what she'd lost, but there was no harm in hoping to create something similar.

Walking up to the office, she analyzed the industrial look of the building. It had gray walls made of metal, and its boxy structure gave it a look more like a warehouse for ambulances than an actual ambulance company. *Maybe that's what they want everyone to think...cookie-cutter medic factory meets medicine.* Once she walked through the light blue glass door, it felt much different.

The front office was vibrantly bouncing with life. The further she walked inside the more she felt her worries fall to the wayside. The woman who sat behind the counter was older, grey hairs speckled throughout the dark blonde that framed her round face. As Reese stepped through the door, the woman's dark brown eyes peered just barely over the counter at her.

"Can I help you?" she pleasantly asked.

"Hi, my name is, Reese Landon. I'm here for an interview today at ten thirty."

"Welcome, Miss Landon. Go ahead and have a seat, Mr. Harris will be with you shortly."

"Thank you."

Reese walked over and sat down in one of the many empty chairs in the waiting area. She pulled out the resume folder she had printed up, just as she did for Dallas Fire. Nervously she shuffled through the papers organizing and re-organizing until she heard footsteps come through the threshold by the desk. A short man with an ample goatee on his face walked over to her.

"Miss Landon, I presume?" he asked with a smile.

"Yes, sir, that's me." Reese immediately stood up and put out her hand. "You must be Mr. Harris. It's nice to meet you."

"Please, call me, Jerry." He reached his hand out and firmly placed it in hers for a handshake. "Right this way." He turned leading her down the hallway to a room across from an office that Reese assumed was his. "Have a seat." He gestured to the empty chair across the table.

Reese once again sat her purse on the floor, and her folder on the desk. It was crazy to Reese that all of her paramedic experience could fit into one folder, although she felt as if she needed at least a large filling cabinet to hold everything that she had learned in her seven years up north. The truth was, the things she's learned really couldn't be summed up on a single piece of paper. This job had taught her too many things to even begin to list.

"So I see from your application that you worked for Auburn Fire Department as a paramedic?"

"Yes, sir, I did."

"Now were you a medic on the engine or on the ambulance?"

"On the ambulance, sir, all of our medics spent time on the bus before being able to transfer over, but for me, I never had the desire to run into burning buildings." She slightly chuckled at herself and so did Jerry.

"Fair enough," he said twisting his thin lips into a smile. "What brought you to Denton?"

"Well, the short version is that I grew up here and I moved back home."

"Okay," he seemed as if he wanted more of an answer, but when Reese didn't continue he moved on. "Name a situation in which you deescalated a conflict."

"Hmmm," Reese's mind raced when a memory flashed of a call her and Kyra went on a few years ago. "Well, in Auburn a few years ago, my partner and I ran on a psych call, a man was barricaded in his house and was afraid to come out. He had been off his meds for several months according to the man's sister. Anyway, the police department was on scene and they were yelling and demanding him to come out. The sister had told me, 'if you talk to him calmly and reason with him we could get much further, much faster.' So, I asked the cops if I could give it a try. Mind you, by this point the man is practically in a tailspin and screaming viciously and acting aggressively. I walked over to the door and started talking to the man, telling him my name and how we were just there to help him out. I ended up being able to bribe him with being able to smoke a cigarette before we left. Once I made the deal he peacefully came out of the room. We walked side by side outside and he was able to smoke his cigarette in full before he got onto our gurney and rode cooperatively to the hospital. Granted, he would still sporadically yell at the voices in his head, obviously there was nothing I could do about that but, just by listening to the sister's advice and treating him like a human being, I was able to accomplish getting him the help he needed without fighting him or possibly hurting him." Reese proudly told that story, and although she knew that type of scenario was hardly ever successful, it was still an event she felt proud of.

"Nicely done," Jerry nodded his bald head as he jotted down some notes. "Okay, next question, what's your five year plan?"

"Oh gosh, to be honest I haven't quite figured that out yet. I've registered for school to start taking a few classes for my general education at the junior college. I've considered nursing, but I'm not convinced that it's for me. I do know that if you hire me, this job will be my top priority."

"Okay," he once again took notes. "What made you want to become a paramedic?"

"Well, when I was a little girl—I believe I was seven or eight—I was in the car with my Uncle Trevor and we got into a pretty bad accident. A car ran the red light and clipped the back of his truck causing us to spin and flip." Jerry's face displayed a saddened familiarity, almost as if he was reliving a similar accident he had had in his own folder of memories. "We were both okay but, I just remember being so terrified. My hands were shaking so bad I couldn't stop them. The paramedic that showed up was a tall blonde woman with big poufy hair. She was so calm, and she helped me to calm down by reminding me that everything was going to be okay. She explained everything to me as they put a c-collar on me and placed me on a back board. Then she took my uncle and me in the same ambulance. My uncle broke his clavicle and couldn't hold my hand, so she held my hand the whole way to the hospital. That was the moment I realized, paramedics are truly larger than life, and to some people, we can even walk on water. I knew this was something that I wanted to be a part of, and I never looked back."

"Wow, that's quite an incredible story! Do you happen to know the name of the medic?"

"It started with an S—I believe—Sandy, maybe?"

"Shelly, I had a feeling that's who you were talking about, she was an incredible medic."

"Well, I hope to live up to her standards, sir."

"She's actually a nurse in the ER now. She left about four years ago."

"Oh wow, so I might see her–if you hire me that is."

"You just might."

Jerry smiled leaving Reese to wonder if he was telling her she had the job in code, or if she's just an over-thinker of everything. Reese chuckled at herself and how ridiculous she was being. *The right door will open,* she reminded herself. Shaking off her thought, she patiently waited for Jerry to stop writing.

"Well, that does it for the interview." Jerry stood up and gathered the papers around him. "It was a pleasure to meet you, Reese. You should expect to hear back from us in about two weeks."

"Awesome, well thank you so much for the opportunity to interview here. I look forward to hearing from you." After gathering her things Reese stuck out her hand, shook Jerry's hand, and left.

Walking out to her car she felt like this was the place she was meant to work. It was a feeling that she couldn't describe, but a sense of home radiated throughout her. Happy with this indescribable feeling and with how the interview went Reese got into her car and drove away with her head held high. She pulled out her phone and called Kyra.

"Hey, Reese," Kyra answered.

"Hey, I just had to call and tell you that my MedStar interview went so good today."

"That's awesome!" Kyra exclaimed.

"Yea, I'm really excited. The supervisor that interviewed me seems really nice, and everyone at their headquarters looked happy. Who knows, maybe this is the right fit."

"I'm so excited for you. I've been hoping that you would find somewhere that makes you happy." Kyra quickly changed the subject, "has Chad called you yet?"

"Chad? Um, I don't think so... That was random." Reese was confused.

"Sorry, I just saw him on our last call. I told him to call you."

"Oh, honestly I didn't know if calling would make this harder, or hurt both of us more. That's why I've just left him alone."

"Yea, I think he feels the same way but, I told him, and now I'm gonna tell you—knock it off! There's nothing wrong with being in each other's lives, and you both miss each other, it seems to me the avoiding each other thing is hurting you both worse."

"You have a point."

"Of course I have a point. I can't help it... I'm always right... and awesome! Or did you forget that already?"

Reese giggled before agreeing with Kyra that she was in fact amazing, there was no argument there. The girls quickly said good-bye when Kyra got toned out for another call. Reese hung up the phone and pulled up Chad's name before turning down the driveway. Once her car was in park she sat as the engine idled and stared at Chad's name on her phone. *Should I call?* Reese's heart ached when she realized just how much she wished he was there. *Screw it,* she hit the call button.

This was a bad idea. Well, you can't hang up now. You'll just look like an idiot. Please don't answer, please don't answer. Send me to voicemail, come on voicemail! The line just kept ringing, and just when she put her guard down thinking that it would go to voicemail, he answered.

"Why hello there, stranger," His voice was like velvet, and butterflies shot through her stomach.

Her nerves began working overtime, "Hey, um, how—how've you been?" She stammered through her words as if maybe she'd forgotten how to speak altogether.

"I've been okay, you?"

Reese imagined his perfect teeth being unveiled in the most luminous smile.

"Um, I've been alright, I guess." There was a long deafening silence that made Reese's heart picked up speed. *Just tell him. Stop being a chicken and just say it.* Reese cleared the nerves from her throat. "I really miss you. I don't know if it's okay to say or not, but I do."

"I miss you too, Reese, like you wouldn't believe." It sounded as if Chad had finally exhaled for the first time since he answered the phone.

The awkwardness seemed to evaporate once they both confessed how they were really feeling. Reese remained in her car while they caught up on each other's lives. Chad told her about how he was almost done with classes to become a detective and has been studying like crazy. Reese told him about her interviews and how she can finally feel the baby move around. Chad seemed just as excited as she was about that. Reese noticed that in just talking to Chad, he seemed to comfort her. Even though he was a few thousand miles away, she felt safe with him on the phone.

"So, I have some vacation time coming up and I was kind of thinking about coming out to see you." Chad sheepishly said.

"Oh my gosh, I would love that so much!" Reese declared.

"Are you sure?"

"Of course I'm sure! How soon can you visit?"

"Next month, I'll let you know the days I can choose from when I know. That way we can plan a time that you're not working."

"That sounds perfect to me."

Reese hung up with Chad after a long and drawn out good-bye with a smile on her face. She loved how things felt easy and warm with him, like a perfect spring day. She was quickly brought back to reality as the humidity and the heat smacked her across the face when she got out of her car. *This is one of the reasons I was happy to leave Texas.* She walked inside to a quiet house.

"Hello?" she yelled for her mom, but no answer.

Shrugging her shoulders she headed down the hall to her room to go change. Her interview clothes were comfortable, but it was just too dang hot. Reese threw on a pair of shorts and a shirt that Penny picked out for her, sat on the couch, and turned the fan on her. She felt incredibly hot as sweat came from every pore just from sitting. Beads of sweat ran down her face and neck, pooling at her clavicles. She felt as if she was burning from the inside out. Suddenly the front door swung open and Maggie walked in carrying a bag of groceries.

"Hey, baby girl, you alright?" She asked as her eyes rested on Reese.

"I think so, I'm just hot. I feel like I may very literally be on fire."

"Let me look at ya," Maggie tossed her keys on the entry way table and came closer, she scanned her eyes up and down. "Yup, you're pregnant!" Maggie laughed.

"Mom, that ain't funny!" Reese whined.

"It's definitely the pregnancy. Shoot, I remember living in front of the fan with you and Soph." Maggie walked into the kitchen.

Reese got up and followed her. "Speaking of Soph, have you heard from her? She hasn't returned any of my phone calls or texts." Reese grabbed a paper towel and wiped the sweat from her forehead and neck. "It's not like her to do that, I'm worried."

"I spoke to her a few days ago, that's it. She has a little one at home, and Paul works outta town. I'm sure everything is fine, Ree."

"Yea, you're probably right." Reese wiped more sweat before realizing that the paper towel she was using was now completely damp. "I'm gonna go back to the fan."

"Give it fifteen, maybe twenty minutes, it'll pass, darlin." Maggie started putting groceries away.

Reese quickly went back to the fan, pulled out her phone, and called Sophie again. The phone rang and rang. It felt like forever before the ringing abruptly stopped, Sophie's voicemail came across the speaker to inform Reese that she wasn't available to take her call.

"Hey, Soph, it's me, you know, your sister, that girl that you used to live down the hall from. I hope everything is okay. I'm not gonna lie I'm starting to worry a little bit here. I haven't heard from you, I mean, I know that you're busy with the baby and everything, but..." her voice trailed off. "I just miss you, call me back, love you."

Reese had a gut feeling that something just wasn't right when she hung up the phone. It wasn't like Sophie to not call her back, and it's not like Piper is a newborn baby. *What if something happened to her?* The screech of the screen door startled her.

"Hey, Reesey Piecey," Rusty greeted his daughter as he walked in and tossed his keys in the bowl, like Maggie had. "Feelin' a little hot there, kiddo?" he chuckled.

"Dad, have you talked to Sophie?"

"Hmm... come to think of it, not recently, why?"

"It's just, I've called and texted her several times the last few days, and nothin'." Reese radiated concern. "I just can't shake this feelin' that somethin' is wrong, Daddy."

"Hmm," Rusty twisted his weathered face as he mulled over what Reese told him. "You're right, that's not like her at all." Rusty grabbed his keys back out of the bowl.

"Where ya goin'?" Maggie asked as she entered into the living room.

"Reese was tellin' me how she's concerned about Sophie, and thinking about it, I am too. I'm gonna head on down that way 'n check on 'em. I'll be back in a jiffy." Rusty walked over and kissed Maggie on the cheek before heading out the door.

The sauna experience that Reese was having had passed about ten minutes after Rusty left, just like Maggie predicted. Once she no longer needed the fan in front of her Reese proceeded to begin wearing a hole in the carpet. She paced back and forth, back and forth. Over and over she paced, fearing the worst, it felt like Rusty was gone forever. Her mind raced from the endless possibilities. *Why haven't we heard from him yet? It's the twenty-first century, Dad. Use that damn cell phone in your pocket!* Reese decided to just text him. Her dad wasn't one to think of shooting a text off to ease everyone. When Reese sent the text, she heard a ding come from the entryway. She walked over to see what it was, and there laid her father's cell phone on the entryway table.

"Hmrph," Reese huffed, displeased with Rusty and his forgetfulness.

It wasn't until she heard the crunching of tires on the gravel that she finally relaxed. Mindlessly, she tapped her foot and fidgeted with her fingers. *Hurry up, Dad!* Finally she decided that she was done waiting for him to come in, so she hastily went out the front door and to Rusty. He had just opened the door to the truck when Reese popped around in front of him, causing him to jump back.

"What in tar-nation?" Rusty threw his hands out in front of him. "Reese, you scared the snot outta me! What are ya doin' out here?"

"Daddy, is she okay?"

"I think that we should go talk inside, Ree."

"Oh God, no, you tell me right now, Rusty Landon!" Reese demanded.

"Reese Elizabeth Landon, knock that off right now. Sophie is fine, but we need to talk inside."

Reese's pulse was beating so hard, she swore that she could taste her own heartbeat. She took a deep breath at the words, "Sophie is fine".

"Fine, let's go inside. Dinner's just about done."

"Good, I'm starvin'."

The two of them walked into the house just in time to go wash up for dinner. Reese could hear mumbles of her parents talking in the kitchen, but she had no idea what they were saying. She assumed that they were telling each other about their day after friendly greetings were exchanged. Or maybe they were dancing in the kitchen like they have countless times before. The most important part was that everything was fine. Sophie was good and not hurt, and Chad was coming out to see Reese soon. Life was kind of falling into place, and everything seemed to finally be settling.

Reese pulled out her chair and sat down at the table with a smile on her face, a smile that wouldn't last for long. Maggie blurted out the news Rusty had and Reese sat there blankly staring at her parents. Her face was frozen in a look of shock and dismay. *That can't be true, they must be lyin'. Soph wouldn't just stop talkin' to me like this.* The confusion sunk in bringing anger to the surface.

"I don't understand why Sophie's mad at me exactly?"

"Well, she's mad at all of us." Rusty tried to reassure Reese that she wasn't alone. "She doesn't think it's right for you to be havin' a baby out of wed-lock, and she thinks we're hypocrites for lettin' you live with us."

"Is that so?" Reese could feel her hands shake with anger. "And just who the hell gave her the right to judge me?"

"Reese, language," Maggie scolded her.

Reese darted a sharp look in her mother's direction before taking a deep breath. "Sorry, Mom," she eventually said. "This is just ridiculous and I don't really understand."

"I don't either," Rusty chimed in. "I tried to explain to her how hard this was going to be for you, and how she needed to think about how she would be feeling if the roles were reversed. I assured her that if she had Piper out of wed-lock we would've taken her in too, but none of that mattered to her."

Reese could feel tears prick behind her eyes as she struggled to hold it back—tears that eventually spilt over and down her face. She quietly excused herself from the table, and tried to walk away, but it felt as if there were miles between the dining room and her bedroom. Sitting on the edge of her bed, she stared at the floor. *How could she just write me off like that?* Reese knew that if the roles were reversed, she could never judge Sophie like she's judging Reese. On her bed, her head sunk low, mourning the loss of her only sister.

She remained in her room until the next morning. When she came out and down the hall, she decided that she wasn't going to let Sophie's negative attitude bring her down. She poured herself a cup of decaffeinated tea and sat down on the couch in her pajamas.

"Hey, kiddo, how ya doin'?" a rough voice asked from behind her.

"I'm okay, I guess. If Sophie wants to not speak to me then so be it. She's entitled to her opinion, no matter how stupid it might be."

"Well, that's one way to look at it." Rusty chuckled, heading for the back door.

"Hey, Dad," Reese called out.

"Yea, sweetie?"

"I love you."

"Love you too, my Reesey Piecey."

The back door screeched as Rusty left for work.

Chapter 9

TWO WEEKS HAD passed and Reese still felt weird not talking to Sophie. She started, once again, being overly critical of everything, trying to figure out how to stop this and how she could fix it, all while knowing damn well and good it wasn't really up to her at all. She smiled at every interview she had in those two weeks and handed over her resume to each supervisor and chief she met with. Reese still hoped that Medstar would call, although as the days passed, it seemed as if her luck had finally run out, when the phone rang.

"Hello?" Reese answered the phone nonchalantly.

"Hello, I'm callin' to speak to, Reese Landon." An unfamiliar female voice said.

"Speaking."

"Hi, Miss Landon, this is Cheryl Glass, at MedStar Ambulance."

"Oh, hi, how are you?" Reese's heart skipped in her chest.

"I'm doin' fine, thank you for askin'." The unknown woman's voice was sweet with a slight twang. "I was callin' to offer you a job here at MedStar."

"Are you kidding!?" Reese exclaimed.

"No ma'am I'm not. We'd like to offer you a full time job here actually. If you're interested, training starts Monday."

"Yes!" Reese declared much louder than intended. "Uh, I mean, yes, I would love to accept your offer," doing her best to suppress her overwhelming excitement. "Do we wear street clothes to training?"

"Well that depends, do you have any tactical pants at home?"

"Uh, I do, but I'm just not sure if they still fit. I'm a little over four months pregnant and none of my old pants fit at the moment." Reese immediately regretted her answer. She hadn't disclosed any of that in her interview.

"Oh, you're pregnant?"

"Yea, I'm really sorry, I was so nervous I forgot to disclose that information in my interview." Reese could feel her heart begin to race as she feared the worst.

"Oh that's no problem at all, congratulations! You're welcome to wear your maternity clothes and we'll make sure we order you some maternity tac-pants."

"Oh, okay, thank you so much. I'll be there Monday morning. What time?

"Class starts at zero eight hundred hours and it'll be here at our headquarters where you did your interview."

"Perfect, sounds good."

"See you Monday. Have a great day, Miss. Landon."

"Thank you, you as well, Miss. Glass."

"You can call me Cheryl, darlin'."

"Okay, thank you again, Cheryl."

Reese hung up the phone and immediately went into a victory dance. She wiggled her body in all different directions and put her hands in the air, dancing like she was the star of the living room. When the front door slammed shut it startled her back to reality.

"What's the occasion?" Trevor laughed.

"I got the job at MedStar here in Denton!"

Trevor didn't say another word; he immediately joined in on the victory dance and let out a Texan, "Yee-haw!"

The next several days were filled with anticipation for Monday morning. Reese felt excited to get out of the house and back to what she believed was a somewhat normal life. Of course, there were some nerves settled in her stomach but, she would never let anyone know it. She remained calm and collected on the outside, and to anyone who didn't know her, she seemed confident and ready for anything life would throw at her. Reality was that she was having an internal panic attack as she pulled up to MedStar headquarters the day of orientation.

Her palms were clammy and her heart raced. She sat down at an empty seat off to the side, alone. Others were trickling in one by one, and every single one of them looked nervous too. Reese's stomach turned and the nausea she hoped was gone made its presence known. *Not now, don't do this to me now.* She begged her unborn child to stop, unfortunately, her pleading fell on ears that were still underdeveloped and briskly found a bathroom.

All of her breakfast was now being flushed down the toilet, thankfully, however, her stomach finally eased up. *Guess you don't like oatmeal anymore.* Reese lightly patted her small baby bump before washing her hands and mouth. When she swung open the bathroom door there was a girl standing in front of her.

"Oh, sorry," Reese had no idea why she was apologizing.

"You okay?" the girl asked.

"Oh, yea," Reese gestured toward the open bathroom door. "Morning sickness," she smiled.

"Oh! Yea, been there and I don't envy you one bit!"

Reese chuckled under her breath as the girl walked passed her and into the bathroom. Reese turned around and headed back into the training room and hunkered down in her chair for a boring day filled with policies and procedures. They were learning the "MedStar way". Reese knew better than to compare Auburn Fire to MedStar, everyone hates the person who shows up stuck in their past. So, she kept her head down and tried to not let her mind drift to the thought of Chad without a shirt on. She was so excited to get his text telling her that he was coming out in three weeks. The timing couldn't be more perfect, she'd be finishing up training by the time he came out. A smile lingered on her lips fantasizing about the fun they would have.

"I would like to introduce to you the EMT E-VOC trainer, Emily Baker," a voice interrupted her sexy daydream.

That's the girl from the bathroom. Emily walked up to the front of the class her dirty-blonde hair bounced full of life. She wasn't wearing any make-up but, Reese could clearly see she was one of those girls that could pull off that look. She remained glued to Emily as she turned to address the new hires. *I wish I had her confidence. I used to be a lot like her. Now, ugh... now I don't even know who I am anymore.*

Emily and Jerry shuttled everyone over to the airport in two company cars where they had set up orange cones to simulate a driving course. *So many orange cones, it looks like a giant threw up carrots everywhere.* Reese made a face of disgust as her stomach turned. *Its official, I'm never eating carrots again.*

"Okay everyone," Emily began. "Each and every one of you is required to pass this course in order to work here. It's our goal that each of you passes today, however, if you do not you'll be able to pick up a check for your time today at the office before you leave." There were several gasps while Reese nodded her head in agreeance with their standards. The gasping from the others disapproval caught her off guard. "Yea, we're aware that this is a tad harsh, but it's our standards, you can either meet them, or leave." Emily stood there staring at them all without waiver. The fact that she probably made some enemies in that moment didn't seem to bother her in the least. "Okay, let's get goin', Gabriel? You're up." She smiled and directed him to the ambulance parked at the start of the cones.

Reese stood there watching these young kids one by one struggle. There were a handful of them that did well in their practice rounds but, not all of them. *They must be green.*

"Look at all those newbies strugglin'." One of the guys said while he popped his chewing gum with over confidence. "It's hilarious!"

"Pretty sure that we were all green once, leave 'em be." Reese snapped at him.

"Well shit, I was just makin' a joke, no reason to get your panties in a wad."

"Excuse me?" Reese whipped around and came face to face with an oversized boy that she wasn't even sure was old enough to be an adult, let alone experienced. "You wanna wipe your tongue and try that again, Opie?" Reese determined his name to be Opie because he looked exactly like the kid from the Andy Griffith show.

"Woah, I ain't tryin' to piss off no pregnant lady!" He threw his hands out in front of him as if he was waving a white flag. "I'm sorry."

"Well, alright then." He popped his gum once again. "Opie," Reese spoke through her gritted teeth. "Either chew the gum quietly or throw it away!"

"Uh...yes, ma'am."

Reese could feel her hands shake and her blood boiled under her skin. She took some slow deep breaths in an attempt to calm her down. *I just wanna rip that jerks head off,* she thought to herself when she felt someone stand next to her.

"Well, that guy's an ass." Emily said loud enough so he could hear her. "But you, you're tough. I like that. I think you're gonna fit in here just fine."

"Oh, thank you."

"Did you do E-VOC training at AFD?"

"Oh yea, we had to do a refresher every two years. But, that wasn't enough for my chief," Reese cracked a smile at the thought of Chief Gibbs. "We trained on E-VOC every year, and most years twice a year."

"So this should be a cake walk for you."

"Well, I wouldn't say it like that."

"Let's see what you got," Emily smiled.

Reese jumped into the driver seat of the ambulance. The overwhelming smell of the diesel engine gave her a headache. She reached up and pulled the seat belt across her protruding stomach and buckled it. Emily walked up next to the driver side window that was rolled down.

"Okay, Reese, what you're gonna do is weave in and out of the cones. Once you get to the end I want you to back through them the same way but in reverse."

"Okay." Reese put the ambulance in drive and took off.

Carefully, yet in a timely manner, Reese weaved through the cones one by one. She concentrated making sure to not hit any of the cones, tightly driving through them like a snake wiggling through the grass. After reaching the end she placed it into reverse and the beeping of the back-up alarm sounded out. Backing her way through, she tried ignoring the back-up alarm that continued to blare.

She made it back to the start without knocking over a single cone. Reese and Emily smiled at each other.

"I told you, my old chief was particular." Reese shrugged her shoulders with a smile.

Emily gave her directions on the other two exercises of the day, which were building up speed before slamming on the brakes, and high speed lane change. Reese of course passed with flying colors. After her practice run Emily and Jerry agreed they would use those as her tests.

"Aye, Opie, that's how it's done, sunshine." Reese winked and smiled before heading off to sit down in the shade.

Emily walked over with Reese to the pop-up tent they had put up out of the way. There were chairs and an ice chest filled with waters. Emily reached into the ice chest and pulled out two ice cold waters.

"Here you go, we don't need you over heating and steam cookin' that baby."

When she grabbed the bottle from Emily's hand, the ice cold chill stunned every nerve on her hand. The water from the ice that had melted dripped down her arms and to the ground as she opened it.

"Thank you." Reese said, chugging the water.

Her body felt instantly cooler within seconds as she filled her stomach with as many gulps as her throat could handle.

"I gotta head back over, you good?"

"Yea, I'm great, thanks!" Reese smiled. *I really think I'm gonna like it here.*

She happily watched Opie and the others from the comfort of the shade.

The week drug on and it was filled with the "MedStar way of life" and how things would be done. Reese chuckled to herself, *this is nothing compared to twenty-three.* She knew it would all be an adjustment to remember that she doesn't have to do her regular routine. *You're not in Kansas anymore, Dorothy,* she told herself as she mindlessly clicked her heels together in hopes that she would be teleported back to station 23.

Disappointed it didn't work, she let out the slightest huff. The final tests were passed out to the class, *ah the exit exam.* Another test required to pass onto the next level, running calls in the real world. Reese quickly rocked her pencil back and forth as fast as she could while reading each question. They were given forty-five minutes, but Reese finished in twenty. She headed up and handed her test to Emily.

"If you take a seat and wait we can grade this real quick."

"Okay." Reese smiled and headed back to her seat.

Opie was the next to turn his test in. *Hmm, he wasn't that far behind me. Either he's dialed in, or an idiot.* Reese looked at his fiery red hair and the freckles that dusted his nose and cheeks. *I think I'm gonna go with option two.* She concealed her chuckle. Just then, Jerry got up from the table and walked back, handing Reese her test. A one-hundred percent was written and circled in red marker. Reese smiled.

"Someone will contact you about your field training by tomorrow." Jerry whispered.

"Perfect, thank you, Jerry."

Reese smiled, gathered her things, and walked out the door. As she was headed to her car she heard clunky footsteps running behind her. When she turned around, she saw Opie running toward her.

"Hey, wait up!" he yelled, out of breath. "Wait up!" Reese obliged out of sheer curiosity. "I wanted to make sure that you know my name isn't Opie."

"Oh, well I know it's not, but you look like his twin, so I went with it."

"Well, everyone's callin' me that now."

"Sounds like you got yourself a Nickname. Congrats, Opie," Reese snickered and turned to walk away.

"Wait, but I don't even like that show."

Reese didn't bother turning around. "Neither do I."

"My actual name is Austin by the way!" He yelled out.

"Whatever you say, Opie..." Reese said as she got into her car.

A week later, Reese started her training on the ambulance. To her relief, Emily was her EMT and Cal was the paramedic training her; he had been a paramedic for only three years. Her training started out with Cal thinking that he needed to show her how to be a paramedic. Reese quietly let him puff out his broad shoulders while internally rolling her eyes. She was left feeling like she was chomping at the bit to start running calls and get out of her "orientation" phase.

"You do know that she's been a paramedic longer than you've been in EMS, right?" Emily snapped at Cal as he was showing her how to feel for a vein when attempting an IV back at the station. "She could probably run circles around you, or teach you a few things, dumbass."

Reese couldn't help but giggle under her breath.

"Oh, um, well, I was just tryin' to do my job." Cal fumbled over his words while he repositioned his hat on his head.

"Your job is to teach her how things are done in this county, not train her like you're her preceptor and she's your intern." Emily rolled her eyes and walked outside the station.

Reese automatically stared at the ground, avoiding eye contact with Cal. She felt afraid to address him, and once again fear of reprimand crept back in. *I have to push passed this eventually.* She forced her eyes off the ground and looked straight at Cal and his bewildered face.

"She's not wrong, you know. I've started more IV's than I can count. I've been a paramedic for almost seven years, and I'm good at what I do." She swallowed the lump in her throat, but her heart continued to feel like it just might pound right out of her chest.

"Alright then," Cal said with intensity in his large brown eyes. "We're done with phase one, effective immediately." Reese could hear the spiteful demeanor in his voice. "Get ready, Landon, you're running the next call."

"Oh, honey, I was ready the second I walked through the door, weren't you?" Her hands quivered.

"We'll see," Cal huffed as he threw himself back on the couch and continued to watch television while obviously bruiting.

Reese got up and headed out the door to find Emily. A sense of endearment developed within her, after all, Emily did inspire her to dig deep and find that attitude she had lost with Alex.

"Did Cal stop his bullshit?" Emily asked before taking a long drag of her Marlboro Light.

"Yea, I kinda told him that you were right, so he threw his hands up and told me that phase one is over effective immediately." Reese chuckled under her breath.

"Are you good with that?"

"Of course I am. Running calls and treating patients here isn't any different than doing it in Auburn. We'll learn each other's moves. Are you good with it?"

"I'm not gonna lie, I'm kinda excited to see what you got, Auburn." Emily smiled before putting out her cigarette.

They didn't have to wait long before the pager activated and dispatch blared out an address. The girls both took off to the ambulance.

"I know the address, get in the front. Cal can ride in the back."

"Okay."

Cal came out of the station door with heavy irritation when he noticed Reese in the front seat. He threw his hands up in the air before reluctantly getting into the back of the ambulance.

"In phase two you're still required to ride back here." Cal viciously said.

"Emily told me to get in the front, I'm sorry." Reese retreated back into the timid girl she was made to be.

"Stop being a dick, Cal." Emily snapped.

I really like her, Reese thought. Cal passively huffed and mumbled a few things under his breath before receding to the back of the ambulance.

"So, we go out on this guy a lot. He's a real nice guy. He usually calls for stomach pain but, he's real hard to get information from because he's really hard of hearing. You basically have to yell at him so he can hear you."

Not to worry, she had a trick up her sleeve for situations just like this.

They arrived at the address to find a small brown house with an American flag hanging off the roof. All three of them jumped out, Reese grabbed her stethoscope from the backpack she brought, and placed it around her neck. They pulled the gurney out and walked up to the house. Once they lowered the gurney to about knee height Reese put on her gloves and grabbed the bag off the gurney. Emily grabbed the cardiac monitor and they proceeded to the door. Reese knocked as hard as she could.

"Ambulance," she shouted, but there was no answer. Reese checked the door, it was unlocked so she slowly opened it. "Ambulance," she yelled again. They found a slightly large old man with a comb-over sitting on the couch. "Hello, sir, did you call an ambulance?" Reese shouted.

"I'm sorry. I'm very hard of hearing," his weary voice said.

"You're gonna have to talk louder than that if you want this guy to actually hear you, Landon." Cal rolled his eyes.

Reese pulled the stethoscope from around her neck with a smirk on her face. "Or, we could save us the headache and just talk to him at a normal level." Cal continued to huff as Reese placed the stethoscope into the man's ears.

"What the hell are you doing?" Cal demanded.

"Watch and learn, son." Reese picked up the drum of the stethoscope, typically used to listen to heartbeats and lung sounds, placed it in front of her mouth and began talking at a normal decimal. "Sir, can you hear me?"

The old man's eyes lit up with excitement. "Why yes I can!" He exclaimed. "I can hear you really good!"

Reese shot Cal a look of arrogance. Every ounce of that smug attitude vanished and his mouth slightly hung open.

"Might wanna close your mouth, dumbass, and work on an apology to her. You owe her at least that much." Emily grinned.

Reese was able to get information that most weren't able to obtain with her little trick, and just like that, the tables had turned.

After dropping the old man, whose name was Darrel, off at the emergency room Cal and Reese came outside. Cal's large feet clunked all the way outside, sounding like a Clydesdale walking through the halls. Cal was tall and broad, and under his MedStar hat sat a mop of messy brown hair. He looked defeated, like a lonely man stood up by his date. There was a pathetic nature about his new found demeanor. His large head hung so low that he could have passed for a hunchback.

"Well? Did you have something that you'd like to say to Reese?" Emily chimed in seemingly eager to kick him while he's down.

"Um," he rested his hat on the back of his head while his messy hair poked out from under it in every direction. "That was pretty genius."

"Thank you," Reese said enthusiastically. "I actually learned that from a nurse at Methodist Hospital in Auburn."

"So are you done being an arrogant prick, Cal?"

"Sorry, Landon, Emily was right. You straight schooled me on your very first call."

Chapter 10

THREE WEEKS OF training flew by much faster than Reese thought it would. She and Emily had begun to build a friendship, and even Cal came around to the shinning new paramedic on the team. They referred to themselves as, "The Wolf Pack", in the last week of her training. Reese continued to be lead on all the calls and, fortunately, her and Cal had found a happy working relationship where they could run the calls together as a team. Reese let her guard down and allowed the two of them in behind the barrier's she'd built. She even told Emily one night about Alex and why she really left Auburn. Emily shared her own story of her ex and the psychological abuse she too had personally endured, and right then and there, a lifelong friendship was forged.

"He controlled every thought in my head. It took me several years to block out his voice in the back of my mind after I left." Emily took a quick drag of her cigarette. "Psychological abuse leaves scars on your soul rather than your body. Sounds like you endured both with your ex."

Reese absentmindedly ran her finger tips across the scar on her forearm. Visions of one of the many nights that Alex had thrown her down came to mind. This particular night she happened to land on her work bag and her trauma sheers ripped the skin open. Because an emergency room visit was out of the question, she was left with a lifelong reminder.

"Yeah, I did. I have scars that can be seen but, I have more that no one knows about. No one really understands. I mean, it's not their fault. I'm just not sure that a person can fully understand unless you've lived it."

"I agree. It's damn near impossible to grasp the magnitude of the damage done. Most will never know just how deep the internal scars can run." Emily said as she threw down her cigarette to step on it.

Emily and Reese became inseparable. Emily even talked Jerry into giving her Reese as a partner, at least one shift a week.

It was finally the day before Chad was coming to visit and it was also Reese's last shift in training. She was only hours away from freedom to spend the next four days with Chad.

"So are you gonna actually show him around, or are the two of you gonna just stay in bed, making up for lost time?" Emily snickered.

"I'm pretty sure that I'm gonna need at least twenty-four hours of pure sex before I'll be able to keep my hands off him long enough to show him around." Reese laughed while she adjusted herself in the recliner she sat in, fluffing the pillow behind her back.

"What are you two laughing about in here?" Cal asked when he came into the station and plopped himself down on the couch next to Emily.

"Reese's hot sex-fest with her boyfriend this week." Emily giggled like a school girl. "So when Reese comes back to work walking funny, you'll know why."

Reese threw the couch pillow she was leaned against at Emily before they roared with laughter.

"TMI, Emily! Next time you think about sharing y'all's personal life with me, do me a favor and don't." He stuck his fingers in his ears, "La-la-la-la-la!"

They ran their last call of the shift, which was Darrel. Cal decided that he wanted to try out Reese's stethoscope trick out. And just as it had when Reese did it, Darrel was able to hear clearly and relay much needed information.

"I can't believe how simple that trick is." Cal hopped in the back of the ambulance. "Y'all ready?"

"Yup," Emily said.

She shut the back doors before getting into the driver seat and heading to the hospital.

"Landon," Reese looked up at Cal. "When we get back to the station all that's left on your paperwork is both of our signatures. Jerry should still be there so I'll turn it in."

"Sweet, thanks!" Reese smiled.

Once she was home, she didn't stop to say hello to her parents, she went straight to the shower as part of her routine. All she wanted to do was wash off the copious amounts of germs that were surely on her body and on her clothes. The baby must've enjoyed the warm water as well because it danced all over the place inside her. With a smile she put her hand on her stomach, and enjoyed the fact she was finally able to feel the movements on the outside. It never ceased to amaze her that she could physically feel her baby, *that's my whole world movin' around in there,* she smiled.

About a week ago Reese felt her first kick, a foreign feeling felt from the outside of her belly. She frantically called for Maggie who came running to her daughter excitedly.

"It kicked, the baby kicked! Mom, you have to come and feel this!" Reese shouted with both of her hands placed on her belly.

Maggie shrieked with pure joy fluttering over to where Reese stood in the living room. She placed her hand on Reese's stomach and Reese guided her hand to where the kicks were happening.

"Right there, you feel it?" Reese smiled.

"Yes, oh my gosh! Well hi there, my little peanut."

Reese and Maggie sat there for the best part of an hour, hands on her belly, and patiently waiting for each kick as they came. They would let out a tiny explosion of laughter and celebration with each kick. Reese smiled thinking about that moment with her mom, and how she must have felt the same way when she was pregnant with Reese. Reese slipped into her comfy stay-at-home-clothes after her shower, as water still dripped from her hair, she swirled it up into a messy bun on the top of her head.

She came down the hall, and as she passed the living room on her way to the kitchen for some water, she noticed there was a man on the couch, talking to Maggie. Reese only saw the back of his head, but she blew it off thinking, *must be one of my dad's business guys.*

"Reese, care to join us?" Her mom hollered after her as she made it to the kitchen door.

Reese didn't even turn around to answer. "Sure, mom, just let me get some water first." With a faint sigh Reese went into the kitchen.

She pulled a glass out of the cupboard and leisurely got herself some water. *I really don't feel like trying to entertain some random rancher dude.* Reese rolled her eyes, took a big gulp of water, and headed back out with her glass in hand. When she came through the door the man on the couch was now facing her. She could recognize that beautiful smile anywhere.

"Chad?" she gasped, almost dropping her cup to the floor. "You're not supposed to be here until tomorrow!"

"I know," he laughed. "I got the day off, so I figured I'd try and change my flight and surprise you." He smiled getting up from the couch, and swiftly walking over to her.

Reese stood in disbelief that he was actually there, standing in front of her. "Well, I'd say you certainly succeeded!" Reese put her glass down on the kitchen table she was standing next to, and threw her arms around Chad.

"I've missed you," he whispered in her ear.

"I've missed you too," she squeezed him tighter.

When their embrace ended they both remained in each other's arms and Reese wanted nothing more than to kiss him. Every fiber in her body was screaming at her to kiss him, *kiss him right now!* She basked in his deep brown eyes and the rest of the world faded into the background. No one else mattered; no one else was even there.

"You must be exhausted from all that travelin'," Maggie's voice barged into Reese's world, reminding her they weren't alone. "Are ya hungry?"

"Oh, no ma'am, I ate on my way over here."

"Well, I'll make us up some sweet tea, there's always room for sweet tea."

"That sounds wonderful, thank you, ma'am."

"Oh please, call me Maggie." She patted him on the shoulder. "But my husband will be home soon, and I'd call him sir if I were you." She giggled.

"Mom, stop it!" Reese weakly demanded with a laugh. "My daddy wouldn't hurt a fly," Reese leaned in and put her mouth next to his ear. "But she ain't wrong about the sir part." She pulled away with a wink and a smile.

Chad smiled, although he looked a tad nervous to meet her dad.

Moments later Maggie emerged from the kitchen bringing a tray carrying four glasses with ice and a large pitcher filled with her famous sweet iced tea. Maggie gently set the tray on the coffee table in the living room, and filled the glasses.

"You're gonna love my mom's sweet tea, its county famous." Reese smiled. "They had a sweet tea contest one year at the county fair. I think I was maybe twelve?"

"You were thirteen," Maggie chimed in.

"Anyway, my dad actually convinced her to enter in the contest. He told her that he's had a lot of different sweet teas over the years, but hers was hands-down the best he's ever had. She finally agreed—after we begged her to of course—and she won!" Reese smiled. "There were over forty people who entered their sweet tea."

"Wow, that's some pretty impressive tea, ma'am."

"Maggie, please, call me Maggie."

"Okay, Maggie, I can't wait to try it."

Maggie handed him a glass and sat back with eager anticipation of his response.

"Oh my gosh, that's really good," he said surprised, "Really, this is the best tea I've ever had." He took another drink.

"Honey, it's not just tea, its sweet tea." Reese corrected him. "Trust me when I tell you that you do not wanna make that mistake in front of my dad or uncle."

"No, no, no," Maggie agreed.

"What's the big deal?"

"Sweet tea is a very big deal in the south. Can you please just trust me on this one?"

"Okay, babe, I guess I'll just trust ya." He winked.

Babe, I like the sound of that coming from him. It wasn't long before Hank, the old hound dog, barked at the sound of Rusty's tires on the drive way, next thing they knew Gracie and Mae joined in.

"Shut up!" Rusty yelled at the dogs, but in good 'ol dog fashion, they just ignored him, and kept on barking.

Reese could feel Chad's body tense up when Rusty's footsteps came closer on the porch. The screen door creaked as it swung wide open and he walked in.

"Hey, Maggs," Rusty walked over and kissed his wife's forehead. "Who's this?" He inquired turning to face Chad who had quickly jumped up off the couch.

"This is my friend, Chad. Remember that I told you he was comin'?" Reese stood up as well next to Chad.

"Oh that's right." Rusty smiled. "Name's Rusty," he stuck his calloused hand straight out in front of him.

"It's a pleasure to meet you, sir." Chad extended his hand and firmly shook Rusty's.

"That's quite a handshake you've got there, son. It's nice and firm." Rusty nodded as he let go of his hand.

"Thank you, sir."

"You can call me, Rusty. Sir always makes me feel like an old man, and I ain't that old yet."

"Whatever you say, Gramps," Reese chimed in with a mischievous grin.

Rusty smiled and chuckled under his breath, "What'ch y'all drinkin'?"

"Sweet tea, it's delicious." Chad looked at Reese looking for approval of the way he referred to the tea.

She smiled, nodding her head to let him know that he had done well. "I was tellin' him all about Mom winnin' the state fair contest."

"Oh, honey, your mamma could win a contest with most of the food she makes. She's got the best peach cobbler I've ever tasted too."

"Peach cobbler is my absolute favorite." Chad smiled.

"Well, Chad I'll have to make you some of mine while you're in town."

"I would love that." Chad sat his empty glass down on the table. "Well, I should probably get going, I'm hoping that my hotel will let me book an extra day, last minute. I got so excited to come out here that I forgot to call the hotel." He smiled at Reese.

Reese saw Maggie give Rusty a sharp look, but when Rusty didn't say anything, Maggie stepped into action.

"No way, that's just silly. Why don't you just stay here tonight?"

"Oh, thank you, Maggie, but I wouldn't want to impose."

"Nonsense, you're not imposin', and I insist. We have a blow up mattress that we can set up in the spare room. Rusty, can you go pull out the air mattress?"

"Sure thing," Rusty got up and headed down the hallway.

"There's no sense in fightin' it, Chad, they ain't gonna take no for an answer."

Chad smiled, "I can see that."

Maggie got up to help Rusty.

"I'm so happy that you're here." Reese said firmly pressing her lips against his.

"So am I." He pecked her lips a few more times while he had the chance.

After everyone had gone to bed and the house was pitch black, silence enveloped her room. She glanced at the clock, *its one twenty-three in the morning.* Everyone was surely asleep but her. She couldn't fall asleep knowing that Chad was just down the hall. Something inside of her wanted him so badly. She didn't know if it was the hormones of pregnancy now that she was into her fifth month or if she just craved for the long awaited intimacy Chad had to offer. She had read in the awful book Kyra gave her that a woman's sex drive can kick into high gear around this time. She wasn't sure if it was that, or if it was the sincerely developed feelings for Chad over the last month since they'd reconnected.

All Reese knew was when she kissed him earlier, she felt a spark within her as if she was now electrified and every nerve in her body pulsated at the thought of Chad. *That's it,* she got up out of bed. *I don't care, I'm going over there.* Reese wrapped her robe around her and tip toed with her bare feet out of her door and down the dimly lit hallway. She pushed the door open gently to ease the sound of it opening. Once the door cracked open just wide enough, it allowed the light from the hall to flood in. Reese could see Chad's back lying in bed with the sheets tucked up under his arm. She admired the way his defined muscles looked as he laid there with no shirt on. It was only a few seconds before Chad rolled over and met Reese's pawning gaze.

"Reese, what are you doing in here?"

"I don't know I just had to come and see you." She went the rest of the way through the door and shut it behind her.

"I can't see anything in here," Reese whispered.

Chad pulled out his phone and turned on the flashlight. *Well that lighting isn't sexy.* Reese searched the room for something better and found the night light she'd bought for the baby so she could see walking in and out in the middle of the night. She grabbed the white plastic night light and plugged it in.

"Okay, you can turn that off." She pointed to his phone and so he did just as she asked.

The dim light brought just enough visibility to the room she could navigate easily to Chad. When she reached the air mattress, she motioned him to scoot over and crawled in bed with him. She snuggled her way into his nook that she fit perfectly in, and rested her head on his chest. Listening to the thumping of his heart, she mindlessly strummed the tips of her fingers up and down on his defined stomach. With each stroke she drew her hand lower until it was hitting the elastic on his boxers.

"Reese, what if your parents catch us?"

"They're not gonna wake up." She sat up and kissed him deeply.

"Baby," Chad stopped her. "Trust me, I wanna do this just as badly as you do, but I would love it if your dad didn't catch me bangin' his daughter on the day I met him."

"Babe, they sleep with a loud box fan going, they won't hear a thing, I promise."

"This bed isn't gonna work, it makes a loud noise every time I move." Chad stopped her from slipping her hand into his boxers. "This isn't right, Reese."

With a heavy sigh she pulled her hand away, "You're right. It's not fair of me to push you. I've just missed your touch so much." Reese snuggled herself back into her nook under his arm and gently rested her head back on his chest.

"Reese, I want you too, and I've missed you like you wouldn't believe. It's just that I don't want to do it like this, where we have to sneak around and be quiet."

"I know, you're absolutely right... can we just lay here like this for a few minutes?"

"I would love that." He kissed her forehead and pulled her even closer.

After snuggling for a while Reese decided it was time to sneak back over to her room before she accidently fell asleep next to him. She passionately kissed his lips and her tongue elegantly danced around his. Chad swiftly ran his hand into her hair at the back of her head, pulling her closer and kissing her deeper. Reese could feel a million different fires being set off in her body as she became electrified. Sparks flew in every direction from her soul and her body tingled, running down her spine and between her legs. Reese knew that he wanted her just as much as she wanted him, but she had to stop.

"I'm sorry," she tried to catch the breath that he stole from her. "I didn't mean to–"

"No, that was my fault."

"I'm gonna go back to my room now." With one last peck, she got up and quietly left.

She crawled back into her bed and rolled over to face the window. She talked herself out of going back over there and having her way with him multiple times. *It's disrespectful... He isn't comfortable... He actually cares about what your dad thinks of him... But, damn it, I want him so bad... No! No, Reese, you can't...* Out of nowhere the door opened behind her. *Shit, they heard me.* Reese slowly rolled over to see Chad standing in his boxers holding his phone flashlight in his hand.

Reese sprung out of bed as he quietly closed the door. Wrapping her arms around him she deeply kissed his lips. Their tongues filled each other's mouth and Reese's body was pulsating with anticipation. Chad removed the oversized t-shirt she slept in and to his delight she had no bra on. He gently pushed her breasts together. Waves of pleasure rippled throughout her body as she concealed a moan. He ran his lips back up her neck and to her mouth. Their lips lightly grazed each other, hot breath gathering between them.

Chad pulled her panties down and used his hand to send jolts of pleasure exploding throughout her body. His fingers were hard at work; Reese tried to conceal her pleasure by muffling herself into Chad's chest. Just as she teetered on the edge of her climax she pushed Chad back and into the wooden chair she used to prop her foot up to tie her shoes. She pulled off his boxers and straddled him. They both quietly moaned into each other's shoulders. Reese tipped her head back with ecstasy. It was building and she felt like she was about to tip over the edge.

"Not yet, baby, wait for me." Chad huffed between breaths.

Reese held it back as long as she could and thankfully it wasn't long before they both reached the pinnacle of pleasure. Neither of them moved a muscle as they caught their breath.

Chad softly kissed her lips. "You're incredible, Reese Landon."

"You're not too bad yourself there, Mr. Platt." She smiled, happily out of breath. "As much as I want to cuddle up with you, I think we will end up falling asleep, and that would be all bad."

"I agree."

Reese removed herself off of him. "I'm gonna go get cleaned up in the bathroom." She kissed him and flitted out the door.

Reese lay down in bed after coming back from the bathroom and tried to make sense of the amount of chemistry there was between the two of them. It was so intense that it put all the sexual feelings Alex had ever given her to shame. Alex seemed almost mediocre in comparison. Reese didn't remember feeling quite this intense with Chad before she left Auburn. *What's changed?* She wondered. *Is it love, or is it the baby?* Reese decided to not get ahead of herself and just let the week take her feelings where it will. She rolled over and closed her eyes and fell into the deepest of sleep.

Chapter 11

OVER THE NEXT four days Reese was the happiest she'd been for a long time. Chad had not only satisfied her body but, he satisfied her heart and soul as well. He made her feel safe and taken care of, always letting her be exactly who she was and he never seemed to mind her flaws. They traveled around Texas and Reese showed Chad all of her old "stompin' grounds". They spent every moment together, blissfully happy. They visited the botanical garden, aquarium, and enjoyed the zoo in Dallas. They even took a day trip down to Austin and enjoyed live music in a few clubs after walking around the city, hand in hand.

Every time the baby would kick Chad would place his hands on her stomach in awe of the fact that they could feel it. Reese would smile and just stare at Chad's face watching it light up with joy with every new kick, wishing that he was the father of this baby. During their day in Austin they had a caricature artist draw them together and he drew them as a family. Chad was holding the baby and looking down with a smile that took up half of his face. Reese was standing next to him with her arm wrapped around his shoulder looking at Chad with sincerity and love.

When the artist handed them the final product Reese stared at the picture with a stinging in her eyes. This was the life that she wanted, not only for her, but for her child as well. She sat there on a bench, and the breeze blew her hair across her face. Pieces of her chocolate brown hair stuck to the tears that now gushed down her face. Chad paid the artist as Reese's strength crumbled. She fought the sobs with everything she had but, her bottom lip quivered with heart ache. Chad gently placed his hand on her back.

"Reese, what's wrong?"

"... It's just—" her words shook from her mouth, causing them to break apart. "This is all I ever wanted, you know? A happy little family, with a wonderful man that loves me for who I am, and instead I got pregnant by the most evil man I've ever known. And then there's you... you in all of your perfect glory and I ruined everything."

"You didn't ruin anything, Reese. I'm right here, and I'm only going to go away if you ask me to." He wrapped his arms around her and held her tightly kissing her forehead. "Are you going to be okay?"

"Yea, I'm fine, I'm sorry. I swear I cannot control these hormones sometimes." She tried to make a joke and brush off her true feelings.

"Look," Chad grazed her cheek with his fingertips before cradling it in his hand. "I have no idea what the future holds, but I would love to be a part of your future, you and the baby are certainly a part of mine."

"Why would you want me after everything?" Reese took a step back from Chad. "I mean," she took a deep breath. "I'm pregnant with another man's baby. Why on earth would you choose that life for yourself?"

"Because you're worth it, Reese," he stepped closer to her, Reese backed away instinctively.

"We should probably get going. I don't wanna get back too late. I have a doctor's appointment tomorrow afternoon. I figured we can hang out for a few hours before?" Reese slowly walked down the sidewalk.

"Is tomorrow just a regular appointment?"

"No, I actually get to find out what I'm having." Reese filled with anguish seeing Chad get excited. *Crap, his whole face just lit up.*

"Would you be alright if I came with you?" He gently grabbed her hand, but once again she stepped back.

"My mom is actually going with me," her voice was monotone.

Guilt hit Reese like an arrow through the heart when she saw his face drop. His eyes, his lips, and even his cheeks hung low with obvious pain as his face ran parallel with the ground. After only a few seconds of despair he lifted his head and gave her a faint smile that was gone as fast as it came.

"I understand. It would probably be weird if I came with you." He wrapped his arm around her, but his disappointment lingered.

Reese was pushing him away, and to her surprise, he was letting her. It left her questioning what exactly she was doing with Chad. Reese knew deep in her heart she wasn't the woman that Chad deserved, yet she didn't want to let him go. There's no way that her broken little soul—that was patched back together using scotch tape—was enough for Chad. He needed someone whole and vibrant, and all Reese could offer was her unnervingly dark past. She had scars that she didn't want him to know about. She harbored hatred in the pit of her stomach. Alex crushed her, and Chad deserved so much more than she could give. Reese worried she didn't deserve a man like Chad. He was pure and an incredible man; she refused to be the girl that let him throw his life away for her.

During their brief ride home Reese envisioned her future with her child. Her lips slightly curled at the ends as she saw them feeding the chickens on the farm and riding the tractor together. As much as she wanted Chad to be in those visions of the future, she knew that she didn't have the right to ruin him; she had to throw him back into the pond for a more deserving woman. Her life was a mess, her heart was mangled, and her thoughts were her biggest enemy.

After Chad dropped her off at home, Reese continued to wrestle with what to do. She knew what the right thing to do was but, she didn't want to do it.

The next morning Reese tried delaying her decision to see Chad before she left for her doctor's appointment. She made excuses of having to fold laundry and sweep the floors. The clock was her main focus as she dawdled through her unnecessary chores.

"What are you doing?" Maggie asked from behind her.

"I'm just doing a few things before I leave." Reese didn't even look back at Maggie or stop sweeping.

"That's just silly, Chad's leaving, sis, you need to go and spend time with him while he's still here." Maggie tried to grab the broom from her but Reese quickly pushed it out of her reach. "Ree, what are you doing? Give me the broom." Maggie demanded.

"No, Mom, I'm almost done, it's fine."

Maggie stepped in front of Reese's sweep strokes.

"Why are you avoiding Chad?" Maggie folded her arms seemingly pleased with herself for finally figuring out what Reese's problem was.

"I'm not."

"Oh, but you are... what I can't figure out is why. Chad is a wonderful man and he seems to really like you. He also doesn't seem to care that the baby isn't his. Is that it? Is that what's bothering you?"

"No."

"Then what is it? Talk to me, Reese."

"It's just–" Reese abruptly stopped, she didn't want Maggie to stop her from what she knew she needed to do, "never mind."

"Pushing him away isn't the answer, Reese."

She ignored Maggie and went back to sweeping around her. Reese knew deep in her soul that this was the right choice, there was no way that she could ever move back to Auburn and she refused to put Chad in that position. She cared about him too much to create a life where they were constantly looking over their shoulders. As much as it broke her heart, she knew what she had to do and she wasn't going to let anyone talk her out of it.

Reese's stomach filled with knots when she lifted her hand and knocked on the hotel room door. When the door opened, her heart fluttered seeing Chad and within a heartbeat transformed into a lingering ache. He was everything that she hoped for in their life. He was exactly the kind of man she wanted as a father for her baby, but her mind was made up and there was no turning back now. With a slow and calculated deep breath she sympathetically smiled and entered the room.

"Hey, beautiful," he said kissing her on the cheek.

"Hey," Reese enjoyed his lips lingering on her face.

"Is everything okay?" he asked.

"Actually, no it's not. We need to talk." She was unable to look him in the eye as she lowered her head.

"Please don't do this, Reese." He placed his hand on the side of her face forcing her to look at him while tears gathered in her eyes. "I'm falling in love with you, I don't care that this baby isn't mine, it doesn't bother me one bit. I want nothing more than to be a family with you, please don't push me away. Pull me close," he pulled her into him and water began to trickle down her face. "I'm here, just talk to me. We can work through this."

"No we can't," Reese pulled away from him. "You don't understand and I honestly don't expect you to, but I'm no good for you. You're an incredible man," her voice quivered, "and I cannot be the woman that you deserve." She wiped the tears from her face.

"You're exactly the woman that I need." He begged.

"No I'm not, I'm sorry." And with no further explanation Reese turned and walked toward the door. "Have a safe flight home, I love you." She whispered without turning around, hearing the devastation of the heart she just shattered.

When the door closed behind her she forced her feet to walk, barely making it to the elevator before she completely broke. She fell against the wall in agony from her own broken heart, finally reaching its limit of pain. This hurt so much more than leaving Alex. She heard the elevator ding through her sobs, thankful that she'd rode the elevator alone. No one was there to witness her vulnerability. As the elevator approached the lobby she wiped her face and pulled herself together the best she could but, the sullen look in her eyes told the world everything they needed to know. She caught the sympathetic looks from the handful of people in the lobby out of the corner of her eye before putting her head down and wistfully walking out of the glass doors.

She drove home in silence, occasionally wiping the stream of tears that continued to fall. Her heart was heavy and her baby must've felt it too, Reese could feel it moving around more than usual. Maybe it was her child's way of trying to cheer her up, and as a faint smile hit her lips it slightly worked. *I did the right thing. I had to let him go... I did the right thing... I know I did the right thing.*

Her hand ever so lightly caressed her stomach. "It's just you and me now, peanut. We'll be okay, don't worry." With one last pat to her stomach, her little one calmed down.

When she made it home, Maggie was sitting on the couch, reading a book. Reese didn't say a word she just walked straight to her room. The last thing she wanted to do was hear a "mom lecture" from Maggie about how she was making a huge mistake. It took everything she had to walk away from Chad and to not go running back into his arms, where she felt safe. She couldn't handle trying to defend her choice to her mom while she was still struggling with it herself. Reese closed her bedroom door behind her and plopped herself down on the bed. She lay down, cuddled a pillow, and didn't move from that spot. She stared at the wall while the flow of unforced tears continued to seep out of her red eyes.

A soft knock at the door startled Reese awake. *I must've fallen asleep,* her foggy mind thought. She cleared her throat and sat up on the edge of the bed.

"Come in." she groggily said.

"Ree, it's almost time to head to the doctor's office."
Maggie poked her head through the door with her voice low
and pleasant.

"I'm up. Give me like five minutes and I'll be ready."

"Okay, sweetie," she softly closed the door.

Reese drug herself out of bed. Once she was on her feet
she shuffled herself to the bathroom and splashed some water
on her face. *I look absolutely terrible,* she huffed to herself.
She didn't have the desire to muster up some sort of false
happiness.

"Forget it," she told the girl in the mirror.

Maggie was waiting at the door for her as she came down
the hallway. "You ready to see our little peanut?"

"Yea."

The thought of seeing her child and finding out what she
was having caused a twitch of happiness deep within her that
had been taken over by grief. It was the only thing that could
possibly make her happy right now. Her sullen face eased with
a slight smile when she passed Maggie and opened the front
door.

"Are you okay, sis?" Maggie trailed behind her off the last
step of the porch.

"Not really, Mom but, I don't wanna talk about it, okay?"
Reese popped open the passenger door.

"Okay, just know I'm here if you change your mind."
Maggie put her hand on Reese's shoulder and turned her
around. "I love you, Ree, and I'm really sorry about
everything."

Reese wrapped her arms tightly around her mom. "Thank
you, Ma," she lost the battle with the tears that fell. "I love you
too."

The car ride to the doctor's office was somber to say the least. Reese stared out her window watching the scenery as it passed her by. Her mind drifted to Chad and how much it hurt her to break his heart. She knew that she loved him but, that was the reason she had to let him go. She couldn't live a life knowing that she had clipped his wings. She still had to put herself back together, and that was something she had to do alone. She knew that she would probably never find a man like him again, and that realization caused her to battle the urge to call him. He was a one in a million and she was forced to just let him go. She hoped that he would find someone worthy of his impeccable qualities, a woman that was a diamond that never stopped shining. As much as Reese wanted to be a woman like that, she was afraid that she would never shine again.

"Reese Landon?" the high pitched voice called out like nails on a chalkboard.

"That's me," she stood up realizing that she barely remembered walking into the office.

"How are you feeling Ms. Landon?" The petite nurse asked.

"I'm fine." Reese said without emotion.

The nurse weighed her and took her blood pressure before leading them to the ultrasound room. Reese stared at the back of the nurses burgundy red hair.

"Okay, Ms. Landon—"

"Reese, please call me Reese."

"Oh, okay, Reese, we need you to get undressed. You can leave on your underwear and bra, and then put on the gown that's on the table. Once you lay down drape the cloth over your pelvic area, under your gown. Do you have any questions?"

"I think I got it, thanks."

"Okay, good luck!" her voice became higher with excitement causing Reese to internally cringe.

When the technician came into the room Reese immediately noticed her incredible beauty. She looked of Native American descent. Her hair was a waterfall of ebony that effortlessly fell around her face and all the way to her waist. Her dark eyes were large and alluring. Her olive skin was flawless, even against the florescent lighting.

"Hi, my name is Aiyana and I'm going to be your tech today." Even her voice was enticing, it was smooth like glass. "Are you ready to see your little one?" Reese could feel her anguish fade.

"Yes," her lips parted and widened across her face in excitement. With a deep breath she let go of her thoughts of Chad. "Let's do this."

Maggie sat up straight and raised her eyebrows when Reese flipped a switch and shoved down her grief. She was still devastated, however, she didn't want her feelings for Chad to ruin this incredible moment. So, she shoved them aside and put them on the shelf next to her unresolved damage from Alex, and left them there to collect dust.

The gel Aiyana dumped onto Reese's protruding belly was warm and it felt weird as she slid the ultrasound device around. The fluttering sound of the baby's heart beat filled the room and an overwhelming rush of love filled Reese's heart.

"Good strong heartbeat, that's wonderful." Aiyana settling the machine in place. "There's your baby." She pointed at the screen to reveal a face that was just perfectly round and the cutest black and white person Reese had ever seen.

"Oh my gosh! Mom, do you see it?"

"I do, sweetie," Maggie grabbed her hand and squeezed.

"Hi there, my love," Reese smiled with the sting ever present in her tired eyes.

Aiyana let the moment linger letting them watch this little miracle move and wiggle around, when suddenly the baby lifted its hand and wiggled its fingers.

"The baby just waved! Did you see that?" Reese exclaimed.

"I did!" Maggie covered her mouth.

"I even got a picture of it!" Aiyana chimed in, seemingly just as excited as they were.

"Awesome! I mean, I know it wasn't an intentional wave but, that was basically the cutest thing ever. My baby is a genius! It's waving in utero!" Reese laughed.

"Okay, ladies," Aiyana said a few moments later. "I'm going to move on. I have to take some measurements real quick. I'm going to move relatively quickly through this part, but I'll point everything out as we go."

"Okay," Reese wiped the tears that had built up in her eyes feeling thankful for the first time today she was shedding happy tears.

Aiyana worked her way through measuring the head, body, kidneys, limbs, and she stopped on the heart for several minutes to check the blood flow. She continually reassured Reese that everything looked perfect. They counted ten fingers and ten toes and the baby was unofficially given a good bill of health.

"Are you ready to find out the sex, Mama?"

Reese squeezed her mother's hand tightly. "Yes, we're ready," she smiled at Maggie and turned her undivided attention back to the monitor.

Aiyana moved the monitor around trying to get it positioned just right. She did it again and again, but the little one was not going to give up its biggest secret that easily.

"I think you've got a stubborn one on your hands here." Aiyana joked. "I'm going to push on your belly and see if we can get this little one to get into a better position."

"No problem," Reese said. "Shocker, it's gonna be stubborn, sounds about right." Reese laughed.

"Just remember, what goes around comes around. You gave me most of these gray hairs, sis, now it's your turn." Reese and Maggie chuckled while Aiyana continued to push on her belly.

"Here we go," she announced. "Do you see this right there?" She pointed to the screen.

"The lines?" Reese asked, feeling stupid for not knowing what that meant.

"Yup! It's a girl!" Aiyana announced.

"A girl? I'm having a girl?" Emotions flooded her body. "I'm having a daughter!" Tears of joy flowed freely from Reese and Maggie's eyes, and Reese was sure that even Aiyana got a little teary eyed. "Oh my goodness! Thank you so much!" Reese covered her mouth with her hand, overwhelmed with happiness. "A daughter," she whispered under her breath as she looked again at the screen with the biggest grin on her face.

Chapter 12

THE FOLLOWING MONTHS were filled with preparation for baby girl Landon to make her debut. Sophie continued to not speak to Reese or acknowledge the baby at all. Even when Maggie threw Reese a baby shower, Sophie refused to attend. So they all made the best of the day and Reese was surrounded by her friends and the family members that could make it. Penny and Emily helped Maggie plan and organize the games and decorations. Maggie ordered a beautiful cake from the local bakery welcoming the yet to be named baby girl to their family. Even Kyra and Jess flew out for the occasion.

All in all, the day was filled with happiness, laughter, and so many blessings, in spite of Sophie's absence. Reese felt beyond grateful to everyone who came because she had un-wrapped almost everything they needed for this little one. At the end of the baby shower she was left with so much advice that she found it hard to process it all, but she felt so blessed for all of the mother's willing to share what they had learned. It helped her feel at ease.

Reese's belly grew by leaps and bounds. She was taken off work around six months along due to the type of work she did and her history of scoliosis, her doctor felt that the curvature of the spine could possibly cause a significant injury when lifting patients. So Reese and Maggie spent their days preparing the baby's room, and running errands. Reese helped her mom around the house with as many chores as she could handle, and they grew even closer in their mother/daughter relationship during these months.

Reese still enjoyed her girl's nights out with Penny and Emily, but for the most part she spent her time with her mom. The baby moved more and more as the space in her uterus became limited. The three of them would stare in awe when they could see the outline of her foot push against Reese's stomach and then move across her belly. Reese joked about how she was convinced that one of these days this baby was going to eat her way out, just like in the movie, Aliens.

Reese sat next to her mom and dad in the pew at church. It was a Sunday morning she won't soon forget. She quietly sat there listening to the pastor preach about forgiveness, and thinking, *what a bunch of crap.* Suddenly she felt a sharp pain in her side. It was sharp enough to take her breath away. She grabbed her side and tried to hunch over, but that was even more painful, so she sat back against the cold hard pew. Maggie looked over at Reese grimacing in pain and trying to breathe through it.

"What's wrong?" Maggie whispered.

"I don't know. It's like she's stuck sideways in there or somethin'." Reese whispered back, talking through her teeth.

"I bet she's turning, you are almost thirty-nine weeks along now." Maggie felt Reese's stomach as Reese continued to quietly grunt in pain. Thankfully they had sat in the back row. "Oh yea, she's sideways alright. Just keep breathin', baby. Let's see if she can turn on her own."

Reese continued to quietly grunt for the next fifteen minutes as her baby slowly made her way through her flip. The sharp pains felt as if her stomach was tearing apart when a sudden release of pressure allowed Reese to fully exhale the breath she hadn't realized she was holding. The pain left as suddenly as it had come on, once she had flipped all the way around. The baby wiggled and moved continuously to finish the positioning for the birth. It was almost time to welcome this little girl into the world, but yet Reese couldn't decide on a name.

She flipped through a magazine and came across a picture of a little girl's room. It was decorated in pink and brown with the cutest little butterflies and on the wall was the little girl's name, Taylor. *That's cute for a girl. If I did Taylor, what would I do for her middle name?* Reese wanted it to mean something to her, *Jan is Mom's middle name and we could call her TJ for short, but Taylor Jan sucks.* She went through a few names and vetoed them all until she thought about Gran.

"Taylor Renee Landon," Reese smiled. "That's it, that's her name." She decided she would need to test it out, so she put on her best 'mom voice' and shouted, "Taylor Renee Landon, get your butt over here right now!" Her face lit up. *It's perfect.* Reese struggled to get up from the couch, feeling like a tortoise stuck on its back. "Mom?" she yelled toward the kitchen once she was finally standing.

"I'm out back with the chickens!" Reese barely heard Maggie yell from outside.

She headed for the back door, much slower than usual, but thankfully her height kept her from waddling like a duck as her stomach was about ready to pop. She yanked at the bottom of her maternity shirt, it was the last one she had that still fit enough to usually cover her large and wide belly. She lived in yoga pants, since she stopped trying to get her maternity jeans on. Yoga pants, stretchy dresses, and oversized shirts were the extent of her wardrobe, but she didn't care anymore. Although it was a brisk forty degrees some days, she remained in her flip flops simply because it was impossible to tie any of her shoes. It was slip on's or nothing at all.

"I think I decided on a name for the baby." Reese announced once she made it out the back door.

"Oh yea?" Maggie popped out from the chicken coop wearing a knitted apron she had made herself with pockets for collecting eggs. "Let's hear it!"

"Taylor Renee Landon," Reese clasped her hands and brought them up to her mouth. Her heart picked up speed waiting to hear Maggie's response.

"Awe, I love it! Is the Renee because that was Gran's middle name?"

"It is," Reese grinned from ear to ear, for her baby girl finally had a name.

"We can call her Tay-Rae for short!" Maggie said, causing Reese to stop in her tracks and look at her mom. "Or, we don't have to if ya don't like it."

"No, I love it, Mom! Tay-Rae," Reese chuckled, "It's perfect!" She went to walk away, but stopped and turned back to Maggie. "Thank you, Mom, for everything."

"Oh, you're very welcome, sis. Your father and I are happy to help you and Miss Tay-Rae out." They both smiled at the use of her name.

"Do you think that Sophie will ever come around again?"

"I'm sure she will, just as soon as she steps down off that high horse she's sittin' on. Just give her some time, sweetie. Sophie loves her family, and we will always love her no matter what happens. All we can do is pray that she will come back into our lives."

"I guess you're right." Not that Reese planned on talking to God any time soon, but she was not about to have that fight with Maggie. "Thanks, Mags," Reese smiled.

"You're welcome, Ree," Maggie laughed.

Chapter 13

FINALLY, IT WAS the morning of her last scheduled visit with Dr. Morris. Reese felt nervous, and yet, she was ready for this kid to finally vacate the premises. She had no idea how to be a mom but, what she did know, she was done baking the bundle of joy in her oven.

"I'm pretty sure you're good enough, seriously, get out already! What are you waiting for?" Reese tried to command her out. "Come on, Grampy will let you have one of his horses if you come out!" She tried bribing, still nothing.

Over the last couple of days she tried everything listed in the books to try inducing her labor, except sex. *You have to actually have a partner to have any kind of sex that's worth having.* Her heart sank thinking of Chad. She even did her best to drink Castor oil in orange Gatorade, but immediately puked it back up.

"I don't know if I'll ever drink orange Gatorade again." Reese's voice echoed in the toilet bowl to Penny who held back her hair.

"Honestly, I don't know that I will either." Penny made grunting sounds.

"You can leave if you need to. I really don't need to wear your puke on my back." Reese joked before dry heaving again.

"I'm just gonna turn my head, I'm good."

Reese tried eating spicy food to encourage labor. Unfortunately, it resulted in giving her the worst heartburn she'd ever had in her life. Luckily she didn't have to suffer alone because Emily and Penny ordered the same thing to be supportive.

"I gotta say, they were right, misery does love company!" Reese joked as the girls grumbled under their breath.

"Shut up," Penny huffed.

"Fuck you right now, bitch." Emily responded in typical Emily fashion, blunt and to the point.

In the midst of all of these, she exercised once a day as well, nothing seemed to get her baby to budge. She drank red raspberry leaf tea, nope, no baby. She ate figs and pineapples, which were the best food suggestions in her opinion; still nothing. Not even a blip on the baby radar.

The morning of her appointment, she sat on her bed in the best mediation stance she could get her legs into, and tried the last method she had found, relaxation. She sat, closed her eyes, and took some deep breaths. It wasn't long before she shifted her body around to try and get comfortable. *Nope, not there,* she moved again, *nope.*

"UGH!" Reese grunted in defiance. *If only I could get comfortable then maybe, just maybe I could relax!* "Just get out! Get out! GET OUT! GET OUT!" She threw her legs over the bed with heavy irritation. "Hmprh, its freakin' pointless, you ain't comin' until you wanna come. Yup, it's official, you're my kid." Reese patted her stomach in acceptance. "Guess I'll just be pregnant forever. It's fitting really," she spoke directly to Taylor. "I'm gonna carry you in there forever like whales do, and consequently I feel and look exactly like a whale. Thanks for that too by the way." Reese chuckled and shook her head at herself. *That's it, Mom of the Year, blame the baby.*

After getting ready, she and Maggie headed off to Dr. Morris's office. Reese was really hoping that he would have good news for her. Maybe her cervix would already be dilating, maybe she was in labor and just didn't know it, or maybe her baby just really liked it in there.

Once they checked in at the office, they weren't waiting very long before the petite nurse with the annoying voice called Reese's name. *I am NOT gonna miss this shit,* Reese thought to herself, plastering on a fake smile to hide her irritation and possible bleeding of ears. Reese knew the routine, but the annoying nurse explained it anyway.

"Yea, I got it, thanks." Reese couldn't take her voice any longer. Besides, she's in her third trimester. *Pregnant ladies get to be as mean as they want in their third trimester, right?*

The well-groomed Dr. Morris came through the door moments later.

"How are we feeling today, Reese?"

"Like shit," Reese bluntly answered. "I'm pretty sure she's boycotting being born."

"Well, I want to talk to you about possibly inducing you."

The whole room stopped and both Reese and Maggie looked bewildered at Dr. Morris.

"Why? Is something wrong?" Maggie asked.

"Is that really necessary? I mean, I want this baby out but, why induce so early? Tomorrow is my due date."

"It's not mandatory at this point, however, your blood pressure is higher than I'd like it to be."

Reese knew what that meant. Hypertension in pregnancy is never a good thing.

"What was it?" Reese asked.

"One forty-four over ninety-four, you're not preeclamptic at this point, however, I think that if we induce now, we can move this process along before your blood pressure increases. You know the risks of preeclampsia: stroke, seizures, heart attack, and you could very easily die from it or even your baby. That's just not a risk worth taking."

"No, you're right, it's not worth the risk, let's induce." Reese confidently said.

"With any luck you're going to become a mommy today." Dr. Morris smiled. "I'll call Labor and Delivery, and let them know that you're on your way.

"Oh, we are doing this right now?"

"Yes ma'am, right this very moment. My colleague Dr. Neely is here, she'll get you started and I'll meet you over there in just a bit."

"Okay," Reese suddenly felt like she was going to throw up as Dr. Morris left the room.

"Oh my goodness, this is exciting." Maggie did a quick and quite clap of her hands before turning around so Reese could get dressed.

"Yeah, but it's also a little scary."

"It's better to do this now than wait and have something go seriously wrong."

"I know, you're right," Reese agreed as she finished getting dressed. "You're good, Mom." Maggie turned around. "I mean,

I know the risks of waiting, but there are risks with inducing too."

"I'll be right next to you the whole time, sissy. I'll call Daddy in the car and have him grab the bag we packed and all the things we'll need, and he'll meet us at the hospital. Everything will be alright, Ree." Maggie kissed Reese on the cheek and tugged on her arm; the increase in the twang in her voice gave her away, she was scared too.

The ride over to the hospital felt like hours had passed while Reese stared out the window, lost in her own thoughts. *What if something goes wrong? Oh God, this is it, my vagina is gonna be ruined forever. How am I ever going to find anyone to love me after this? Ugh, is it shallow of me to even care about this? Most women don't seem to care then again, most women are married to men who are forced to love them and their vaginas, no matter what happened to it during labor. This is ridiculous, Reese, you're having a baby! This is supposed to be exciting... Then why can I only think about how much it's going to ruin me? I look like I got into a fight with a cat and it attacked my stomach—so many damn stretch marks this kid has given me! Now, I gotta push her out of my hoo-ha. Not to mention the fact that I have absolutely no idea what I'm doing. What if I traumatize her? What if she gets hurt on my watch? Everyone will judge me like, oh that poor stupid girl, she can't even care for a baby right. Oh gosh, what if MJ hears that I ruined my baby, she would have a freakin' field day with that one. What if I can't get her to sleep? What if she hates me? Is that possible? Can babies hate their mommy's for being irresponsible? Will she hate me for the choices I made to protect her? I hope that one day she will understand why I did what I did, and I hope that she believes me when I tell her about her dad. Oh shit, what if she tracks him down? Oh shit. I can't... I can't do that... I can't deal with that...*

"We're here!" Maggie announced pulling up to the hospital.

"Oh, that went really fast."

"Are you alright, Ree?" Maggie scrutinized Reese's weary face.

"Yea, Mama, I'm fine. I was just lost in my own thoughts there for a minute." Reese got out of the car. "Do you think Taylor will understand when she gets older?"

"Understand what, love?"

"Why I ran away from Alex," Reese cradled her belly in her arm. "Or do you think that she'll end up hating me forever?"

"Well, I honestly don't know, Ree... all we can do is pray she'll come to understand one day."

Pray, just the thought of the word made Reese angry. *I certainly won't be asking God for anything any time soon. He let me down, He handed me this life.* She huffed a sigh of irritation. As her pregnancy progressed, her anger with God grew. She never doubted the existence of God, for He had revealed himself to her long before life kicked her down. She knew that God was real; she was just infuriated with Him. She blamed Him for Alex and everything that transpired because of their relationship. It was never about not wanting Taylor, it was about wanting Taylor with a man capable of being a father to her. She wished so badly that God had allowed Chad to be her father, now Chad was gone, and that was just one more thing to hate Him for.

Reese situated herself on the bed in her pale blue gown that tied in the back. The nurses came in and got her hooked up to all of the monitors. They adjusted the elastic waist bands around her mountain of a stomach until they could hear the whooshing sound of Taylors heart beat loud and clear. They explained in far more detail than necessary that one band had a sensor to measure her contractions, and the other band had the sensor for the heartbeat so they could monitor the baby as her labor progressed.

A tall, thin, and rather distinguished looking woman walked into the room. Her mocha hair was slicked back into a tight bun at the base of her head. Her eyes were light blue, almost white, and commanded attention. She walked with a confidence that Reese desperately wanted back in her life, and only after rounding the bed, the woman finally looked up from her chart.

"Hi, Ms. Landon, I'm Dr. Neely, and I'll be starting your inducing today." Her voice was silky smooth, with not even the slightest twang to it.

"Dr. Morris told us that you'd be helping us out. You can call me Reese, by the way. Ms. Landon makes me feel, well, like my mom." She turned to Maggie, "no offense, Mom," she shot her a quick smile.

"You're lucky that you're havin' my grandbaby or I'd smack ya for that one." Maggie joked.

"I think you two just might be my favorite patient and family of the day." Dr. Neely gracefully chuckled. "Well, let's get the ball rolling, shall we?" Reese nodded her head. "First we are going to get an IV in you and we'll start what's called Pitocin. That should help to kick off the contractions. After the contractions have begun, we'll give your water some time to break on its own, but if it doesn't, I'll come back in and break it for you. That should actually kick your body into overload and really bring the contractions through. Do you guys have any questions?"

"Nope, I think you covered everything." Reese said with a smile. "Mom?'

"I think I'm good for now." Maggie agreed.

"Great," she gave a thumbs-up. "The nurses will be in shortly to get that medicine going for you. See you in a bit." With one last smile, she was gone.

Within a few minutes, Reese had an IV placed and Pitocin running rough her veins. She hardly felt a thing. *Maybe this won't be as bad as I thought.* She swallowed her fear of the pain that was surely headed her way and masked it with false confidence. *There's no turning back now.*

Time passed as slow as molasses, and still, her water had not broken on its own.

"So the nurses tell me that things are not progressing in here at all." Dr. Neely gracefully walked into the room, putting on a pair of latex gloves. "I think it might be time to break your water and kick this into overdrive."

"Sounds good," Reese anxiously agreed.

Shortly after Dr. Neely broke Reese's water it quickly amped up the velocity of her labor, just as she said it would. It wasn't long before Reese was clinched to the railing of the bed. Her fingers held so tightly that she lost feeling in them. Maggie tried to rub her back when the back labor started but, every time she touched Reese the pain increased unbearably.

"Mom, please stop," Reese pleaded.

"Ree, just let me–"

"No, Mom, don't." Reese grunted as another contraction took over her body.

"Let me just–"

"Maggie, don't freakin' touch me!" Reese snapped.

"I'm sorry," Maggie raised her hands in surrender.

"I'm sor—ugh, shit, another one."

"There's only a few seconds between each contraction for the last two minutes now. You've had seven contractions... hmm... that can't be right." Maggie walked over to the recorder and looked at the print out of Reese's contractions. "I'll be right back, sweetie."

"Kay," Reese pushed the words through her clinched teeth before hearing the door shut.

A moment later, the door opened and she heard the clicking of Dr. Neely's high heels on the floor.

"Reese, I'm going to turn your Pitocin down, it is up way too high." Reese could hear several beeps from the machine her IV was hooked up to. "It'll take a while for the contractions to slow down but, while I'm here, let me check to see how dilated you are." Reese rolled to her back, grunting through the pain of the back labor for a few awkward moments while Dr. Neely checked her cervix. "You're not even dilated to one." a hint of concern in her voice.

"Is everything okay?" Maggie asked.

"Well, this is her first baby—it might take a while for her body to start opening up. We usually don't do an epidural until you're dilated to at least a four but, since you've been enduring this for a while now, I'll call the anesthesiologist." Once again the clicking of her heels echoed through the room and out the door.

Sweat accumulated on Reese's brow. Her knuckles were white as a ghost. She gripped the bed rail to endure yet another contraction. It felt like an eternity before the door opened and a cart followed a woman into the room.

"Reese Landon?" A raspy voice asked.

"Yes, ma'am," Reese groaned.

"I'm Lilly, and I'm here to do your epidural."

"Oh thank God. Thankfully the contractions have slowed down a little bit." Reese grunted as another contraction came on, "but not much."

"Okay, breathe through this one, I'm going to get set up and we'll have you sit up right after your contraction so that I can get as much time in between as possible." Reese nodded her head, agreeing to Lilly's plan. "Is this print out accurate?"

"Yes ma'am it is." Maggie answered her.

"That's a lot of very hard contractions in a short amount of time!" Lilly sounded shocked. "This all makes a lot more sense now."

Reese could hear the rustling of paper and supplies being quickly moved around on a metal surface. She prayed it would be done soon so she could finally breathe. It felt as if someone was trying to rip her body in half every five to ten seconds. She was already exhausted as she white knuckled her way through another contraction. Two more contractions passed before Lilly was ready for her.

"Okay, it's done." Reese announced as she fought to pull her worn out body up off the bed.

Her arms quivered but, she managed to sit herself upright and swing her legs off the edge of the bed. She was facing the wall with her back to Lilly, just as she instructed her to do. Reese continued to follow Lilly's smoky voice and the orders she was giving her.

"Tuck your chin to your chest and lean over as far as you can."

Reese did as she was told, just in time for another contraction to cause most of the pain to shoot throughout the right side of her pelvis. She had visions of Tay-Rae thrashing around in there, wondering why Mommy was smashing her like that. *I'm sorry, sis, we're almost done...I hope.* Reese instinctively placed her hand on her belly, trying to calm Taylor the best she could.

"Got it in, now you're gonna feel a warm sensation as I start the medicine to numb you."

"Okay," Reese said, feeling the pain melt away. It felt as if someone was pouring hot butter down her spine and to her legs. "I didn't even feel you poke me." Reese laughed.

"You were a tad preoccupied."

"I feel so much better! Oh my God, thank you so much, Lilly!"

"You're welcome."

"No, I don't think that you understand. You're my freakin' hero right now!" Lilly chuckled at Reese's statement. "Seriously, I'm not a lesbian, but I could totally kiss you right now!"

Lilly and a nurse helped Reese lift her nonfunctioning legs up and into the bed before the nurse got a Foley catheter ready.

"You'd be surprised how often I hear that!" Lilly giggled with delight. "I've even had a few marriage proposals, in front of their husbands."

"I bet!" Reese chuckled.

"Well, Reese, good luck with everything, and congratulations!" Lilly exited with a smile.

"Thank you so much."

Shortly after the epidural was finished, Rusty and Trevor showed up at the hospital. They sat and visited with Reese and Maggie for about an hour.

"Ain't an epidural cheatin'?" teased Trevor.

145

"Cheatin'? Are you kiddin' me?" Defiance shot up within her. "Let's have a donkey kick ya in your balls a few times and let's see if you wanna "cheat" too!" Reese snapped.

"I was jokin' Ree." Trevor put his hands out in front of him in surrender.

"Well, it ain't funny."

Maggie smacked Trevor on the back of the head, "What the hell is wrong with you?"

"Sorry, ma'am."

"I ain't the one you need to be apologizein' to." Maggie put on her mom voice. It was something Reese hadn't heard in a long time.

"I'm sorry, Reese."

"It's okay, it's just, you weren't here, and you don't know how bad it was. I didn't ask for an epidural, they suggested it. I ain't no sissy."

"I know you ain't." Trevor got up and kissed Reese on the forehead. "I didn't mean nothin' by it, I promise."

"You're lucky that you're my favorite uncle." Reese smirked.

The boys headed out of the room when Dr. Neely came in to check Reese's cervix again. She pulled her limp body up in the bed, her legs felt like two tons of bricks that she couldn't move, no matter how hard she tried.

"You're fine like that, Reese."

Reese noticed an odd look on Dr. Neely's face when she was checking for longer than the other times, and concern swept through her like a gust of wind. *What if something is wrong,* Reese worried.

"Is everything okay, doc?" Reese asked as calmly as she could.

"Well, you're still not dilating. When I told you that you were at a one earlier that was being generous, it's more like a half."

"I'm not even at a one? After all of that, my cervix is still basically closed?"

"I'm sorry, Reese, it looks like this is going to be a very long labor."

"Ugh!" Reese grunted.

Hours went by. The boys had left and came back a few more times before making themselves comfortable in the waiting room. Contraction after contraction, still numbed by the epidural, there was still zero progression. With each passing check of her cervix, Dr. Neely appeared to hide her concern less and less. Reese felt worried with one thought running through her head, *don't ignore it.* Over and over it played in her mind.

Nineteen hours in, and still zero progression, Dr. Neely continued to tell them not to worry but, her body language screamed that even she was feeling panicked. She pulled her phone from her pocket as the door to the room closed behind her.

"Do you think something is wrong, Mom?" *Don't ignore it.*

"I honestly don't know, love. When I had Sophie, my labor lasted thirty-six hours, and with you it lasted twenty-eight, but you're not even dilating. That doesn't sound right to me."

Don't ignore it, "Me either." Reese ever so slightly winced with a quick sharp pain.

"What's wrong?"

"I think that contraction broke its way through the epidural."

Reese pushed the button on the machine to deliver a little extra, just as Lilly had told her to do.

Another hour went by before they heard a knock at the door. When the door opened, it was Dr. Morris who came walking through.

"Dr. Morris, no offense but, you have gotten much uglier since I saw you an hour ago." Reese joked, trying to distract herself from her own terrifying thoughts.

"Ha, ha," he chuckled. "So, I hear, you're not progressing very well."

"That's what she tells me." Reese absentmindedly bit her bottom lip. "Is everything okay? I feel like after this long I should be progressing at least a centimeter or two!"

"Well, every woman is different, which makes this very difficult. Although, I am surprised, we usually see this slow of progression in a more petite woman. No offense, Reese, but you are tall and you're hips should be able to withstand childbirth without issues like these." He casually ran his fingers through his salt and pepper hair, furrowing his brow as he read her chart. "Let's just give it some more time."

"Are you sure? I can't really explain it but, I just have this gut wrenching feeling that something is wrong."

"Well, you're a paramedic, so you're used to seeing the one in a million type calls. You're used to being a part of some of the most horrific moments in people's lives but, you've never gone through labor before, trust me, you're fine."

Dr. Morris left the room, his words didn't put Reese's mind at ease. No sense of calm. If anything, the voice in her head got louder, *don't ignore it.*

Time carried on and it wasn't long before that sporadic tinge in her right side came back. It was so faint that at first she chalked it up to gas, but with each contraction it became more and more predominant. This time, Reese chose to not push the button for extra medicine to numb the pain, she decided maybe it was best to see how it played out on its own. The feeling something was wrong continued to grow stronger with each passing minute.

It wasn't long before the consistent pain in her side had increased ten-fold. Reese was once again on her left side, with her fingers numb around the bed rail. Sweat poured from her forehead.

"Mom, something's wrong, I'm telling you, something is wrong!"

"I agree I'll be right back."

Maggie left Reese's side and in less than a minute she was back with a doe-eyed nurse who looked like it was her first day, maybe second at best. Her brown eyes were as big as saucers when she saw Reese hunched to the side, drenched in sweat, and trying to fight back the tears that poured down her face.

"Is everything okay?" her lips quivered when she spoke.

"Does everything look okay?" Reese snapped through her teeth. "Get Dr. Morris, now!" She demanded.

If the doe-eyed girl said anything Reese couldn't hear her over the screech of her shoes on the floor when she took off running for the door. It was a few moments later when Dr. Morris calmly walked into the room, a look of confusion came over his face when he noticed the full extent of the situation.

"What happened?" He asked.

"I told you something is wrong." Reese forced the words out. "The right side of my pelvis, it feels like its breaking."

"Well, everything has to–"

149

"No!" Reese cut him off. "My pelvis opening up would not be so painful that the epidural no longer works!"

"I'm sorry, Reese, but how would you know? You've never had a baby."

"Have you?" Reese snapped back. "I'm telling you that something is wrong, it's my body, it's my baby, why won't you listen? Take her out, take her out right now!" she demanded.

"Reese—"

"Dr. Morris," a stern voice cut into the argument. "You need to look at this."

"What is it?" Reese could hear him snap the paper from her hands.

"D-cells," the woman tried to whisper so that Reese wouldn't hear.

"I told you, doc, are you gonna listen now?" Reese laid back and felt dizzy. "Mom?" she reached her hands out to feel for Maggie.

"I'm here sweetie, I'm right here."

Reese felt Maggie's cold hand slip into hers as darkness began to close in around her. The voices of those in the room became a blur and quickly faded out, until there was nothing but black and silence.

Chapter 14

THE DARKNESS REMAINED as Reese heard the faint sound of repetitive beeping. *What is that?* Although she tried, she could not speak. The world around her was lost in a sea of black—she was trapped, unable to move, unable to see. She heard the faint muffle of people talking, as if she was in a trance and the conversation was in the room next to hers. It was as if black paper thin walls surrounded her, separating her from the world around her.

Slowly the muffles became more distinct, and she could make out the occasional words, "stable for now", and "not out of the woods yet." Reese felt stuck in a nightmare that she couldn't force herself to wake up from. Wake up, Reese! Wake up! Please, just wake up! It seemed the harder she fought, the less she could understand the world around her. She struggled to make sense of everything. Is that sobbing? She heard the distinct sniffling of someone crying.

"She'll be okay. She's got to be okay..."

Mom, is that you? Is Dad here too?

"She's a strong woman, Mags, she won't give up." The smooth calm voice of Rusty sent ripples of hope throughout Reese's body.

Taylor? Where's Taylor? Wake up, Reese! You have to wake up and find Taylor! Oh God, what if something happened to her! Oh God, no, please, no. The world around her quickly dissipated and she was once again swallowed by darkness.

What felt like seconds later the beeping had returned, this time it was louder, and much more annoying. Reese felt the tips of her fingers move. She tried opening her eyes but, they felt like someone had super glued them shut. She continued to try and slowly they started to break free, and before long she opened her eyes. The first thing she saw was Maggie's relieved face shoot over the top of her.

"Reese?" Maggie quickly turned her head. "Rusty! She's wakin' up! Get the nurse and get in here!" Maggie flashed back into view. "Reese? Can you hear me?"

Reese tried to talk but she couldn't get out more than a few low grumbles. *My throat's on fire.*

"Mags, I'm here, the nurse is comin'. How's she doin'?" Rusty's face joined Maggie's over the top of Reese. "Ree, it's Dad, can ya hear me?"

Reese still couldn't muster up the energy for words. *Where's Taylor?* She heard the quick shuffling of feet enter the room. It sounded oddly close to a herd of elephants wearing tennis shoes as they rounded the bed.

Dr. Morris' face shot into view. "Reese, nod your head if you can hear me." Reese was barely able to move but, she was able to nod enough that he knew she could hear him. "You gave us quite the scare there." *Good,* she thought. "I'll explain everything to you when you have more strength, just rest for now." *Taylor, tell me about Taylor!* Her mind pleaded with her to speak. "We'll be back to check on you shortly. Take your time. Just promise me you'll take it easy, you lost a lot of blood."

What the—? How did I loose blood? What the hell happened? Why is no one telling me about my daughter? Anger boiled just enough under the surface.

"Wait," a crackled and weak voice fell from her lips. "Taylor," was all she could get out.

"We'll talk when you're able." Dr. Morris tried to leave.

"No, now," she quietly demanded.

"Okay," he turned around and walked back to her bed and his face came back into view. "There were some complications, she's currently doing great but, she'll need to be monitored in the NICU for a while, just to make sure that she's okay."

"When can..." her voice trailed off, she tried to force the words, but she wasn't able to.

"When you're strong enough, you can see her; you need to rest. Don't worry, she's not alone."

Dr. Morris walked away and Reese drifted off to the clicking of his dress shoes on the floor.

The next time her eyes popped open with ease, she was able to move her arms and legs much easier than before. She turned her head to see Chad asleep in the chair next to her bed. *Chad? What the hell is he doing here?* She looked around the room and noticed Kyra curled up in another chair, and Stump who was standing at the foot of her bed.

"Hey, kiddo," he softly said, "how ya feelin'?"

"I'm..." Reese stopped to clear the mucus from her throat, causing the others to stir. "I'm okay. I feel a lot better now."

Her voice was still raspy but, it sounded much stronger than before. "When did y'all get here?" She sat herself up in bed.

"About two this mornin'," Stump took a sip of the coffee he held in his hand, and he looked up at her, wide eyed. "This doesn't bother you anymore, right?"

Reese was able to muster up a faint chuckle, "No, you're good. Actually, that smells really good, can I have some?"

"Sure," he handed her his cup.

She took her first sip of bold coffee in what felt like forever. The steam tickled her nose when she inhaled the aroma. The warm feeling trickled down her throat and into her stomach. It was black with just a hint of sugar in it, and although Reese would've loved to have some flavored creamer in there, she thoroughly enjoyed the full flavor of the rich roast.

"Mmm... God I've missed you." She looked directly into the cup with a smile, before enjoying another sip. "Here, take this from me, before I drink it too fast and throw up or somethin'."

"We saw enough of that back at twenty-three, we don't need anymore." Stump chuckled.

Reese stuck out her tongue.

"You gave us quite the scare, kid."

"I don't even know what happened. Dr. Morris refused to tell me." Her voice was less scratchy after the coffee.

"Well, we all wouldn't be here if it hadn't been bad. You've pretty much been out for forty-eight hours."

Reese was taken aback but, she would eventually get to the bottom of what happened and hear the details soon enough. She had lost forty-eight hours of her life, and she had the good sense to know she was lucky to be alive. But, all she wanted in the moment was her daughter by her side. She wanted to hold her, and see her face for the first time. She hasn't even touched her or kissed her or told her it was going to be okay. She missed her, which was an incredibly weird feeling to have. She missed a child that she had never technically met but, one that she knew like the back of her hand.

She knew that every time Carrie Underwood would come on the radio, her daughter would dance. She knew that she always woke up in the womb at least once in the middle of the night to play the conga drums on Reese's insides. And she knew that she was already a thumb sucker because most of the ultrasound pictures Miss Taylor had a thumb in her mouth. Reese couldn't keep thinking about Taylor, or she would go insane. She needed a distraction.

"Why is Chad here?" She whispered to Stump.

"You're Mom called him, and he's the reason we are all here, actually."

"What do you mean?"

"Well, he told me what you did when he was here, dick move by the way but, we'll get back to that. He said that Maggie was in tears and all she kept saying was that something happened and that it was bad. She asked him to call us for her."

"First of all, I can explain my reasoning for what I did, and second of all..." Reese paused and let the defensive tone go. "I really am glad that all y'all are here."

"He said you might be pissed but, he didn't care." Stump nodded his head toward Chad, "explain."

"It's complicated, Stump. First of all, he lives in Auburn, and I live here now. He's the most amazing man that I've ever met but, distance never works, and I can't move back to Auburn, not with Alex there."

"That's not the reason." Stump folded his arms and stared at Reese, obviously not buying her story.

"That's the truth," Stump just stared, "I swear!" He refused to break eye contact with her. "Okay, fine... here's the real reason... He really is the most amazing man that I've ever met. He's thoughtful, and loyal, and funny. We have the most amazing time together, and he treats me the way I've always dreamed of being treated. He doesn't put up with my crap but, he also gives me space to be exactly who I am. And if I'm being honest here," she stopped to exhale. "I love him with all of my heart." She lovingly looked over at Chad.

"So what's the problem?"

"I don't want to bring him down. He's that one in a million guy, you know? He deserves a woman who is worthy of that, not some chewed up and damaged toy that comes with a boat load of baggage." Reese dropped her head.

"You are not chewed up and used." He said lowly, sadness quivered under his words.

"Yes I am, and all I want for him is to be happy."

"I understand that, but you can't choose his path to happiness for him, Reese."

"But—"

"No, but's, that's his choice to make. By all means, if this is how you feel then you need to back off from dating each other right now but, don't close that door. You two are perfect for each other. At least entertain the idea of being friends and keeping the possibility open."

"How did you get so wise? Is it because you're ancient?" Reese tried to divert the conversation with a joke; Stump just stared at her.

"I'm serious, Reese."

"I know... I'll fix it, I promise."

A knock at the door startled Chad and Kyra awake. Before they had time to say a word, Dr. Morris, and a woman in an expensive looking pant suit walked in.

"Good morning, Reese, I'm glad that you're awake."

"Cut the crap, Morris, what the hell happened?" Reese demanded answers.

The door opened once again when her parents walked into the room, followed by Penny and Emily. Reese was surrounded by people she loved and she felt more determined than ever to find out the truth.

"Reese, I would first like to apologize on behalf of myself and Northwest Medical Center. What happened was something that we couldn't've predicted."

"Let me guess, I was right, and something was in fact wrong."

"Yes."

"Spill it, and I want to know every detail."

"Well, just before you passed out, Tami, the nurse in the room, pointed out that the baby's heart rate kept dropping with every contraction. Your blood pressure dropped to seventy over thirty-six. We rushed you down to the O.R., and once we got you open we realized what had happened. Your baby hadn't flipped all the way around, so the reason that you weren't progressing was because she was trying to come out of the opening of your hip rather than the birth canal." Reese's heart picked up its pace. "In the midst of her head being wedged in the opening of your hip, your uterus tore little by little with every contraction. When you passed out, it was because you had already lost so much blood that your blood pressure dropped rapidly." Reese stared wide eyed at Dr. Morris when a warm hand slipped into hers, and she looked up at Chad and squeezed his hand. "We were able to repair your uterus wall. As for Taylor, everything appears to be perfect at this time. We've run some tests, and at this point it doesn't appear that she was damaged in any way during the incident."

"Will I be able to have more kids in the future?"

"Yes, there shouldn't be any complications down the road."

"And what if Taylor does have damage, what then? I mean, we both almost died because you wouldn't listen to me."

"We here at Northwest would like to reassure you that Taylor is doing fine." The woman in the overpriced suit spoke.

"With all due respect, ma'am, I wasn't talking to you." Reese stared at her stone cold face and golden blonde hair that was slicked back into a low ponytail.

"Ms. Landon," she continued, "I am the lawyer for this hospital, and I'm here to ensure that we try to find a compromise in every situation."

"I'm sorry did you say compromise? He almost killed me and my daughter, and all you want is to solve this right here and now?" Reese stared at the lawyer with fire raging in her eyes and pure disbelief on her face. "I want to see my daughter, now."

"We really need–"

"I don't give a shit. I haven't even held my daughter yet because of Dr. Morris and his ignorance. This meeting is over. Please have someone either take me to her, or bring her to me."

"Yes, Ma'am," the lawyer retreated out of the room with Dr. Morris.

Chad turned his full attention to Reese, "Are you doing okay?"

She looked up at him with sadness in her heart for how things ended with them. Stump was right, she could've handled it better than she did, and maybe she needed to keep the possibility of a friendship on the table. After all, he did just fly a few thousand miles to be by her side.

"I–" she felt at a loss for words. "I'm okay, thank you." She squeezed his hand, "Thank you for coming... I'm glad that you're here."

"There was no way I wasn't coming. You almost died, Reese." He gently brushed the hair from her face.

For a brief moment, Reese had forgotten about the room full of people surrounding them. When she looked up and noticed that everyone was trying to give them some space but, that's not possible in a tiny hospital room.

"I know." She said shyly, quickly changing the subject. "... Can someone find a nurse, and make sure they're bringing my baby, please."

"I'll go check," Kyra announced and promptly left the room.

Moments later, the door swung open, and a nurse followed behind the portable bassinet wheeled in the clear plastic bucket that held the most precious thing in Reese's life, her daughter. She looked absolutely perfect as she peacefully slept. Her body was wrapped in a cocoon of blankets and her head covered in the tiniest beanie Reese had ever seen. The nurses made a bow out of a second beanie so Taylor had a bow the size of her head attached to her hat. Her thin little lips pursed together in her sleep. For the first time in a long time, Reese didn't fight the sting in her eyes and embraced the happiness in her tears. Her broken and damaged heart was filled with more love than she knew what to do with.

"Hi, my love, I'm your Mommy." Reese gently stroked her finger across Taylor's puffy cheeks. "I've been waiting for so long to meet you." Tears broke free and down her face as happiness swirled around within her. "I'm so happy that you're okay."

"I'll get her out of there for you. The doctor doesn't want you getting up quite yet." Maggie ever so gently reached in and pulled Taylor out and handed her to Reese.

Before this moment, Reese was worried about not knowing what to do, or how to hold Taylor. She didn't want to be the only mother in the world who felt at a loss on how to hold her own child. The fear had grown by leaps and bounds as her due date approached; all of those fears seemed to melt away and drift into distant memories as Reese embraced the new found love she had for this newborn baby girl. Reese confidently reached her arms out and cradled her daughter in her arms for the very first time.

The rest of the room faded away and her world finally felt complete. She gazed upon her daughter's perfect face. Reese's eyes danced with overwhelming joy as her body naturally conformed to Taylor's. It was a beautiful thing. *How is it, something so sweet and so innocent can come from such a dark past?* Right then, a perfect child brought happiness to a broken mother and filled the void she had been missing.

Chapter 15

THE NEXT FEW days quickly passed as Reese entertained a parade of visitors from her hospital room. In no time at all she was able to get up out of bed, taking the most rejuvenating shower she had ever had, all on her own. *Sponge baths just don't feel this good.* She relished in the hot water cascading down her body. It was finally her last day in the hospital and by nine the following morning she and Taylor would be released to go home. She had spent a total of seven days in the hospital and she was more than ready to go home to start her new life.

Reese had even come to an agreement with the hospital; the entirety of her hospital bill would be compensated to make up for the mistakes that were made, and she had an open invitation to come back if any developmental problems came to light with Taylor. Reese felt that she could've easily won in a lawsuit against Dr. Morris and Northwest Medical Center but, it wasn't worth the fight. She got a sincere apology and her bill taken care of. The only thing she really hoped was in the future, if another woman were in her same position, they would be willing to listen to a mother when she's telling them something is wrong.

Before Reese left the hospital, Dr. Neely had come into her room offering an apology and an explanation. Dr. Neely explained, due to the multiple times, over a short span of several hours, she had called Dr. Morris to alert him of Reese's decline in health, to no avail; despite Dr. Neely determining Reese needed surgery immediately after seeing her blood work. Dr. Morris had brushed her off and stated he would speak to their supervisor if she continued to get in his way, "preventing patient care," was how he explained it. Dr. Neely wasn't present during the birth and after care of Reese and her daughter because she wasn't allowed to enter the room to help Dr. Morris. After things went really south with Reese and the risk of death due to negligence had become apparent, Dr. Neely turned in her resignation. She had decided to work in another hospital; Dr. Neely didn't want to be associated with a hospital and staff that commonly and very blatantly ignored patients. Moreover, she didn't want colleges who made it a point to ignore symptoms or diagnosis' if they didn't come up with it themselves first; she'd be damned before she worked with another doctor willing to put pride before a patient.

Everything had been settled and after the last night in the hospital, it would finally be time to go home and adjust to the new normal.

Taylor was proving to be one of the best babies ever. She was extremely content and happy as could be in her blanket cocoon. She would routinely get up like clockwork at three in the morning, every morning ready for a change and to be fed. Luckily, she would eat, and go right back to sleep. Reese was in love with her perfect bundle of joy, and she felt like the words "I love you" were inadequate to how she truly felt. Her whole world had shifted the moment she looked into Taylor's eyes.

The crew from Auburn had used up all of their vacation time and had to leave. They came in one by one and said their good-byes. Reese was convinced that Stump had orchestrated this whole thing so she and Chad would have a moment together before he had to get on a plane and leave. Kyra and Stump each took their turns holding Taylor before they gave Reese long lasting hugs and the tears shared among them were bitter sweet.

When Chad was the last one to say good bye, Reese didn't know if she was truly ready. She knew Stump was right, the way she handled things before was all wrong. There was a faint knock at the door, before it creaked slightly open.

"Reese?" she could recognize Chad's voice anywhere.

"Come on in, Chad." She smiled through the nerves that had taken over her body.

Taylor lay fast asleep next to her in her bassinet, and Reese quickly adjusted her messy bun the best she could. She knew that she looked terrible but, there wasn't enough time to get cute as Chad walked into the room. He looked handsome as he smiled at her, holding a bouquet of Sunflowers.

"Awe, those are beautiful." Reese smiled.

She had chosen them to be her new favorite flower—Alex had ruined lilies for her forever. She never wanted to receive lilies from another man as long as she lived, and she vaguely remembered telling Chad sunflowers were her favorite the day before she tore his heart right out of his chest. Heartbreak fluttered through her body.

"You think? I got them for the woman down the hall." Chad smirked and laughed when Reese raised her eyebrows and turned her eyes into lie detectors. "Of course they are for you." He leaned over and kissed her on the cheek before laying the flowers on her tray. "You look absolutely beautiful, Reese. Motherhood suits you quite nicely." He smiled his lovingly beautiful smile.

"Thank you," she said lowering her eyes and putting her head down. "I need to talk to you for a second, if that's okay. I just want to explain before you leave and end up hating me down the road."

"Why would I hate you?" Chad looked bewildered.

"The way I ended things with us was..." her voice trailed off, trying to find the right words. "Well, it was bullshit, and I'm really sorry."

"You don't have to—"

"Yes I do," she cut him off. "You deserve..." her voice cracked, "the world Chad Platt. And I don't want to be the reason you don't get it." She wiped the single tear that slowly trickled down her face and grabbed his hand. "I need to fix myself before I can be the woman you deserve. Now, I don't know if you and I are meant to be together or not but, I do know I have never felt this way about anyone, ever. I love you so much, Chad but, I'm broken. My heart is a mess, and that's not fair to you."

Chad sat down by her side on the bed, and placed his other hand on top of hers.

"I love you too, Reese. I know you think you're saving me from something terrible but, all you're doing is keeping me from the life I so desperately want, a life with you and Taylor."

"I want that too but, I'm just not ready for it, not yet anyway..." Her voice was almost a whisper, trying hard to keep the damn of tears from breaking, "... can we just be friends for now?"

"Of course, Reese... all I want is for you to be happy."

They leaned into each other holding their foreheads together before Chad pulled himself away just enough to be able to focus on her face. They stared lovingly into each other's eyes, and Reese couldn't help herself. She pulled Chad toward her and kissed him deeply.

"Well, that was unexpected," he grinned

"Probably wasn't fair to you, I'm sorry." Reese looked to the ground.

"You don't have to apologize to me all the time, Reese."

"Oh, sorry..." she said quickly, "Geez, there I go again!" she huffed." Seriously though, I shouldn't have done that but, I just really miss your lips on mine." She faintly ran her fingertips across his lips. "Is it unfair to ask you to wait for me?"

"I'd already planned to," he softy pressed his lips into hers. "No rush, Reese. You work on you, and in time I have no doubt that things will work out."

They talked for a few more minutes and Chad kissed her one last time before leaving and heading back home to Auburn with Stump and Kyra.

Reese sat alone in her empty hospital room, just her and Taylor; her and her daughter against the world.

Reese was so lost in her loving gaze at Taylor she barely noticed the knock at the door. The wide door was slowly pushed open, catching Reese's full attention. She wasn't expecting anyone else for a while.

"Hello?" she called out, shifting herself in bed and wincing at the pain from her C-section.

"It's me," a voice called back.

"Emily?"

Her blonde hair was the first thing to enter the room, followed by a box of chocolates, and Reese happily accepted the company.

"Come on in, Em." Reese said with delight.

"Is she sleeping?" She whispered.

"Girl, she's always sleeping," they both laughed.

"You really scared us all, you know." Emily's voice trembled.

"I know, I'm sorry about that, I'm doing great now, and Taylor is perfect." Reese beamed as she looked down at Taylor.

"Well, thank God for that! I really like you, and I just don't know what I would do if you left me all high and dry like that!" Emily gushed out feelings in a way that Reese had never seen before. Emily was always so tough, crass, and incredibly confident, in this moment she seemed almost vulnerable. "So don't ever do that again, you crazy bitch." Emily wrapped her arms around Reese and Taylor, *ah, there's the Emily I know,* and Reese smiled.

"I'll do my best," Reese vowed.

"Oh," Emily pulled away quickly reaching for her purse. "This is from all of us at MedStar." She handed the box of chocolates over along with a card.

"Mmm, these look delicious, we'll hafta open them up here in a minute." Reese pulled the card and placed it on top of the chocolates. She opened it with ease, expecting it to be signed by Emily, Jerry, and maybe even Cheryl from the front office; never in a million years did she expect so many signatures.

Disbelief took over her face as she read the countless get-well-soon wishes. Reese was surprised to learn everyone she worked with at MedStar cared so much for the new girl. There were so many passages of care they had to sign the back of the card as well. "Wow," Reese said under her breath.

"You've made quite an impact on the people around here. Not just with your knowledge of this job but, with your undeniable charm. I know that you say you've been through hell and you wish you could go back to being the girl you used to be but, the girl that you've become is pretty great too, don't forget that. We all love you, Reese, and we're so happy you're okay." Reese had tears building up in her eyes, threatening to spill over when Emily waved her hands back and forth in front of her, drying the tears from her own eyes. "Okay, now that's enough of this mushy crap. Who the hell was the hottie that came out of your room before me?"

"Ah yes, that, my dear, was Officer Chad Platt himself."

"Damn, just damn."

"I know, right?" Reese laughed.

"I saw Kyra in the lobby, I kinda figured it was the infamous Chad, I had to make sure you weren't keeping hotties stock piled in your room or somethin'."

"Nope, no other hotties here!" Reese laughed; just the idea of it seemed ridiculous.

"Because," Emily continued, "if you were trying to keep them all for yourself and not share any with me, I'd have to smack ya!" Emily smacked her hands together one time as hard as she could, and they both burst out with laughter. "Seriously though, have you come to your senses about that boy yet?"

"Not you too," Reese shook her head. "Stump already lectured me about it." She looked down at her perfect little girl that still slept peacefully in her arms. "Stump was right, the way I handled things with him was crap but, I still stand behind why I did it. I'm broken, Em, no matter how much I want to deny it, I am. I just think I might be a little too broken to love Chad the way he deserves to be loved. Who knows what the future holds, trust me when I say, I hope my future contains that beautiful, sweet, lovable man. If it doesn't, I'll know I did right by him."

"I see your point, Reese, but now it's time for you to hear mine. Yes you're broken and damaged and scared, I know, I've been there! Being broken doesn't mean you deserve to be thrown out. When I was a kid, I had this cute little dollhouse. When the door would open it made creaking sounds, and when I pushed a button the husband would yell to his wife, 'Honey, I'm home!' I played with it so much and so often, I wore out the batteries on a regular basis. One day, it stopped working all together. My dad changed the batteries but, it still didn't work. He told me there was nothing he could do to fix it, and it was broken for good. To say I was devastated doesn't even come close to how I felt. I decided since it was broken, it was time to part ways, so I gathered up all of the pieces and went to dump them in the trash. Well, my little brother, Tommy, stopped me, and begged me to let him have it. I told him, there was no point in keeping it because it was broken. He begged me to let him keep it anyway, and so I finally caved. That little boy was so excited to have this broken toy. He jumped up and down thanking me like a million times. I wish I was kidding about that part but, I'm not, it was really annoying." Reese cracked a smile. "He ended up transforming the broken dollhouse headed for the trash, into a garage for his Hot Wheels cars. Do you see my point?"

Reese just looked at Emily, unsure of what she was getting at. *What does a dollhouse have to do with me?* She tried to come up with a plausible answer but, nothing instantly came to mind, she shrugged her shoulders instead.

"My point is you see yourself only as a broken dollhouse right now, to Chad, you're a shiny new garage. I know you think because Alex intentionally broke certain pieces of you, you'll never work right again but, maybe it's alright if you don't. Maybe those pieces had to be broken so you could stop being a dollhouse. Maybe you were always meant to be someone's garage."

"Holy shit, Em, that..." Reese's voice trailed off.

"That was crazy deep, right?" Emily puffed out her chest, pleased with her epiphany. "I say some pretty smart shit sometimes. You should really listen to me more often."

"Between you and Stump, I feel more confused than ever." Reese shook her head before stopping to look at her daughter. "Can I adjust to being a mother before we try tackling my love life?" She begged, "Please?" she said with a smile.

"Ugh, fine," Emily reluctantly agreed. "But you know I'm right, and I'm not gonna let you brush this under the rug forever."

"I would expect nothing less from you." Reese winked.

Chapter 16

THE NEXT DAY, Reese was finally able to take Taylor home. She bundled her in a beautiful cream colored sleeper that had pale purple flowers hanging from pale green vines. The print reminded her of Gran, and Reese felt pain in her heart knowing Taylor would never get to meet the woman who inspired Reese in so many ways. Taylor would never get to hear Gran's infectious laugh that brought a smile to everyone's face. She would never hear her loud southern voice yelling down the street that super was ready. Taylor would never get the opportunity to learn from a woman who rose above the hard times, and rolled with the punches life brought her way.

"Are y'all ready?" Maggie's voice pierced into Reese's memories. "Is our little Tay-Rae ready to come home?"

"I think so," Reese fought back the ache in her heart.

"Now, we've got a week to help you adjust before we take off on our trip."

"I still can't believe you're going to leave me with a new born baby all alone for a whole week, just so y'all can go on some vacation?" Reese packed her bag with her back to Maggie.

"Well, sis, there's no sense in gettin' mad over it again. This trip was planned a year and a half ago, and it's non-refundable. You'll be fine." Maggie sounded matter of fact.

"But what if I'm not, I mean, y'all are trustin' me an awful lot here, don't ya think?"

"Baby, you're this little ones mother. It's not about us trustin' you; it's about the fact she's yours."

"I'm not ready, Mama, I can't do this without you, not yet anyway."

Reese zipped up her overnight bag and turned around to face her mom. Her eyes were wide with fear at just the mere thought of doing the mom thing with a newborn on her own.

"Nonsense," Maggie waved off Reese's comment. "You'll be fine, you hear me?" Maggie placed her hands on Reese's shoulders. "The day you become a mother, God grants you a few 'mom privileges' so to speak. It'll take you some time to get them finely tuned but, you've got 'em, right here inside of you." She moved her hands to each side of Reese's face. "You'll know what to do, just breathe."

Reese took a deep breath in to help calm her nerves. "Not all of us trust God to take care of us, Mom." Reese exhaled.

"What exactly is that supposed to mean?" she said, clearly confused and skeptical.

"Look at the life I have right now, it's in shambles! God allowed me to get pregnant by a monster, no less! He allowed that man to father a child. How is God on my side?" Reese became defensive as her feelings she'd been holding in poured from her. "Maybe this is just God's way of punishing me for not following the rules, either way I didn't deserve a monster."

"Reese Elizabeth, you listen here, and you listen real well, missy. God did not do this to you. God did not make this happen, you did! Your choices led you to this life you have now. You chose to be with a monster. Although, you didn't deserve the things that he did to you, you chose to go back for one night which resulted in this beautiful little girl. You've been quietly blamin' God for all of your sins, and that needs to stop. You're not the victim here, Reese, you chose this path, whether you like it or not." Maggie tugged at the bottom of her shirt and stood up straight. "Now, I'm gonna go make sure that Daddy's got the car seat in the car correctly. You get that sweet baby ready." Maggie opened the door to walk out of the room, she paused a moment and turned to Reese one last time, her voice soft and less direct. "You should probably think about apologizing to God, more importantly, you need to learn to forgive yourself for the role you've played in the events that put you on this path. I cannot imagine what it must be like in your shoes, Ree, what I do know is you're here, and there's no turning back." Maggie looked down at Taylor, "... and what he's given you looks pretty darn perfect to me. I love you, sissy, you're wrong about Him." Her eyes met Reese's and without another word she walked out.

The door softly closed behind Maggie, leaving Reese to stare at the floor behind tear filled eyes. She looked at Taylor, who peacefully slept in the car seat that practically swallowed her whole. Reese never blamed Taylor for coming into existence but, she certainly spent the better half of a year blaming God for all she had endured.

"Is she right, Tay?" Reese skimmed the bridge of her nose with her knuckle, the same way Maggie used to do to her when she was a kid.

Reese stared at Taylor, her mind raced a hundred miles a minute thinking about what her mom had said. Realizing, no matter how much she didn't like it, Maggie was right. Reese hadn't taken full responsibility for the role she played in guiding her feet to this path. However, she still felt angry with God. She wasn't ready to let Him off the hook quite yet but, maybe she could find herself on the path towards forgiving herself. *I just hope one day, you can forgive me too.* Reese looked down at her daughter.

"Are you ready to go, Reesey-Piecey?" Rusty asked, bursting through the door without warning.

"Yup, we're all ready." Reese smiled when Rusty took the car seat out of her hands and looked at Maggie. "I'm sorry, Mama. You're right. I've been blamin' God rather than taking responsibility." She hugged Maggie tightly. "I'm not making any promises but, I'll work on forgiving myself and God." They released each other and smiled.

"That's all I ask, sis." Maggie wrapped her arms around Reese one last time. "I love you, ya little twerp."

It had been a long quiet car ride home. Reese felt odd sitting in the backseat of her own vehicle but, she also didn't want to leave Taylor in the back seat alone. Dust flew off the back wheels of the car as they turned down the driveway approaching the house.

"Is that Sophie's car?" Reese asked a small ray of excitement in her voice.

"Looks like it." Maggie said, less excited and more skeptical.

Reese got out of the car and stepped back so Rusty could pull the car seat out of the car for her, because she wasn't able to yet. Reese wasn't allowed to lift over ten pounds for six weeks after her surgery, and even though she wasn't thrilled about it, her parents wouldn't let her lift a finger.

Once Rusty pulled the baby from the car, Reese took the car seat out of his hands.

"I got her, Dad. I want to be the one to carry her in the house for the first time."

"Just be careful, Ree, you don't wanna rip your stitches."

"I will, Daddy, I promise." Reese kissed him on the cheek and turned on her heel, heading toward the house. "Soph?" Reese called out, there was no answer. "Sophie? Come meet your niece!" Reese slowly walked up the five treacherous steps. Pre-surgery, these same steps were a piece of cake, even at nine months pregnant. Post-surgery, they were her Everest. Reese finally reached the front door, and pushed it open. "Soph?" Reese looked up to see her coming down the hallway. "Do you wanna meet your niece? This is Tay—"

Sophie walked right by Reese, as if she wasn't standing there. She ignored the very existence of her sister and her niece. Reese felt like an unwelcomed guest in her own home. Her heart filled with rage, appalled that her own sister would dismiss her child like that. *Who in the hell does she think she is?* Reese stewed in her thoughts. *I would never do that to her! You know what? I'm not going to allow her to ruin this incredible day. Screw her and the high horse she rode in on.* Reese took several steps forward and set her daughter on the dining room table.

She carefully unfastened the seat belts that hugged Taylor keeping her in place, and untangled both arms before pulling her out of the seat. Taylor bent her arms and arched her back, contorting her tiny lanky body into a reverse C. Reese didn't think she could love this little blessing any more than she already did, with each passing adorable moment, she fell that much deeper into the trance Taylor put her in. Every time she looked at her, Alex and her past no longer existed. She felt more put together than she had in a long time just staring at her daughter's beautiful face. *Her eyelashes are so long,* Reese examined Taylor, thankful that the marks on her head had already faded so much she couldn't even tell they were there anymore.

"I don't care what anyone thinks, you are the most special baby in the world." Reese bent over and gently kissed her button nose. "Did I ever tell you you're a God send?" Reese slowly walked around the dining room and into the living room. "There's only a small window every month a woman has to get pregnant in, and my small window had long past. My body created two windows in one month, which is something it's never done before. That's why I was so angry at God. I know He has a plan for you, sweet girl, I just hope that I can protect you in the meantime." Her finger tips grazed Taylor's puffy cheeks. "I hope you know I tried to do right by you. I've always tried to do right by you. I hope one day, when you get older, you can see that. You're my whole world, and I gotta say, I'm kinda startin' to understand His plan. All I've ever wanted was unconditional love, and God gave me just that." Reese peered at her daughter through tear-filled eyes before kissing her on the forehead. She softly sang, "As the Deer," the same way her Mom used to when she was a baby.

Chapter 17

THE FIRST WEEK home with Taylor went better than Reese expected. She expected to feel like she'd been blindsided by a freight train, instead, she was managing quite well. Taylor was proving to be the absolute easiest baby around. She slept the majority of the time and when she did wake up, she would eat, stay awake for a bit, and right back to sleep she would go. At night she would go down at ten, wake up at three, and sleep again until seven in the morning. *I've had worse shifts at work than this.* She laid her back down in her crib at three-fifteen sharp. *This kid doesn't mess around. Let me eat so I can go back to sleep.* Reese smiled.

The next morning Reese got up before Taylor did. She shuffled down the hallway, still trying to fully wake up when she noticed the suitcases sitting at the door.

"It's not too late to change your mind, you know."

"Ree, you're gonna be fine. That is the easiest baby I've ever seen."

"But what if—"

"You'll be fine."

"But, what happens if—"

"Reese," Maggie looked at her with the up most certainty. "Women have been suffering the same growing pains for centuries as they've adjust to motherhood. You'll be fine!"

"Okay," Reese meekly said.

It wasn't long before Maggie and Rusty said their good-bye's to Reese and Taylor and whisked away on their glorious vacation, leaving Reese to "suffer the growing pains" alone. *This is a terrible idea.* Reese looked down at the tiny bundle in her arms with her eyes wide and fearful. With a slow deep breath she told herself, *I got this,* she wasn't sure she actually believed it.

"Well Tay-Tay, I'm gonna say as long as no one dies, this will be a success. That's called setting our bar incredibly low, so we have a better chance to succeed." Reese laughed at herself. "We got this, kiddo. You and me, against the world, right?" She paused as if she was waiting for Taylor to actually respond. "Right, Mom," Reese's voice was high pitched and squeaky as she spoke on Taylor's behalf. "Plus, you're the best mom ever! This is gonna be so much fun!" Reese gasped and placed her free hand over her chest. "Well, bless your heart, aren't you just the best baby in the whole wide world."

With a final chuckle, Reese went about her morning. Grabbing the bouncer off the dining room table she carried it with them into the kitchen.

"Coffee, Tay-Rae, coffee is liquid gold. Learn it. Love it. Make your peace with it." Reese set the bouncer on the counter next to the coffee maker and strapped her into it, like she had been doing it for years. "There ya go, see we got this, we're gonna be fine."

Taylor slept while Reese tried to convince herself she had the whole mom thing under control. She drew a deep breath in, enjoying the aroma of freshly brewed coffee while patiently waiting for her K-cup to finish. Reese was one of the lucky mothers, she hadn't been up all night with a screaming baby, after all, she had her mom to help her any time she needed. They tag-teamed the three a.m. feedings and even Rusty was caught sleeping with Taylor on his chest. Reese didn't feel that impending demand for coffee. She felt functional, and maybe a little entitled to being well-rested.

Taylor and Reese went about their day. She enjoyed her coffee and zoning out on the television while her baby slept. Taylor would wake up hungry, Reese would feed her, but for some reason, Taylor kept falling asleep after half of her bottle. *She must be really tired.* Shrugging her shoulders she laid Taylor back down into the bassinet. Reese got up and loaded clothes into the washer and washed her dishes from the coffee and cereal she had for breakfast.

Lunch time was still a ways off when Taylor began crying again. *That's odd, she's waking up two hours before she normally does.* Once again, Reese shrugged her shoulders, and tended to her newborn baby. Taylor again fell asleep halfway through her bottle. *Am I doing something wrong?* Reese tried to tickle her. *I've seen Mom do this a few times,* Taylor didn't budge. Reese moved on to gently blowing in her face and softly poking her cheeks. Still nothing, *great...* Reese laid her down in her bassinet so she could grab some lunch.

She made a quick sandwich and grabbed a handful of potato chips from the pantry, and sat down on the couch next to the bassinet. As she took her first bite, Taylor ever so slightly started crying again.

"What's wrong?" she asked knowing she wouldn't get a clear answer. "Are you hungry again?" Reese changed her diaper before making another small bottle with formula. Taylor fell fast asleep about thirty seconds after getting the bottle in her mouth. "Seriously?" Reese huffed, unsure what to do.

She went back to her sandwich after laying Taylor back down, after a few bites, Taylor fussed once again.

"Uuugghh," Reese groaned.

Grabbing the bottle she scooped up Taylor with frustration pouring over her. She took a breath and placed the bottle back into Taylor's mouth. Once again, Taylor was back out within a minute.

"Why are you doing this to me?" She pleaded.

The rest of the day moved like molasses, with the struggle the same. Taylor wouldn't eat much before falling back asleep. It wasn't long before the sun fell and darkness enveloped the world around them. Reese felt exhausted. She was ready for this day of motherhood to be over. *I don't understand what I'm doing wrong.* Reese questioned as she changed her diaper and clothes. *It's nine, one more hour and hopefully you'll sleep until three like you always do.* Reese tried feeding her one last time but, after only a quarter of her bottle, Taylor was fast asleep. *Thank God,* Reese laid her in the bassinet she moved next to her bed.

As quietly as possible, she crawled into bed allowing the softness of her mattress to swallow her whole. She shut her eyes and was blissfully asleep within minutes. Everything remained dark and finally quiet.

Nooooo, Reese cried to herself when Taylor cried out. It wasn't a whimper this time, but a full on cry. Reese tried to rock the bassinet back and forth in hopes that the motion would put her back to sleep, with no such luck. Taylor continued to cry, projecting her sound louder and louder with each breath. *Damn it,* Reese huffed, throwing the covers off of her and turning on the light.

"Why are you crying?" Reese's voice sounded like she wanted to cry.

She was so tired that she could almost taste the tears she was choking back. *It's only eleven? Are you kidding me?* Reese stared at the clock as if she was anticipating it to jump up and say, "Sike! Just kidding!" Scooping up Taylor she paced around the moonlight room. There was a chill in the air, leaving Reese to wonder if Taylor was warm enough. She headed down the hall and changed her into a warmer sleeper, unfortunately, it didn't do any good.

"I'm not sure what you want. Are you hungry, again?" Taylor's blood-curdling screams now echoed throughout the entire house. "Okay, okay, I'll feed you for the thirtieth time today."

Frustration and exhaustion was setting in, Reese was in clear denial of what her night had in store for her. She made a bottle as fast as she could while Taylor screamed at maximum capacity.

"Okay, shhhh, Okay, here you go," Reese tried to calm her as she shoved the bottle in her mouth. Taylor latched on to the bottle like a shark grabbing its prey. She drank the formula as fast as she possibly could—as if she hadn't eaten in days. "I think it's safe to say you were hungry! We'll get the hang of this, baby girl," Reese felt a sense of calm knowing she had finally gotten something right today.

Unfortunately, once Taylor was full, burped, and dry, she was wide awake and ready to party. Reese tried to rock her, she tried to sing to her, she even tried walking the layout of the house in hopes that Taylor would get sleepy. Reese sat in the chair and put on Baby Einstein videos her mom had. Reese fought exhaustion while Taylor remained mesmerized by the colors on the television.

A few hours and another feeding later, Taylor was fast asleep as dusk rose outside. Reese's eyes burned with sleepiness. She laid Taylor down and fell into her bed and the abyss of a dreamless sleep. Her brain was too tired to organize subliminal messages, let alone some random moment in time. Maybe she dreamed of sleeping and that's why it was so peaceful. It's just too bad it couldn't last longer.

Two hours later, Taylor was once again crying and grunting. Reese made subtle forced pouting noises of her own before sitting up. *Whyyyy?* Reese got up and could smell exactly why. Shuffling her feet down the hall she changed her diaper, again. Reese could hear the pitter patter of rain falling on the roof. Rain was common for Texas in January. Thunderstorms would typically roll in one after another. Reese was thankful it wasn't tornado season, not yet, anyway. She certainly wouldn't want to be forced to endure that alone with a newborn baby. Of course there was plenty of stock down in the basement at all times because the weather can be unpredictable. Rusty had even put a container of formula, bottled water, and baby food down there before leaving, just in case.

After changing her diaper, Reese tried to lay Taylor back down with no luck. She continued to fuss and grunt while attacking her hands with her mouth.

"You're hungry, again?" *Damn it,* Reese shuffled her feet to the kitchen.

Reese made a bottle and fed Taylor with one hand while turning on the Kurieg with the other. She pulled down her coffee mug from the cabinet and tapped her fingers on the counter trying to death stare the machine into warming up faster. After one day with no help she was already wishing she could fast forward to next week when her parents would be home. Her mom could fix whatever she screwed up with this child.

As the week drug on, Taylor managed to flip herself completely around and stayed up all night long screaming and fussing like she was being tortured. Maybe she was, by the new mommy who had no idea what on earth she was doing. Reese lived off of coffee and tears during the week, and it wasn't until the day before her parents came home that she had any refuge.

In the early morning hours of the day before her parents were scheduled to be home, Reese sat on the couch holding Taylor bringing them face to face. Reese could feel the salt burn her tired eyes as she sobbed.

"I'm so sorry, I'm a terrible mom. I have no idea what I'm doing here. Are you broken? Did I break you? I don't know why you won't stop crying. You barely eat and then you're screaming at me like I'm starving you. I know you're a baby but, I'm desperate here, Tay. I need you to tell me what you want. I don't know." Tears effortlessly fell from her cheeks and onto the blanket Taylor was wrapped in. "Please, just tell me," she sobbed.

Reese looked at the clock, counting down every second left until her mom would finally be home, and can fix this broken child. *She has to be broken. I must've done something—I just wish I knew what.* The seconds ticked by at snail speed. Taylor had finally fallen asleep when there was a knock at the door. It startled Reese, *was I expecting someone?* She puffed her cheeks out with a sharp exhale. *I'm not sure that I would even want to entertain Jesus himself right now.*

Reese reluctantly cracked the door open to see Penny standing there holding up homemade cinnamon rolls.

"Ree," Penny gasped. "Are you okay?"

"No," Reese cried out opening the door to reveal the full extent of the damage.

Reese's hair had an "Albert Einstein had a break down" kind of look to it. There were dark circles under her eyes and her skin was pale and pasty. Reese's clothes were covered in spit up marks and coffee spills. That wasn't even the worst part. As Penny walked in she could see the mess of dirty diapers thrown on the floor and the collection of dirty bottles on the coffee table. Basically, Reese had all of the battles wounds of a first time mother, baring the pains of adjusting to motherhood.

"When's the last time you showered, Ree?"

"Um, I honestly have no idea." Reese's red eyes pooled with water.

"Okay, I've got Taylor, you go shower and change your clothes. I promise you, you'll feel better. Afterwards, we can have some cinnamon rolls and you can tell me what's wrong and I'll see if I can help you fix it."

"Oh my God, Penny, thank you so much." Reese grabbed her and squeezed her tightly.

"Oh whoa, make sure you scrub really well while you're in there, okay?" Penny suggested before letting Reese go, pulling back with her nose scrunched up.

"Okay, um, the formula is in the kitchen. Well, it's in the pantry actually. I can get it for you, hang on." Reese went walking toward the kitchen and grabbed the formula bottle from the pantry. "So she does four ounces when she eats which is two scoops of formula and then fill the water to this line."

"Reese, I have a son, I know how to measure formula," Penny huffed a laugh.

"Right, I'm sorry." Reese shook her head. *Who am I to tell a mom how to take care of a baby?* She started to walk away when she abruptly stopped and turned around. "Oh, Taylor is prone to spitting up."

"I can see that," Penny pointed at Reese's formula stained shirt.

"I'm just saying. If you pat her back too hard she will without a doubt vomit on you. So what I do is I rub up and down and do little pats in between."

"I got it," Penny smiled.

"I just don't want you to get puked on."

"She'll be fine," Penny promised. "She probably won't even wake up."

"Oh no, this child knows my parents are gone and has officially turned into the demon spawn of Denton."

"I was convinced Dominick was the demon spawn of Denton too when he was a few weeks old. Go shower, I'll be here when you get out."

"Are you sure?" Reese felt guilty leaving her baby, even for a moment to shower.

"I know this is hard, but go, she'll be fine with her Aunt Penny."

Hearing Penny refer to herself as "Aunt" made Reese miss her sister. She was so afraid Sophie would never forgive her, even though she didn't feel she had done anything wrong. Brushing off the thought of her sister she swallowed her guilt and jumped in the shower.

Reese fully understood Penny's crinkled nose and push for a shower. As she stripped off her clothes she could smell the mix of her unpleasant body odor and formula vomit. It caused Reese to crinkle up her nose as well and helped her make peace with her guilt of leaving Penny tending to her child.

The steam from the shower surrounded her as she stepped into the hot water. It felt as if the water was erasing the dirt and grime of battle. It was the battle of the newborn versus the mom who doesn't know squat about how to be a mom. The battle smells of "not enough deodorant in the world that can help" ran down her sore body and into the drain. Maybe, just maybe, this new mommy will live to fight another day.

Reese felt rejuvenated coming down the hall with her wet hair flowing freely around her face. Penny was right, a shower made a world of difference.

"Hey, look at you!" Penny boasted.

"You were totally right, that shower just changed my life!" Reese ran her fingers through her dark wet hair. "But, I still need more coffee."

"Already made you some," Penny smiled, pointing to the steaming cup on the now clean coffee table.

"You cleaned!" Reese announced.

"I figured you could use the help," she patted Reese on the shoulder with her voice sweet and non-judgmental. "Now come, sit down, and tell me what's goin' on with you, darlin'."

"Okay," Reese felt like a teenager headed to tell her guidance counselor all about how her mean math teacher is keeping her from reaching her full potential. If only this tiny noisy human would cooperate, then Reese could be the mother she'd always imagined she'd be. It's the kid's fault, she's broken, take her back to the baby factory and exchange her for one that's not broken. "Well," Reese hesitated unsure if she really wanted to go the blaming her child route. Tears stung her eyes as she was at her limit. A shower indeed helped but, it didn't erase the amount of hell she had been in all week long. "I think I broke her!" she cried out.

"Oh goodness," Penny scooted closer to Reese and wrapped both arms around her. "Why do you think that?"

Reese sniffled, wiping her tears as she pulled away from Penny. "She won't sleep, she won't stop crying, and she won't eat! She keeps falling asleep. I try to wake her up but, nothing works!" *Apparently I am the mom that blames the kid.* "I don't know what she wants from me. I've asked but, obviously she's just a baby, she can't tell me. I promised to buy her the biggest dollhouse on the block if she'd just go to sleep, that didn't work. I bribed her with more formula. I even offered up Buckie, my dad's best horse, still nothing." She reached up and wiped the tears from her cheeks. "She wasn't like this when my parents were here, so it's gotta be me. I did something wrong, I just know it!"

"Okay, slow down, sweetie, and take a few deep breaths." Reese followed her advice. "Good, that's perfect." Is Penny coaching me off the ledge the way I've coach countless others? "Reese, I promise you that you did not in any way break your baby."

"How do you know?"

"Because I've been exactly where you're at right now and I would cry to my husband about what a terrible mother I was. After I called my mom in tears at two in the mornin' she came straight over and helped me get Dominick flipped around. I will help you, are you ready?"

"Yes," Reese felt an overwhelming sense of eagerness. *Show me your magical ways, Penny.*

"First things first, when you're feeding her, do you let her wake up all the way?" The confusion staring back at Penny was all she needed to move on. "Okay, so before you feed her, let her fully wake up first. Let her cry for a bit before you get her food."

"Isn't that mean?" Reese felt like her heart break just thinking about it.

"For your sanity, trust me, she'll be fine."

"Okay," Reese reluctantly gave in. *I'll try anything at this point.*

"Now, the biggest thing my mom helped me with was getting Dom on a schedule. Taylor is brand new, so you're gonna want to modify it to fit your life. A routine will seriously save your life, no joke."

"A routine...?" Reese still felt confused.

"Yeah, you want to get her up at the same time, every day. You put her down for naps at the same time and you feed her at the same time. She will pick up on it rather quickly. That's probably what your mom was helping you do, you just didn't realize it."

"Oh..." *thanks a lot for not tellin' me, Maggs.* Grunting and whimpering came from the bassinet. "Oh great, she's waking up. Can you stay here while I go make a bottle?"

"Let's let her wake up first." Penny put her hand on Reese's leg. "This is the hard part, Mama."

"What do you mean, 'hard part'?"

Twenty minutes later, Taylor was now screaming worse than ever and Reese curled herself into a ball, rocking back and forth on the couch fighting tears.

"Now?" Reese pleaded with Penny. "Please can I feed her?"

"Yes, now you can go in and make a bottle, but don't–"

Reese didn't wait for Penny to finish her thought. She shot up from the couch and sprinted into the kitchen, thankful to make the magical formula that makes the crying stop. *I just want it to stop.* Reese dumped two scoops of formula into the bottle, spilling clumps of powder on the counter and with shaky hands she measured the water level. Screwing the cap back onto the bottle as fast as she could, she once again sprinted back to the living room. Penny was sitting there, un-phased by the sound of a screaming baby. She wasn't frazzled or devastated, she was just sitting there, almost peaceful. She even giggled at Reese as she raced around the couch and to the bassinet.

Scooping Taylor up, Reese quickly placed the bottle in her mouth, silencing the tiny banshee in her arms. *Ah, the sweet sound of silence.*

"I'm proud of you, Reese." Penny calmly said.

"How in the hell are you so calm and unaffected by what just happened?"

"Because, like I already told you, I've been exactly where you are, it'll get easier, I promise. She should stay awake for a few hours after she's done."

Penny was right. Shoot, Penny was right about everything. She stayed with Reese all day to help her manage the "let her wake up" method. Penny ordered pizza for lunch and even made soup for dinner.

"I really appreciate you doing this, Pen but, where's Dominick? Won't your husband be wondering where you are?"

"Josh is at home with Dom, and he knew I was comin' to help you. I texted him while you were in the shower I was going to be here until this evening. You needed me more than they did today."

"Thank you, seriously. Thank you."

"You're very welcome."

After dinner was put away and the dishes were cleaned up, Penny decided to head on home. Reese was handling things much better, and another storm was making its way toward Denton.

"You will get the hang of it Ree, I promise." Penny hugged her tightly.

"I really hope so."

"You will," Penny continued her embrace. "I felt like I was losing my mind," she released Reese, "and then one day— boom—everything clicked into place."

"I don't know, Pen, I feel like I'm not equipped with the 'Mom gene' you know?"

"I do know, and I promise that you are. Remember, deep breaths."

"Okay," Reese took a long drawn out breath. "Drive careful, and let me know when you get home."

"I will."

Penny headed out into the dreary evening filled with mist in the air. Reese stood on the front porch until she could no longer see Penny's tail lights. She finally receded inside into the calm and quiet house. Reese felt so thankful that Penny had come by to save her from herself.

The remainder of the evening was uneventful, and both Reese and Taylor were fast asleep by ten that night and Taylor finally slept soundly until three in the morning.

When Rusty and Maggie made it home that afternoon, Reese filled them in on the horrifying and painful merge into motherhood. She wore her wounds proudly and she also gained a new found respect for the women out there who don't have a Penny or a Maggie in their lives.

Chapter 18

REESE WAS IN the full swing of motherhood, she was starting to accept her fears of doing the wrong things and making mistakes; believing her worries were a sign of wanting to be the best mom she could possibly be under the circumstances. Reese knew as long as she followed the plan Taylor would sleep all night, except for her one feeding at three in the morning. She finally had their routine down and it was fool-proof.

"Hopefully it will be easier to get her to sleep through the night since you only have to break one feeding." Maggie mindlessly spoke while Reese washed bottles at the kitchen sink.

"I think it might be time to add a little bit of rice cereal to her last bottle of the night and see how she does." Maggie suggested.

"Isn't it a little early for that? In all the books I've read–"

"Oh, psh," Maggie cut her off. "The books change every couple of years. When you and Sophie were little, this is what I did with you both. By eight weeks y'all were sleepin' through the night."

"I just... maybe we should... she's so tiny, Mom."

"I know this feels scary but, you'll be going back to work before you know it. You won't survive twenty-four-hour-shifts and coming home to being up all night with a baby. You have to get her sleepin' through the night, or it'll kill ya."

Reese knew Maggie was right, it didn't mean she liked it but, definitely had a point. "Okay, Mom, can you put rice cereal on the list?"

"Already done, sis," Maggie smiled.

That night Maggie showed Reese how to go about putting the rice cereal in the bottle after she used an ice pick to make the hole bigger in the nipple of the bottle. Reese scooped up Taylor from her swing and into her arms, gently sitting back in the rocking chair Rusty had bought her a couple weeks prior. She sat admiring her daughter as she lay comfortably cradled in her arms.

"Okay, sister, I'm gonna tell you what's going on so that you know what to expect."

"What are you doing?" Maggie laughed.

"I'm talkin' to her so she knows what's goin' on." Maggie laughed some more and Reese turned back to the sweet baby in her arms. "Mama's gonna have to go back to work soon, and when I do, I can't be gettin' up at three in the morning with you every night. Mama's work is hard and exhausting. I love you so much but, I need you to start sleeping through the night. We're gonna drink this bottle and then we're gonna go to bed. It's ten o'clock now, and once I put you to bed I won't be back in until seven o'clock in the morning, okay?" Taylor made cooed and gurgled sounds as she smiled and tried to eat her hands. "I'll take that as a signal that you understand."

Maggie laughed as Reese turned Taylor and cradled her in her arms. Once the bottle was secured in her mouth Reese turned to Maggie.

"Why are you laughing?"

"I just think it's adorable that you think that's gonna help, it's going to take at least a week or so to get her use to the rice cereal."

"It'll help, you'll see. She'll be sleeping through the night in no time at all!"

Within two days, Taylor was sleeping through the night, and Maggie was shocked. She apologized to Reese for making fun of her methods because maybe there was something to it after all. Life for Reese had settled into a new normal and now that Taylor was sleeping through the night, life was much easier to manage. No more middle of the night shuffles to the kitchen to make a bottle in her sleepy daze and then to shuffle back to the bedroom. Taylor was also out of the bassinette and in her crib in the nursery, and Reese was glad to have her room to herself again.

Before Reese fell asleep, her mind fluttered back to the night Chad came into her bedroom and they spent the most electrifying night together. The chemistry between them was undeniable. Thinking about that night sealed the deal in her heart and soul that her feelings for him were worth fighting for.

The next morning, Reese called and made an appointment with a therapist. With time and work, she would be able to love Chad the way he deserved to be loved.

Twelve weeks after the baby was born, Reese returned back to work. She felt nervous, *what if I forgot how to be a good paramedic, what if I make a huge mistake?* She worried during her drive to work. Pulling up at the station her stomach twisted into one giant knot. The knot grew bigger when she walked in and saw the board. She was scheduled with an EMT she didn't know.

"Great," she mumbled under her breath.

"Welcome back, Reese! We're all so glad that you're okay." Jerry stood behind her, and the steam flowed out the top of his coffee stained mug.

"Thank you, feels good to be back. Do you know who Vasquez is?"

"You're scheduled with Vasquez for your first shift back?" His brow rose up to mid forehead.

"That's what the board says." Reese pointed to her shift.

"Well look at this bitch! Surprised you remembered how to get here!" Reese smiled, when she turned around Emily stood next to Jerry, packing her fresh pack of cigarettes, smacking them against the palm of her hand.

"I missed you too, wench." Reese laughed and hugged Emily. "Besides, I just saw you a few weeks ago, so knock it off."

"Psh, details." Emily waved off her comment. "You can't put her with Vasquez, that guy's an idiot."

"Is he that bad?"

Reese usually wouldn't care, she'd worked with plenty of newbies in her day but, this wasn't just any other day. Reese hadn't ran a call in almost eight months between being taken off early because of back issues she was having, post coma and C-section time, and then her additional weeks of baby bonding time, it had practically been a lifetime since she even held a needle in her hands, let alone started an IV driving down a bumpy road.

"Yes, he's that bad." Emily looked at Jerry. "Tell her."

"I don't know what you mean? I value each and every employee here at Medstar, and I'm happy to work with them."

"Oh stop that shit! You and I both know this last batch of EMTs we hired, are completely worthless, and should probably go back to school! Cut the supervisory diplomatic bullshit."

"I can't," he said in a level tone and a serious face. "That would be considered playing favorites, and here at MedStar we don't do that."

"Bullshit," Emily contested. "Look, I'm on a transfer car today. It's a shift that's easy money and in an environment that Vasquez can't really screw up. Switch us. I'll work with Landon so at the very least she has a competent partner to work with."

"If Vasquez agrees... then yes, you can do that." Jerry leaned over to Reese and whispered. "For the record, Emily isn't wrong."

Reese's eyes widened, "What if he won't switch?" Reese asked Emily.

"Oh, he'll be switching."

Emily made a B-line for Vasquez the second he walked through the door. His uniform appeared freshly pressed, his boots shinny enough to do your make up in the reflection, and yet he looked meek and timid. *She's gonna eat that boy alive.*

"Vasquez," Emily sternly said. "I need to talk to you."

"Um, oh—okay," his voice was soft like a mouse.

"This is Landon's first shift back after maternity leave. She's been out for a really long time and she's a little wobbly and nervous."

"Okay?" he said it more as a question, unsure of what Emily's point was.

"I'm going to switch with you. She needs someone she can trust today, no offense but, she doesn't know you and you're still really green. You'll be on the transfer car with Campbell." Emily didn't ask, she told.

"Oh, yea sounds good."

"Thank you for understanding," Reese smiled from behind Emily.

"No problem."

The girls grabbed their belongings and loaded them into the ambulance.

"I went through this ambulance last night," Jerry came out and stood at the open back doors of the ambulance where Reese and Emily were going through their regular check-off routine. "Everything is good to go. All your batteries are fresh and you have spare batteries for the monitor and gurney. I really need y'all to go in service, levels are low."

"You got it, boss," Reese said, passed the lump in her throat.

The girls hopped in the front of the ambulance and arranged their belongings.

"Want to do the honors?" Emily asked handing the mic of the radio to Reese.

"Sure," Reese smiled and grabbed the mic. "Medic seven log on."

"Go ahead," a scratchy voice came over the radio.

"Medic seven, log on, Paramedic Landon, EMT Baker, physical unit one-one-four."

"Copy, Medic seven, I show you now as the closest unit to priority one traffic. Nine-four-nine south Robin Street. Priority one for a cardiac arrest, CPR's in progress."

"Shit, are you kidding me?" Reese filled with panic.

Emily grabbed the mic from her hand, "Medic seven responding," she secured the mic back in its slot. "I know where this is."

Reese heard Emily's words but was too busy going over protocols in her head like a brand new medic whose ink hadn't even dried on her card yet. Panic hit the pit of her stomach.

"You got this, Reese. It's like riding a bike," Emily's confidence carried them both through the drive to get there.

"I know, I just thought I would have a second to ease into it, you know?"

"Well, the EMS gods feel differently, so suck it up buttercup, and do your job the way I know you know how."

"You're right, we got this." They shared a quick fist bump as they rounded the corner directly behind the engine. "Oh thank God, we have a good fire crew." Reese mumbled to herself.

They pulled the gurney and a backboard from the ambulance before heading inside to find an elderly woman on the floor in the hallway, where the fire department was preforming CPR.

"Reese," The Capitan sternly called out. "This is all you, tell us what you want, Boss." His handlebar mustache wrapped tightly around his hidden mouth.

"Let's get her on the monitor and see what we are dealing with here." She flipped around to Emily who was already handing her the airway bag. "I'm gonna step over so I can intubate real quick and then I'll move back for the IV. Keep doin' CPR until I tell you to stop."

"You got it," the pudgy out of breath firefighter said between compressions.

"Is the monitor on yet?" She asked.

"Yea, let me turn it around," Emily answered.

"Hold CPR," Reese analyzed the rhythm, reaching across the woman's lifeless body to charge the monitor to deliver a shock of electricity through her heart. The monitor made a noise indicating that it was booting up power. The sound started low and as the volts increased in the charge it became high pitched until it rang out with an alarm indicating it was ready. "Everyone clear?" she asked.

"We're all clear."

"Shocking," Reese pushed the button and watched the lifeless body quickly convulse and immediately go limp on the ground. "Continue CPR for two minutes, can you time it, Cap?"

"Sure thing, starting two minutes..."

Reese put all thoughts out of her head, except one—*do what you can for her.* She slid the tube down the patient's trachea with ease. *Just like riding a bike,* Emily's voice called out in her head. After securing the tube, she noticed a nice vein down her neck.

"Two minutes," the captain's deep voice rang out.

"Stop for a rhythm check," everyone paused, watching Reese for direction. "Still in V-Tac, charging," once again the monitor sang out its warning. "Everyone clear?"

"Clear."

"Shocking," again the lifeless body slightly jolted from the current. "Start CPR, two more minutes, Cap."

"You got it."

"Hand me an eighteen gauge," Reese directed Emily in what she needed.

"Here you go," Emily reached over the top of the action stretching her short body to its limits toward Reese, handing her the opened green package with the handle of the needle facing her.

It's like riding a bike. She took a sharp breath in and exhaled as blood filled the chamber. The tube advanced effortlessly into the vein and they had beautiful flow in the IV.

"Two minutes."

"Rhythm check," Reese immediately followed the time alarm. All efforts stopped. "Charging again," she called out followed by the alarm sounding. "Everyone clear?"

"Clear."

"Shocking," the twitch seemed bigger this time. "Continue CPR, two minutes."

Reese then pushed the meds through the IV. Now was the time to wait, She picked up the trash around as the fire fighters continued to rotate doing compressions and breathing for her. Two minutes never felt so long. This was always the part where the medic feels like twiddling their thumbs as the seconds ticked by at snail speed.

"Two minutes," all motion stops at the captain's alarm.

"That looks like sinus, do we have a pulse?" She asked the firefighter bagging air down the tube in her throat.

"I—Yes, I feel a pulse."

Reese let go of the air she held in her chest, "Excellent," she pushed one final drug through the IV. "Let's get her on a board and get outta here."

They placed the still lifeless woman onto a backboard and carried her to the gurney. Emily drove as fast as she could to the emergency room, and the woman remained alive. Reese gave the report to a room full of nurses and doctors, giving them a play by play of what had happened and their findings.

Walking out of the room, she felt like she had just had an outer body experience. *Well I'll be damned,* she smiled to herself, *Emily was right—it really is just like riding a bike.*

"Nice job, Landon," the captain gave her one firm pat on the shoulder.

"Thank you, Mac," Reese smiled.

He was her favorite captain to run with in Denton. She couldn't have asked for a better crew on her first call back.

"I heard welcome back is in order."

"Yea," she laughed, "first shift, first call."

"Well, you'd never know." He smiled. "Did you get the card and flowers from all of us?"

"I did, I planned on coming by to tell all y'all thank you today but, fate stepped in. I really appreciated it, it honestly means so much that the department would do that for me."

"You're one of our favorite medics 'round here, Landon. When we heard what happened we wanted to do something. A whole mess of us had come down to the hospital but, you were still unconscious. Once you had woken up, there were so many people coming in and out, we thought we'd just leave the flowers and card, and let you spend time with your family. I'm really happy you're okay, we all are."

Reese choked back the tightness in her throat. Without any sense of fear she reached out, wrapped her arms around Mac, and tightly hugged him.

"Thank you so much," she whispered in his ear.

For a brief moment Reese was shocked she didn't feel any guilt over hugging another man that wasn't Alex. She knew that each day she was getting closer to the woman she once was but, interacting with men still felt like a huge hurdle to clear. She stumbled a lot, even with Uncle T's friend Robert, whom she saw regularly. She always felt a lingering feeling of guilt, like she was doing something wrong, and she was constantly pushing through the shame the way her therapist told her to. Chad and Stump were the only two to break through that so far, and now Mac. Oddly, he reminded Reese of Stump. Mac was a little taller and his hair was darker but, the build and personality were the same.

The next several months passed as Reese continued to run stat call after stat call. Typically, most of the calls in EMS are filled with the flu, stomach aches, and the rare and occasional significant call that requires fast interventions and a code three transport. Lights and sirens to the hospital does not happen for everyone, except in Reese's case, most of her calls were transported to the hospital as fast as she could. So many stat calls in such a short amount of time.

Taylor continued to grow and get bigger by the minute. Reese would come home after a forty-eight hour shift and swear that Tay-Rae was a completely different baby. She started crawling at a mere four months, and even took off running at nine and a half months. Reese loved the sound of her daughter giggling while running as fast as she could up and down the hallway. Her teeth began to poke through and with each check-up Reese thanked God that her daughter didn't show any signs of damage from the traumatic delivery.

Reese had even managed to find time to patch things up with Sophie. She came by the house to apologize to Reese and let Piper meet her new cousin. Piper and Tay-Rae instantly became best friends, which made Reese so happy. Penny would bring over Dominick and the three of them would happily play together.

Reese was gradually patching her life back together. Thanks to her therapist, she felt stronger, more confident, and even found some of her sass again. She no longer felt guilty talking to men, or hugging them for that matter. The shame that had been hardwired into her mind had dissipated and seemed to have left for good.

She stayed in contact with Chad over the last year and they had become closer than ever, as friends. After a trip to Seattle with Chad and his friends, Reese felt that she was almost ready to finally take things to the next level with him.

He had finished up his classes for detective shortly before Taylor's first birthday and when he came out to Texas to celebrate the birth of a little girl he already considered his own, they celebrated his accomplishment as well. Reese took him out to a fun little honky-tonk bar that served the best barbeque in northern Texas. They ate, they drank, and they danced the night away, consummating their relationship that night in his hotel.

Reese finally felt whole again, and ready to start an entirely new journey—a new chapter in her life that finally didn't involve Alex.

Chapter 19

IT'S MARCH SEVENTH. Reese was up early to go for a much needed run. She cracked open the door to Taylor's room, just enough to see that she was still fast asleep. *God I love you, little one.* She softly closed the door and headed out. She took off down the dirt driveway, curving around onto the road. She decided to run down to the stop sign and back which was about two and a half miles. That morning she chose to leave her earphones at home and enjoy the time alone with her thoughts. She felt at ease thinking about Chad and their possible future together. She softly smiled, reliving several of the moments they shared over the last few years; her favorite was when she woke up in the hospital and found him sleeping in the chair next to her bed.

Her love for Chad had grown by leaps and bounds from that moment on. They had gotten to know each other on a much deeper level than Reese ever expected. She was brutally honest with him when it came to her struggles and the fears Alex instilled in her. Best of all, Chad never judged her for it. Instead, he was understanding and forthcoming with advice or reminding her she's not doing anything wrong. He helped her work through her fears, and helped her heal, rather than discarding them all together. Sometimes Reese would catch herself being cynical, thinking Chad was too good to be true. *No man could possibly be this perfect, could they?* But, she was honest with him about her fears and he promised her he was genuine, and he reassured her that one day she will know it without a doubt.

They both hated the distance between them but, Chad told her he wasn't in a hurry.

"We have our whole lives to get to where we're going." He would remind her.

Two weeks ago, he called Reese to tell her his transfer was finally accepted and he was officially promoted to detective. The following week he would be starting in homicide. Reese jumped up and down with delight and Taylor clapped her hands together and squealed.

"Even Tay-Rae is happy for you, baby! God, I am so freakin' proud of you!"

"I love you guys!"

"We love you too, babe. Tay and I will have to figure out a time to fly out so that we can properly celebrate."

"That would be great! I want nothing more than to see my two favorite girls."

"I have some vacation time saved up, I know we are short medics since three of our guys left in the last month but, let me see if I can swing it."

"Okay baby, I gotta go, the detective training me is calling me."

"Love you."

"Love you, too."

The phone clicked and Reese could feel all of the pieces of her life finally falling into place. She wasn't sure as to how or when but, she knew all she wanted was to grow old with Chad. She wanted to sit hand in hand together on a front porch swing, with their skin wrinkled and hair turned white, and just love him until her last breath. He was her forever, and there was no doubt in her mind about that anymore.

Rounding the corner onto the driveway, her lungs burned and beads of sweat rolled down her temples. She couldn't believe today was Chad's first day as a detective. She got back inside the house and quickly showered and got dressed before Taylor woke up. As she poured her coffee she could hear the faint babbling of Taylor, almost a toddler now, and was talking to the stuffed giraffe Chad had given her. Reese opened the door and poked her head in Taylor's room.

"Well, good morning, princess."

"Hi!" her sweet voice answered.

"Hi, my love," Reese picked her up from her crib. "Are you hungry?" Taylor nodded her head yes. "Let's get you changed and I will make you some breakfast."

They came down the hallway and headed into the kitchen. The sun was shining outside in the beautiful blue sky. The weather was predicted to be wonderful with a slight early spring breeze. There were puffy white clouds that hung in the sky like they had been placed there by a professional artist.

Reese made them a quick breakfast of yogurt and strawberries with a handful of cheerios for Taylor. As they ate Reese's phone went off with a text.

CHAD: *Good morning, beautiful. 7:05AM*

Reese looked at the time.

REESE: Good morning, handsome. You're up early. Nervous about your first day? 7:06AM

CHAD: Yeah, but that's not why I'm up early. I'm headed to a crime scene. Another dead girl was found in a field just on the outskirts of town. Detective Stone thinks it's connected to the others they've found over the last few months. 7:09AM

REESE: Oh my God, I can't believe that. Be safe out there, Detective Platt. We love you. Xx. 7:10AM

Reese sent a picture of her crouching around Taylor, who had yogurt all over her face.

CHAD: Those beautiful faces, I cannot wait to kiss you both. I love you girls too. What are your plans for the day? 7:12AM

REESE: I think we're gonna head to the park. The weather here is perfect and I don't want to waste it staying inside. 7:12AM

CHAD: I wish I was there. I gotta go, I'm almost there. I'll text you later when I can. 7:13AM

REESE: Ok xx.

Reese and Taylor met up with Penny and little Dom at the park, and even Emily decided to tag along. Her kids were teenagers now, so she came to soak up the sun and some little munchkin love. Taylor enjoyed the swings more than anything else at the park. She ran straight to them and pointed, making begging noises doing her best on learning how to talk.

"Peeass... up.... peeeass," she pleaded.

"Okay, sis, let's swing." Reese lifted her into the baby swing that held her tiny body on all sides, and began to push.

She laughed and squealed with excitement. The sound of her laugh melted Reese's heart every time she heard it. She pulled out her phone and sent Chad a few candid pictures she caught of Taylor on the swing and coming down the slide. She knew he was busy but, when he was able to look at his phone it would make him smile amidst his not so easy morning he was surely having.

When their perfect day started to wind down, Reese double checked her phone for messages from Chad, there was nothing. *He must be slammed. Hopefully they caught a break in the case. Ugh, those poor innocent girls. I hope they catch whoever it is.* Picking up her phone she took a quick video of Taylor sitting up in her pajamas on the changing table in her room.

"Say night, night to Chad, sissy," Reese said off camera.

At just the mention of Chad's name, Taylor's whole face lit up.

"Nye, nye," she then blew kisses from her hand to the camera for Chad.

She sent the video to him and wrote a quick note attached to it.

REESE: I know you're busy but, I thought the pictures earlier and the video would cheer you up when you had a chance to see them. I hope everything is going okay with your case. Fingers crossed y'all caught a lead. Xx 7:15PM

The next morning Reese woke up early for work and found a text from Chad he sent in the middle of the night.

CHAD: I'm so sorry, honey, I'm not ignoring you. It's a long story, one I promise to explain when I can but I can't talk about it. Chief has put a gag order on Stone and I. I love you both. Thank you so much for the pictures and the videos, you have no idea how much that made my day better. If you only knew what I've had to watch and comb through all day, I'm going to try and sleep. Be safe on your shift tomorrow and give that sweet girl kisses from me. I love you so much, Reese. I

*want so badly to tell you everything that happened today. Just
know that I'm so sorry I can't. Please forgive me. 1:36AM*

Please forgive me? She wondered, confused. *Why on earth
would he say that?*

*REESE: Please don't apologize. I completely understand. Just
know that when you are able to tell me, I will be here. I know
how tough this case has been, and this is the first scene you've
been to with Stone. You do what you have to do. Please don't
ever think that you have to apologize to me for doing your job.
6:45AM*

Reese got ready for work and quietly slipped out of the
house. She drove to work in silence trying to decode Chad's
text, and before she knew it, she had pulled up to the station.
She and Emily were scheduled to work together this morning.
Once she came back off maternity leave, Emily and Reese were
working a minimum of two shifts a week together, which Reese
was thankful for, *nothing like Emily's blunt demeanor to get me
through a tough shift.*

They went about their morning routine of checking off the
inventory of the ambulance. Reese was so far in her own head
she didn't notice Emily staring at her.

"Spill it," Emily's sharp voice demanded.

"Uh–there's nothing to–"

"Bullshit! Don't you dare start lying to me now... Something
is obviously wrong, so spill."

"It's Chad," Reese caved. She wanted to talk to someone
about everything but, she felt like she was being dramatic
about the whole thing. However, there was an undeniable
wrench that sat deep in the pit of her stomach, a wrench that
felt like a warning but, a warning for what? "It's stupid."

"If it's bothering you this much, then it's not." Emily said with sincerity.

Reese handed Emily her phone and let her read through his last text. She sat in silence confused. Reese could see her eyes reading the text over and over, the same way that Reese did when she got it. *At least I'm not alone in my confusion.*

"Did you ask him why he's apologizing?"

"I didn't want to push the issue. I'm sure it's about the Auburn teen killings. Chad started working under Detective Natalie Stone. She's one of the best homicide detectives in Auburn, and Chad got roped into an ongoing investigation. Stone thinks that all of the young girl's body's they've found over the last six weeks are connected and it's the same person responsible for all of their deaths. So, she's been working that angle since the second victim was found. Chad had said he was on his way to another crime scene of a young girl that was found dead. After that was when I got that odd text. It's almost like it's encrypted but, I have no idea what he's trying to tell me, without actually telling me, and it's driving me crazy."

The puzzled look on Emily's face remained. "I—," she paused, "Well shit, I got nothin'."

"That's exactly the problem, I've got nothing too."

"I'm sure when he can finally explain he will and it'll all make sense..."

"You're probably right." Reese sighed. With a slow and steady exhale, she pushed her insecurities to the back of her mind, and continued doing inventory.

"We're all good here," Reese pointed to the cabinets in the ambulance. "You ready to log on?"

"Sure."

The day moved along rather quickly as the girls ran several calls, Reese was thankful for the distraction of work to aid in not obsessing over Chad's cryptic message. However, Reese couldn't help herself in the ER, big screen televisions hung behind the nurse's station set to the national news station; made her wonder if she would catch a glimpse of Chad and the case with the dead girls. If they found more bodies it wouldn't be long before it caught the attention of the media, and maybe then everything would make sense. *Knock it off.* She shook her head and finished her paperwork just in time to be pulled away to another call.

"What's it for?"

"It's priority three for an ill twenty-six year old female."

"Seriously?"

"Yup, this is gonna be complete bullshit so, gear up, sister." Emily laughed.

When they arrived on scene, there was a young woman sitting on the front porch of her small apartment, texting on her phone.

"Wanna go see what's going on before we bring our stuff in?"

"Absolutely," Emily smiled.

The girls strolled up the walk-way together and met the young woman who barely acknowledged their presence.

"Did you call for an ambulance?" Reese asked unable to conceal her irritation.

"Oh, yea," she popped the gum in her mouth and finished the text she was typing before continuing. "So, um, like my stomach hurts." She popped her gum again.

"And you called for an ambulance, why exactly?"

"Because it hurts," the woman stared at Reese like she was an idiot.

"So?" Reese countered.

"Well, isn't that like, your job?"

"We aren't an Uber you just call up and use to shuttle you around." Reese could feel that anger simmering just below the surface.

"But, my stomach hurts. I need to go to the emergency room."

"Not by an ambulance you don't."

"But I don't have a ride."

"And so you decided the best option was to take an ambulance out of the system to chauffeur you to the ER? You know, there could be people calling nine-one-one who actually need us, and we are here wasting our time with you."

"You don't have to be a bitch about it."

"Apparently I do, because you don't seem to understand what an utter waste of resources this is!" Reese hissed. "If you wanna go, get in, you're going to the waiting room."

"No, I want a room!" she demanded.

"It doesn't work that way," Reese took a deep breath and pulled back her tone. "You'll go to the waiting room. It's not up for negotiation."

"What the hell? Forget it! I'll call my mom and go to Urgent Care."

"Good choice. Next time, do that and don't call us, unless it's a real emergency." Reese ripped her gloves off her hands as she turned around and headed back to the ambulance with Emily on her heels.

When the doors shut, Emily didn't waste any time. "Where the hell did that come from?" she laughed.

Reese sat forward and put her head in her hands. "I honestly don't know."

She ran her hands down her face and rested them over her mouth before both of them began laughing uncontrollably. Neither of them could speak, they were laughing so hard they pulled over and parked the ambulance once they rounded the end of the street. After several belly laughing minutes, they took some deep breaths to help regain their composure.

"Where to, woman?" Emily asked, breathing through her giggles.

"I gotta go back to the ER. I just gotta print out some documents, shouldn't take more than a minute." Reese said wiping the tears of laughter, trying to gain her composure. "Man, I haven't laughed like that in forever."

"Me either," they shared one final chuckle before being on their way.

When they pulled up to the ambulance entrance at the emergency room, Reese got out and headed to the automatic doors. She typed in the code and the doors sprung open, leading her through the brief hallway to the nurse's station in the middle of the emergency room. With a light step and a smile on her face, she glanced at the large flat screen televisions that hung on the wall behind the desk.

Reese immediately recognized the pictures on the screen, the small town she had lived, in what seemed like a lifetime ago, being reported on. Panic, fear, and disgust rose up in Reese as a familiar face came onto the screen.

"This is Amy Cho reporting live here in Auburn, Washington. We are currently standing outside of the Auburn Police Station where they are bringing in the man alleged to be the Auburn Schoolgirl Killer." In the background Reese watched in horror as Chad walked Alex handcuffed into the station. "It has been reported that Auburn PD believe Alex Cunningham, a local resident of Auburn, to be responsible for the rape, torture, and murder of several local teens. We don't have very many details yet, Auburn PD have not yet released an official statement but, we plan to continue with non-stop coverage until we know more on this case. Again, this is Amy Cho, reporting live for NCN—back to you, John."

With a sharp inhale Reese felt the world around her become a faint memory. She stopped dead in her tracks, her eyes focused on nothing but the story unfolding before her eyes. The Toughbook laptop computer slid from Reese's hands and clattered to the floor, the whole world went silent as her focus laid solely on the broadcast. It wasn't until she heard Emily's voice in the back of her mind, "what the fuck was that?" Emily's hands were on Reese's shoulders then waving in front of her face, forcing her to look at Emily's face.

"Holy fuck, isn't that your ex?!" Her voice cut through the emergency room noise causing a wave of silence to roll through the halls.

Everyone stopped—they stared at the television screen periodically looking back at Reese with shock on their faces. The noise didn't return to normal in the halls, instead Reese stood horrified as whispers filled the air, like a far rumble of thunder. Reese didn't want anyone to ever know about Alex, and how horrible he was. Unfortunately, there she was, standing in the middle of her own nightmare looking as guilty as him.

Reese barely made it out the doors of the emergency room when she burst into a full blown panic attack. Tears effortlessly fell from her eyes and she felt her world begin to spin. A tingling sensation replaced her fingertips as she heaved herself over and crouched forward with her hands on her knees. *This can't be happening. Wake up, Reese, wake up!* She grabbed a piece of the pale skin from her wrist, and pinched it as hard as she could.

"Damn it," she forced the words through her breathing.

Reese heard clumpy footsteps running toward her.

"Are you okay?" Emily placed her hand on Reese's back.

"No, I'm not okay!" Reese stood up and shifted Emily's hand off of her. "No thanks to you."

"What the hell is that supposed to mean?"

"Really!? You had to come in and make the announcement that it was Alex on TV? Why not tell them that it was my current boyfriend walking him to the squad car in cuffs? Why not tell the entire ER that my ex, was arrested for torturing, raping, and killing those girls? Why didn't you just tell them that he has been deemed the Auburn Schoolgirl Killer? Oh wait, you've already done that!" Reese wiped the steady stream from her cheeks.

"I'm so sorry, Ree, I was so shocked, I didn't think—"

"Obviously," Reese cut her off.

"I really am sorry. It was an honest mistake. Please! I'm so sorry, Reese." Emily begged.

Reese gradually caught her breath, looking away from Emily, taking a few minutes to gather her thoughts, and realized none of the new predicament was Emily's fault. Reese stood leaning over the hood of the ambulance, silent a few more drawn on moments.

"You're right, I'm sorry too," her shaky voice was barely audible.

"Maybe we should call Jerry and at least tell him what's going on."

"I'm fine." Reese said trying to steady her voice.

"Reese, I can literally see you shaking. It's okay, I know Jerry will understand." Reese looked at Emily, concern painted across her face. Reluctantly she agreed, knowing it wouldn't be long before Jerry heard about the hospital incident anyway. "I'll call him. After we leave, we'll go drink... a lot. Your mom has Taylor until tomorrow, right?"

"Yea," Reese stared off at nothing.

She could barely hear Emily on the phone explaining to Jerry what was going on. Reese sat silently in the passenger seat of the ambulance thinking about how ridiculous it was for her to have actually believed Alex would no longer be involved in her life. *Everyone is gonna know, there's no stopping this now. The whole country knows. Shit.* Reese knew nothing would ever be the same and longed to go back to yesterday, everything had been so perfect then—what a difference one day can make.

Her heart soon shattered for her daughter. Reese knew the world around her would judge her relationship with Alex, she didn't care. What she did care about was the world judging her little girl. All she hoped for now was Taylor would never be accosted for the actions of a father who was never present in her life. Tears stabbed the back of her eyes before lazily streaming down her face.

Reese knew she would have to tell her daughter the truth about her father one day, and on that day she would have to shatter her daughter into a million pieces right before her eyes. *God, please let that day be when she is old enough to handle it... Who the hell am I kidding? I'm twenty-seven and I can't handle this right now.*

She felt empty and hopeless sitting in the passenger seat while Emily drove them back to headquarters.

"When we get back, I don't wanna see anyone or talk to anyone. Can you run interference for me?" Reese's voice was lifeless as she continued to stare straight ahead.

"Of course," Emily replied.

"Thanks."

Emily did the best she could to run interference when they walked in the door but, she couldn't stop Jerry. The owner was there right by Jerry's side and both were purposefully walking toward Reese.

"Can we talk in my office, please?" Jerry asked.

Reese didn't say a word she simply nodded her head in reluctant agreeance. She walked in the room and Jerry pulled over a chair for her to sit. The owner, James Fischer, closed the door behind him before sitting down in a chair next to Reese. Jerry casually leaned against his desk across from her and sympathetically stared into her broken eyes.

"Are you okay?" James's raspy voice asked.

Reese shook her head no. She was using all of her strength to hold her emotions together, rendering her speechless.

"I will cover all of your shifts this week. I think it's best to give you some time to process everything." Jerry stroked his goatee as his brows hung low over the concerned look on his face.

Reese again nodded in agreement.

"If you need anything, you call us, okay?" James offered.

Reese nodded in silence, internally she was screaming, begging for the day to be just a horrible nightmare she could wake up from—*any minute now,* she pleaded to herself. She couldn't bring herself to speak. She just sat, staring at the floor. It was the only constant in her life at the moment, staring so hard as if she could magically will the carpet to become a body of water she could drown in.

"You can go," Jerry motioned at the door and without hesitation Reese popped up and swiftly left the building.

All of her focus was on her car. She didn't notice that Emily had pulled up beside her.

"You're not driving anywhere, get in." Emily tore through her trance.

Without a word Reese opened the door, threw her purse into the back, and got in. They sped off and out of the parking lot, driving straight for the bar.

It was a rundown wooden shack of a building that probably wouldn't pass a health inspection but, it would do. When they walked in the somber ambiance of the room seemed to fit her mood. Reese was joined by a handful of others at the bar on a Thursday afternoon, drowning their sorrows. She slid onto a bar stool, and with Emily by her side, she ordered the first of many whiskey shots.

After a few shots Reese felt off balance and tipsy. Her palms felt sweaty and her head in a fog. Her physical state officially resembled her emotions.

"How can this be happening?" Reese slurred.

"I don't know, honey." Emily tried to console her.

"Do you have any cigarettes?"

"I do," Emily hesitated. "Do you want one?"

"Yes."

"I didn't know you smoked."

Reese didn't feel like herself anymore, as if she was watching a horrible movie play out. She pushed the heavy front door of the bar open—the brightness of the sun burned her blue eyes. She walked straight for the designated smoking area with Emily following close behind.

"I don't smoke, well not anymore." Reese put the cigarette into her mouth and fumbled with the lighter. "I smoked occasionally back in Auburn." Her words were muffled by the round white paper filled with tobacco. She flicked the lighter to life and inhaled the sweet sting of nicotine in her lungs. "I usually smoked when Alex would make me angry or after he would hit me, it seems only fitting to have a smoke now since he's once again wreaking havoc in my life."

Emily sparked her cigarette to life, "I can only imagine what you must be feeling, Reese..." she said between a long drag, "I hope you know none of this is your fault."

"Not my fault?" Reese scoffed. "The fact my daughter's heart is going to shatter one day when she finds out who her father is, is one hundred percent my fault. I chose to be with a monster, and I chose to go back for a one night stand, and it's my choices which got her psychopath as a father."

"Why not just lie to her about who her father is?"

Reese pondered Emily's question for a good long minute. She sucked in the smoke and held it before giving a steady and winded exhale.

"Everyone deserves to know where they came from, Em, even if it's from the devil himself."

"Are you sure that's the best way?"

"Wouldn't you want to know the truth?"

"I suppose."

"Even if it was the worst news of your life and it was terribly awful and devastating?"

"Honestly... yea, probably." Emily said defeated.

"And wouldn't you be violently angry at your mom for lying to you when you found out the truth?"

"Without a doubt, I would be furious but, I hope I would realize my mom was only trying to protect me in the end."

"You would hope but, how we hope to handle a situation isn't always how we actually handle it."

"I see your point."

"I know I would want the truth, and I'm sure Taylor would too..." Reese practically choked on the words as they fell from her mouth.

They each lit up a second smoke and enjoyed the euphoria it brought in silence together.

Once they made it back inside the bar, Reese indulged in several more shots. It didn't take long before she was unable to pronounce syllables, and Emily had to help her walk to the car.

Chapter 20

WHEN REESE'S EYES slowly opened, she was surrounded by darkness. *Where the hell am I?* Her bloodshot eyes burned as she tried to let them adjust to the darkness, making out a statue on the table next to the couch she was sprawled out on. Her aching feet hit the ground and the room spun out of control. *Oh God,* she placed her head in her hands and rocked her intoxicated body back and forth trying to calm the storm raging in her stomach. It wasn't long before she leaped off the couch and took off in hopes to find a bathroom.

She ran into a bookshelf and a wall but, luckily the first door she found was in fact, a bathroom. With a flick of the switch the light immediately filled every part of her path to the toilet, and quickly heaved her body over rejecting the copious amounts of alcohol she had consumed that afternoon. She didn't even have time to close the door behind her.

Reese felt a cold hand swoop her hair up and out of her face as another hand rub her back.

"You drank quite a bit."

"Emily?" Reese heaved again, relieved to hear a familiar voice.

"I left a bucket next to the couch, guess you didn't see it." Reese slightly shook her head no. The slight movement caused her to puke again, "you poor thing."

Reese could feel the pull of an elastic band being placed to hold back her hair and then heard footsteps of Emily walking out of the bathroom. She reached out her limp arm begging her to come back.

"I'm just getting a couple of wet washcloths." Emily told her.

The shock of the cold damp washcloth on the back of her neck was more welcomed than she thought it would be. It seemed to help ease the dizziness into a gentle sway. *I can handle this,* she lied to herself.

"I'm so sorry," Reese's voice echoed into the toilet bowl.

"Don't apologize, you're fine."

It wasn't long before everything became hazy and darkness swallowed her whole.

Reese's eyes involuntarily broke opened making her painfully aware of the cold hard surface her face was on. Pushing her tired body up off the floor of the bathroom she felt warmth disappear. *Who put this blanket on me? Wait, am I actually at Emily's or was that a horrible dream?* Taking in her surroundings, she realized she was in fact at Emily's, at least she was about eighty-five percent sure it was Emily's house.

Peeling herself off the floor she wrapped the warm blanket back around her icy body. She glanced into the mirror and was horrified at her reflection. *You're so worthless! You can't even handle a little bad news. If only Chad could see you now.* The voice she thought was long gone was back in full force. She thought she had gotten rid of Alex taking over her thoughts but, sadly, she was wrong.

Stumbling out of the bathroom she came down the hallway.

"She lives!" Emily shouted. Reese winced at the noise and instantly became fully conscious of the pounding in her head. Placing her hand on her temple she pushed in as hard as she could muster. "Oh shit, I'm sorry, honey." Emily whispered.

"No, I'm sorry. I never drink like that!"

"No need to apologize." Emily was filling up a glass of ice water. "Your phone is on the coffee table. I hope you don't mind but, I answered your mom. She had called you about a half-a-dozen times, I explained everything. She seemed to understand."

"Shit," grabbing her phone she pulled up the eighteen text messages her mom left.

MAGGIE: Reese, I've been tryin' to call you. Please answer your phone. Daddy and I saw somethin' on the news and I need to talk to you right away. 5:25PM

MAGGIE: Please answer your phone! 5:48PM

MAGGIE: We know about Alex, and you need to call me back ASAP! 6:00PM

MAGGIE: At least let us know if you're alright! 6:14PM

MAGGIE: Reese Elizabeth Landon... CALL ME BACK RIGHT NOW!!!!!! 6:22PM

Reese stopped reading after that since Maggie just continued to repeat herself multiple times.

"I figured she was worried about you." Emily offered an unnecessary explanation.

"I should've called her," Reese lowered her head. "I gotta go. Can you take me to my car?"

"Sure, but, take this first." Emily slid Tylenol and Advil across the table to her.

"Thanks," she popped them into her mouth and swallowed a gulp of water. "Let's go." She grumbled.

Reese gathered her shoes and belongings with the same urgency as she did the morning after she conceived Taylor. She wanted to get the hell out of there that morning with Alex, and this morning, she just wanted to hold her baby girl.

"Where in tar-nation have you been young lady?" Maggie met Reese out on the porch when she got home, hands on her hips.

"Don't talk to me like I'm some teenager who stayed out past curfew, Mom. Where's Taylor?"

"She's sleepin', we need to talk about this."

"Mom, I don't want to talk about this, okay?" Reese tried to walk past Maggie but. was stopped by a firm grip to her arm.

"You can't just run away from this, Reese."

"Do you honestly think I don't know that?" Reese broke into tears and ripped her arm from her mother's grip. "This is not me running, Mother, this is me trying to just process it all! Besides, even if I tried to run from it, I can't because everyone knows! The whole damn country knows! There will be no escaping it, so excuse me for trying to escape it for just a few more hours."

Maggie's mouth hung open as water flooded Reese's face. Reese felt regret storming off. None of this was Maggie's fault. Reese could barely wrap her head around the reality of the chaos yet to come; there was no room left for dealing with her mom and her relentless pushing. Reese opened the door to Taylor's room. She didn't just want to see her daughter, she needed to.

Gently scooping her out of the crib she was left with a nagging sense of urgency, and pulled her to her chest. Tears continued to flood her face as she stood there holding the love of her life. She knew that things would never be the same; there was no going back now.

"Mama?" she heard Taylor's sweet voice.

"Hi Tay, Mama loves you so much!"

"Cry'ng?"

"Everything's okay baby, everything's going to be okay."

Reese was not only talking to Taylor but, to herself as well. After all, she had pieced herself together once before, she could do it again. She swayed her body ever so gently back and forth mindlessly humming a melody. She wished Chad was there with them, he could hold them both and tell them everything was going to be okay, and she would believe him. It all made perfect sense now... the text, the lack of response from Chad. They had caught a break, they found a lead, and it led them straight to Alex. *How could Alex do this? How could I have not seen it?*

She replayed their relationship again and again. *I guess the warning signs were there, I just don't understand how I didn't think to investigate. God, I hope he wasn't doing this when we were together. Oh my God. What the hell am I gonna do?*

She changed Taylor's diaper and put her feet to the ground, and followed the lively toddler into the kitchen. Reese placed her into her high chair for breakfast.

"Reese," Maggie softly said, "can we talk?"

"I don't know what to say, Mom. I don't know what to think, so I don't know how you expect me to talk."

"Come," she placed her hand on Reese's shoulder, "sit." She motioned toward the stool at the bar in the kitchen.

Reese walked to the stool with her head down. *You're such an idiot, Reese. Blind as a fucking bat.* Alex's voice rang in her ears. She could just picture his smug chiseled face with his signature smirk on it. She felt a shiver down her spine thinking of him sitting across from Chad with that exact look. That was the same look he used to have on his face after he would hit her. That look echoed "What are you gonna do about it, bitch?" *Ugh,* his voice rang louder with each passing minute.

"I know you're not okay," Maggie started, "... but, I want you to know you're not alone."

"I know, Mama," Reese gently smiled at Maggie.

"Did you know his girlfriend got arrested with him?"

"What?" Reese's voice went up about three octaves.

"Yea, I think her name was Vanessa?"

"Holy shit! I didn't know that."

"Language, Reese!" Maggie snapped.

"Mom, we are way passed that right now."

"I guess you're right..." Maggie rubbed her hands together and pools of water formed in her eyes.

"Mom?"

"It's just..." Her voice trailed off behind the sniffles. "That could've been you!"

"Mom, I would never–"

"Of course, not now but, the way you were when you were with him. You've told me the awful and horrible things he did to you! Who's to say he wouldn't convince you to do this too?" Her voice hiccupped between the staccato breaths she took.

"Well, let's just be thankful it isn't me."

Reese easily knew it could've been her. He made her watch underage porn and out of fear she didn't say a word. He raped her on multiple occasions and never once did she try to fight him off. Her fear of him was much bigger than her fear of the consequences from everyone else. She tossed her friends aside, isolated herself from anyone he didn't like, and had become someone she never imagined she would ever be. She believed, at the time, she acted the way she did to save them but, soon found, it was more so to save herself. She just never saw it before now.

"Mom?"

"Yea?" Maggie asked, wiping her eyes and cheeks.

"I'm sorry."

"Why on earth are you apologizing?"

"I'm sorry I ever put you through any of this."

"Oh baby," Maggie moved closer to Reese and put her arms around her. "This is not your fault."

"There were signs, Mom." Reese broke down. "Had I said something, or done something, those girls would still be alive right now!" Reese forced the words through her breath.

"You can't think like that!"

"But it's the truth!"

"No it ain't," Maggie released her hold and looked Reese in her eyes. "No one can predict the future, sis. Hind sight is always twenty-twenty; we can't always see in the moment things that are happening. Reese, you barely got yourself and Taylor out from his grasp, let alone anyone else."

"Those poor girls, Mom, they didn't deserve any of this."

"No they didn't, baby, that ain't your fault though."

"But I left him!" Reese screamed. "I left him to wreak havoc, and now... Oh God..."

"Shh," Maggie held Reese as tight as she could.

Reese felt another set of arms around her holding her as tightly as they could.

"I'm so sorry, Reesey." Rusty whispered, causing Reese to cry harder than she thought possible.

Guilt had swallowed her up without even batting an eye and left her for dead. *I should've been stronger, I should've tried harder. This is my fault. It's my fault those girls are dead. I would endure a thousand more beatings to fix this if I could. I would endure whatever I had to as long as they could live.*

Forty minutes later, Reese felt exhausted. Her eyes purged so many tears—they were unable to produce anymore for now. She sat on the couch staring off at nothing. Her eyes were puffy and sore, her nostrils beat red, and her lips continued to quiver. Maggie took care of Taylor as Reese just sat. She felt lost and couldn't seem to find her way to a map that told her where to go from here.

Her phone buzzed over and over again. One by one her family from Auburn called her, they texted her, and they called her again. It wasn't until Chad's name flashed across her screen she felt compelled to answer it. She picked up her phone and slid the arrow across the screen to answer. She held her phone to her ear but, couldn't bring herself to say anything.

"Reese, are you there?"

"Mm-hmm," she was able to faintly answer.

"Baby, I'm so sorry. I don't know what to say. I wanted to tell you but, I couldn't. My boss specifically named you in the people that couldn't know about any of this. I didn't know what to do." Silence fell between them. "Reese, please say something!" he begged.

"I'm not mad at you," she whispered.

"You're not?"

"No."

"Are you okay?" There was a brief pause. "That was a stupid question. Of course you're not okay."

"I–I–" Reese stopped to gather herself. She cleared her throat and shook off the trance she was in. "I don't know how to even begin to process this. How do I wrap my head around any of it?"

"I don't know, baby." Reese could hear the disappointment in his voice.

"Are you sure it's him?"

"Are you sure you want me to answer that?"

"Yes."

"I am one hundred percent sure. We were anonymously given a flash drive with multiple videos on it, and he's in every single one."

"Shit."

"I know. Is there anything I can do? I feel like you got blindsided because of me."

"You couldn't tell me, you didn't have a choice."

"I love you so much. I wish I could be there to just hold you right now."

"Me too, babe, I love you."

"I gotta go, babe. Are you gonna be alright?"

"Yes, I'll be fine," eventually, she quietly sighed

"I'll call you when I can."

"Okay."

They hung up the phone and Reese decided sitting there, staring off into oblivion, wasn't going to change a damn thing. She got up off the couch, wiped the remainder of tears from her eyes, and decided to carry on her life. Her baby girl needed her mother, not a lump on the couch who stares off into space. Reese refused to let a monster take her focus off of her daughter anymore. Although she couldn't shake the overwhelming guilt she had within her, she could certainly shove it down, and deal with it later.

Chapter 21

THREE DAYS LATER, Reese was ready to go back to work and was dealing with everything the best she could. She felt confident, like she could face everyone without breaking. Her puffy and bloodshot eyes had finally returned to normal. Without thinking, she tossed her work bag into the back of her 4Runner and headed off to work. When she finally pulled up to headquarters she could feel her confidence cracking.

The kid from the new hire class she nicknamed Opie was standing there. Reese would normally tease him with some friendly banter and he would notoriously fire back. She had actually grown to like the red headed jerk from the class. Once he got on an ambulance and ran a few legit calls his whole attitude changed, and Reese could see him for what he was; a scared boy out of his element. Things were different this morning though. Opie seemed to be searching for the right words to say with a bewildered look on his face. He seemed unsure of how to interact with her. *Look, there she is the ex of a monster.* Reese immediately broke eye contact and put her head down.

"Reese?" he hollered after her.

"Yes?" she didn't bother turning around.

"I'm really sorry," he sincerely said to the back of her head.

"Thank you," she mumbled walking through the door to the station.

Inside she was met by a hallway filled with faces that looked exactly like Opie's did. Sorrow and confusion overwhelmed them all. Reese could practically see the questions written all over their faces. Last week they all smiled and hugged her, today, on the other hand, she might as well have the plague. When Reese needed it the most, it seemed that no one was there to offer up a hug.

"Reese, can you come in my office, please?" she heard Jerry ask.

She walked in and closed the door behind her when he asked her to. She limply sat in the chair across the desk from him but, couldn't bring herself to look at him. She wasn't the one sitting in a jail cell but, she certainly felt on trial within minutes of arriving to work.

"Are you doing okay?" Jerry politely asked.

"As good as can be expected, I guess."

"I have to ask—they sure this guy did those things? Do you even know? If they aren't sure, maybe this will blow over soon?"

"They are one hundred percent, no doubt, sure." Reese's voice remained somber.

"Oh," Jerry shot his glance down to the desk and appeared embarrassed for asking.

"It's fine that you asked. I know everyone has questions, hell I have questions, and there's no blowing over quickly, not with this. I'll always be the girl that dated a killer... a monster. He was a terrible human being when we were together, and he did unspeakable things to me..." Her voice was stuck in her throat, *I can only imagine the horror those poor girls went through.*

"You don't have to explain. Yes, people will accept it all in time. It'll blow over."

"Sure it will," Reese didn't try to hide the sarcasm in her voice. "Is that all?"

"Yes."

She shot up out of the chair and out the door as fast as she could. She went over to the board and saw she and Cal were working together as dual-medic today.

"You ready, Cal?" she sternly asked.

"Yup," he shot a glance back at the group of people he was talking to before catching up to Reese. "Are you..."

"I'm fine."

"Are you sure?"

"Cal, I said I was fine, drop it."

She pulled herself into the driver seat and wasted no time in speeding off. Cal barely got his door closed before her foot pushed down on the gas pedal.

"Shit, Reese, don't kill us!" Cal howled.

"Oh relax, princess, I ain't gonna kill us."

Those were the only words they spoke as they sped across the city toward one of their stations. During the drive, Reese could feel the burning of Cal's eyes on her. His stare was making her angry. Everyone was staring at her as if they were trying to figure out if she's just as guilty as Alex is, or if she was an innocent bystander. Reese wanted to scream at them she didn't know anything but, what would that honestly change? You can scream at someone until you're blue in the face but, the reality is, they will only hear what they want to and forget the rest.

She slammed the rig into park, "What, Cal? For the love of Christ and all things Holy, what the hell do you want?"

"Are you–" he stopped. "I'm sorry this is happening to you, Reese."

She immediately felt terrible for biting his head off.

"You get three questions."

"Huh?"

"I know everyone has questions, and I also know if I don't answer some, people are going to find their own truth. So, fire away, three questions, nothing's off limits."

Cal shifted in his seat to face her better, and Reese did the same to face him.

"Did you know?"

"Of course not!"

"Did he do that when you were with him?"

"Honestly, I don't know." Her voice shook.

"Is it true that the one who arrested him is your current boyfriend?"

"Yes."

"Oh man, must be awkward. He couldn't slip you a heads up?"

"That's a fourth question but, I'll answer it anyway. His Captain put a gag order on him and the detective training him. He couldn't tell me, no matter how much he wanted to."

"And you believe that?" Cal huffed.

"With all my heart, it took me a long time to realize Chad is not Alex. Chad is honest, caring, sweet, trustworthy, and so many more things. I had to work through all of my past issues to get to the point of seeing that with him. Lord knows therapy certainly helped. I trust him with every fiber of my being. I trust him more than anyone on this planet, besides my parents, of course."

"That's quite a bit of trust."

"Yes it is but, he's earned it."

Their alert tone ripped through Cal's lingering thought.

"Ambulance seventy-one; priority two; one-six-four-three West Cameron; difficulty breathing, forty-six year old female." Dispatch advised.

"Ambulance seventy-one responding," Reese said through the mic.

"You're driving so I'll take this call."

"Are you sure?"

"Yea."

Cal directed Reese to the address while the siren bellowed through the air.

When they arrived on scene, Cal took charge rather quickly with the entire family standing out in front of the house, screaming at the two of them.

"Hurry the fuck up!" an irate man screamed.

"Oh yea, they're taking their sweet-ass time," a woman said on the phone to God knows who.

"You should be running!" another angry man yelled.

"We don't run, sir, where is she?" Cal sternly asked.

"She's inside, hurry up."

Reese could see Cal starting to let the panic of the family seep into him. He started walking faster, and almost tripped on the steps outside of the house. *This is why we don't panic, kids.* With a deep breath she calmly followed Cal into the house to see a woman in her mid-forties sitting on the couch rapidly breathing. There were another ten family members inside the house, surrounding her.

"What's going on?" Cal asked.

Reese stood back and listened as six different people cut each other off, one after the other, trying to tell them what was going on.

"Okay, wait, hold on," Reese cut in. "One person, one person gets to stay and explain, the rest of you need to step outside." She unapologetically said.

A few of the woman who left the room right away called her various names in Spanish under their breath.

"Puta," the last woman forced under her breath.

"I'm not a bitch," Reese turned around and came face to face with the woman.

"Excuse me?"

"You heard me, just like I heard you. We can't do our job properly with this many people screaming at us. Let's remember you called us, so don't get mad and call me a bitch under your breath because you assume I won't understand you. You called us for help, and that's what we are doing. Just because we aren't doing it the way you think we should doesn't warrant all the screaming at us and name calling." Reese stood her ground and refused to break eye contact with the woman.

The woman's chubby cheeks puffed out as she pursed her lips together in defiance. Folding her arms across her ample belly she shifted her weight to the side. *Is she trying to intimidate me?* Reese wondered, not breaking her stare. It was clearly a battle of wills and Reese refused to loose. Not today.

Eventually the woman caved and muttered, "No me digas," and walked off to presumably tell everyone what a puta Reese was.

After she walked away, Reese was able to re-join Cal, doing the duties of the EMT. She took the woman's blood pressure, put her on a heart monitor when Cal asked—although Reese didn't feel she needed it—she even did all of the heavy lifting into the ambulance. Reese felt confident the woman was only experiencing anxiety. The sudden onset of feeling like her heart was racing, shaking, difficulty breathing, chest pain, and the hum-dinger, tingling to her hands and face. All of these symptoms, of course, were made worse by the amount of people surrounding her. Reese had seen this same scenario a hundred times at least, happening to an array of people from all walks of life.

When they arrived at the ER, nerves seeped into the pit of her stomach. The last time she faced the ER staff was when her nightmare unfolded on national television. Reese punched in the four digit code and stood in fear as the automatic doors opened wide and everyone stopped to see who it was. Those who noticed her nudged the others next to them who didn't, it wasn't long before she stood there and was seemingly the focus of everyone's attention.

This is what Reese was afraid of. She hated the feeling of being exposed and vulnerable.

Everyone looked at Reese with such distain, as if she wasn't the girl they had all grown to love but, someone who was carrying some highly contagious incurable disease. Reese took a deep breath and did her best to hold it together. She tried to picture the day before her world changed, pushing Taylor on the swing with a warm breeze on their faces. She tried to hear the laughter they all shared that day and embrace the love she felt, it all seemed so far away now.

As they walked down the hallway, everyone's heads turned in unison to carry on with their work. She had seen the pity in a few of their eyes but, pity wasn't what she wanted.

Conversations ceased to continue as she walked back down the hall toward the exit. Whispers filled the background noise around her. It was like the faint buzz of a bumble bee, barely audible on a spring day, almost unnoticeable... almost. Reese was used to being the one everyone liked and got along with, not the girl they all talked about behind her back. She didn't know what to think but, she knew that she didn't like it.

"Hey, Reese," a woman's voice startled her.

Reese turned around to see Carrie standing there with concern filling her eyes. Her thin jaw moved up and down a few times as she tried to speak but, obviously didn't know what to say.

"Hey," Reese offered up an exhausted smile.

"Are—um—well, I saw—" Carrie tucked a piece of her blonde highlights behind her ear.

"Yea, I'm sure everyone has seen it by now... that's what I'm guessing since everyone is staring at me like I've contracted the plague."

"I just wanted to make sure that you're okay."

"Oh," Reese was taken aback by her kindness. "I'm fine, I guess," the lie fell from her lips so effortlessly Carrie seemed to believe it.

"I just—it's so crazy! Did you know?"

"Do you honestly think I knew?" Reese's voice cracked. "Is that what everyone thinks?"

"I don—"

"Do they think that I knew all about who my ex was and I just let it slide? I mean, hell, maybe I was holding the camera for him, huh? Sure, yeah, I knew all about it." Reese sarcastically huffed before storming away.

The doors closed behind her and finally the buzzing of the whispers stopped. Reese felt as if she was walking around with a target on her back. She heard the doors to the ER open and assumed it was Cal coming outside.

"Reese!" Carrie shouted as she jogged after her.

"What do you want, Carrie?"

"Reese, I didn't mean it like that! I would never think that!"

Reese stopped and looked up to the sky letting out the breath she was still holding, "I'm sorry," Reese put her head down ashamed of her reaction. Carrie had become someone that she adored in Denton, and the two of them had become friends. "This whole thing is just crazy and it has me feeling like I'm losing my mind!" Reese tried to fight the tears that burned in her eyes.

Carrie grabbed Reese and wrapped her thin arms around her waist, "I'm so sorry!"

"Thank you, I needed that!"

Reese knew, had she just picked up the phone and called Kyra, Jess, or even Stump, shoot, had she just called anyone from Station 23, she would've found the support she not only wanted but, she needed right then. Carrie walked back inside, and Reese pulled out her cell phone and decided to FaceTime Kyra.

"Reese! Oh my gosh! It's about time you called me back! We've all been worried sick about you." The heartbreak in Kyra's eyes was ever-present as she twisted her strawberry blonde hair between her thin fingers.

"I know, I'm sorry, I wasn't really up for talking."

"I get that, we all do but, we are just trying to be here for you."

"I just don't really know what to think right now."

"Chad said you seemed at a loss when he talked to you last."

"Yea, I'm afraid he thinks it's because I'm mad at him but, I'm really not mad at him. I don't blame him one bit for not telling me."

"He did say he was worried about that."

"Well he shouldn't be." Reese shook her head back and forth. "You know what I keep thinking?"

"What's that?" Kyra leaned into the phone.

"How could I not know? How could I not see him for what he is?" Water spilled down her face.

"Reese, please don't blame yourself."

"Well it's pretty easy to do that when everyone here is staring at me like I'm just as guilty as he is."

"Wait, what?" the irritation in Kyra's voice was easy to notice.

"It's nothing, its fine, I can handle it."

"Um, no it's not nothing! Do I need to come down there?"

"No, God, it's fine. Don't come down here!"

It's not often Kyra came to someone's defense but, when she did, it wasn't pretty. Kyra appeared scrawny and non-threatening but, mess with someone she cares about and she'll take them out, even if they were eight feet tall—she'll make damn sure to take out their knee caps.

"Okay, all you gotta do is say the word and we'll all be on a plane as soon as we can."

"I know, and I appreciate it. I gotta go, girl, my partner is headed this way and I still gotta put the rig together."

"Why aren't you running calls?"

"We're dual medic today."

"Oh, that makes sense," Kyra laughed. "Call me later."

"Okay, bye."

As much as Reese intended to call Kyra back, her day wouldn't allow it. Reese and Cal ran call after call and unfortunately, every trip into the ER created more and more gossip. Carrie did her best to break through the humming of the whispers that filled the hallways but, it didn't stop people from asking various questions when they passed by Reese.

"Did you know?"

"How did they find him?"

"Did you turn him in?"

"Were you a part of it when you were together?"

"How on earth could you not know he was like that?"

These questions haunted the free time she did have. No matter how many questions she answered, it never seemed like enough. Reese's thoughts continually went back to the innocent girls who were raped, tortured, and brutally murdered at the hands of Alex. *They must've been so scared. What I'm dealing with right now, fails in comparison to what they went through. I wish I could just hug their families and tell them how deeply sorry I am.*

"Hey," Cal broke into her thoughts. "You alright?" he lifted and repositioned his ball cap on his messy hair.

"I'm fine, I was just thinking about all of the girls Alex hurt."

"Don't do that to yourself, Reese."

"Do what to myself?"

"Torture yourself like that, it's not fair."

"You're right." She forced the words out.

"Let's go get ice cream, it's on me."

They never made it to the ice cream shop, instead, they ran more back to back calls, and before they knew it, they were watching the sunrise outside of the hospital. A new day was breaking, and Reese vowed to suffer in silence—was the least she could do to honor the girls who Alex had murdered.

Chapter 22

A S THE DAYS sluggishly passed by, Reese started to embrace her nightmare. Sure, everyone around her was talking about her and judgmental eyes followed her down the hallways in the ER and at work. The fire department never said anything on calls with her but, they didn't have to. The looks on their faces were enough to prove the breaking news had taken over Reese's world. Alex was a monster and Reese was too stupid to see how big of a monster he truly was.

Her nagging guilt grew by leaps and bounds, worried her feelings would never dull. She knew she needed to find a way to work through it but, no one seemed to want to listen to her guilt. Everyone reassured her before she was done talking that none of this was her fault. The only person she thought might listen was Chad but, he was up to his eyeballs in evidence as more had come to light.

Reese sat at home and watched the press release of the details of the case on the news station. Detective Stone stood next to Captain Ward and Chad stood behind them. Detective Stone looked somber with her light chestnut hair slightly moving with the steady breeze, and her thin lips weakly pursed together. Exhaustion enveloped them all, especially Detective Stone, they all looked on wearily as the details of the case continued to produce more evidence. Reese felt concerned as she focused on Chad, noticing the dark circles under his eyes. *They're all working so hard to piece everything together.* Reese knew there was no way Alex would graciously confess or tell them anything useful. The only thing left for them to do would be to break Vanessa—who was also in custody now—or back to more digging.

"Good afternoon, I am the Captain of homicide, Bart Ward, and I want to thank you all for joining us today. We called this press conference to share with the public what we can, and also to ask for your help. As of today we have two people in custody in association with the Auburn Schoolgirl Killer. Alex Cunningham and Vanessa Alvarez are both being charged with the kidnapping, torture, rape, and brutal murder of multiple young girls. We have strong evidence linking the two of them to all the crimes involved, unfortunately, I won't be able to comment on anything further seeing how this in an ongoing investigation." Bart straightened his papers and subconsciously cleared his throat. "We at the Auburn Police Department would like to urge anyone who knew either suspect to come forward and speak with us if they have any information regarding these girls or aspects of this case. We will be calling in all known associates of these two to conduct interviews in hopes to get answers. Again, thank you for coming out this afternoon. We will do our best to keep you updated with what we can as we move forward with this investigation."

Bart grabbed his things from the podium he stood behind and walked off the stage, ignoring the multiple hands of reporters that reached as high as they could into the sky shouting out various questions in the hopes to get more information. It wasn't long before the stage was empty and the thin Asian reporter came onto screen.

"There you have it John. Captain Ward confirms there are two in custody now. However, he was unable to confirm if they, in fact, have video evidence linking the two of them to the victims, or how they were able to lure the girls. Coming to you live from Auburn, Washington, this is Amy Cho with NCN News—back to you, John."

The screen flashed back to an older gentleman in a well-tailored pin-striped suit, and Reese fell into her own thoughts. *We would like to urge anyone who knew either suspect to come forward and speak with us... We will be calling in all known associates of these two to conduct interviews... Does that mean they are gonna call me? What if they bring up Taylor? What if they think I knew! But I didn't know!? What if they plaster my picture across the NCN screens?* She could just hear Amy Cho reporting on it now, *Ex-girlfriend claims to know nothing—Is she negligent, or just plain stupid?*

She pulled out her phone and text Chad.
REESE: Hey, my love, I just saw the press release. Y'all look exhausted. If I was there I would bring you all coffee. Chad... what do I do? I don't know anything but, I also don't want to answer questions about Taylor. I don't know what to do. Do I call and set up an interview? I cannot handle being plastered all over NCN though.

She sat staring at the text, unsure if she should send it. *What if that puts him in a messed up position?* Before she could ponder things further her phone rang. The caller ID said it was Auburn Police Department. *Crap.* She thought, *maybe it's Chad.*

"Hello?" Reese answered.

"Hi, is this Reese Landon?" A female voice came through the phone.

"Yes, this is she."

"Hi, Reese, I'm Detective Natalie Stone with the Auburn Police Department."

"Oh, yea, Chad has told me so much about you."

"He has?"

"Yea, he really admires you, and he says you're the best detective in all of homicide."

"Wow, that's so–" Natalie cleared her throat. "Miss Landon, do you know why I called you today?"

"Um–" *I know exactly why but, I'm not admitting anything.* "No, I can't say that I do."

"It has come to my attention you dated Alex Cunningham for a few years and that the two of you lived together, is this right?"

"Um yea, that would be correct."

"We actually have a few questions for you but, we would need to conduct the interview in person."

"Uh...well, I live in Texas now."

"Miss Landon, I am calling you out of courtesy to Chad but, if you'd like I can certainly haul you in for questioning."

"On what grounds?"

"There've been statements made Miss Landon, statements that would give me the right to bring you in. You have forty-eight hours to get here."

The phone went silent as they were disconnected. Reese sat in horror with the phone up next to her ear. *Statements!? What the hell is she talking about?* She looked at the screen of her phone and wanted so badly to call Chad but, couldn't bring herself to do it. She stared at the screen unsure of where to go from here. When the phone rang out she almost dropped it to the floor.

"Chad?" she timidly answered.

"Reese, thank God. I'm so sorry, Stone wasn't supposed to call you. She was supposed to let me talk to you. Shit, babe, are you okay? What did she say to you?" There was a sense of panic in his tone.

"She said that there were statements made..." Her broken voice trailed off. "...Statements... what does that even mean? I don't understand."

"It's so stupid. Fuck. I wish she hadn't come at you like that!"

"I don't know anything, Chad, I swear to God," Reese cried. "You have to believe me."

"I do believe you, I do! Just get on a plane as soon as you can and I will explain everything when you get here. Just try to breath, babe."

"I'm trying."

"I know you are. I love you, Reese. Everything's gonna be okay."

"I love you too," she forced the words through her tears.

What kind of statements could've possibly been made? Do I know something and I don't realize it? Her head fell into her hands.

Maggie came through the door to find Reese rolling out a suitcase.

"What's all of this?"

"Auburn Police Department called today." Reese grimly stated.

"What did they want?" Maggie's voice filled with the twang of concern.

"They are making me come in for questioning. They told me I had to come in person." Maggie's eyes widened. "Chad

246

said that everything will be fine," Reese continued. "I guess they need to ask me some questions about statements that were made."

"Statements!? What does that mean?"

"I don't know, Mom." Reese lowered her head. "But, they said it wasn't optional."

"Do you need us to come with you?" Maggie clinched her hands together.

"I'll be alright, Mama. Chad will be there. Can you keep Taylor? I don't really want to bring her with me in the midst of all of this."

"Of course, yes, Daddy and I will keep her safe and sound."

"Thanks, Mom," Reese grabbed Maggie and hugged her as tightly as she could.

"I love you, Ree Ree. Chad's right, everything will be okay." Maggie released her grip around Reese's body. "You let me know when you board the plane, and when you land in Washington."

"I will, Mama, I promise."

Reese grabbed her carry on suitcase and rolled it right out the front door. Sadness hit her as she closed the door, hoping this wasn't the last time she would see her family. Reese didn't know what she was walking into, or how big these so-called statements would be, and although Reese knew she was innocent, she just might have to fight to prove it to the world.

Chapter 23

WHEN SHE MADE it outside of the Seattle-Tacoma Airport, the frigged and refreshing air lightly caressed her face. She'd forgotten how much she loved the cool crisp air of Washington. She noticed Chad standing next to his car in the pick-up zone right away. When Reese caught his eye, against his olive skin, a smile illuminated his face. The darkness Reese had seen on his face during the press release seemed to have melted away with each step Reese took toward him. Her heart felt incredibly full with love for him, and for a few moments she had forgotten all about why she was back in Washington. When he scooped her up into his arms and kissed her, her worries were non-existent.

She felt electrified by his lips on hers. It had been far too long since they were able to actually see and touch each other. Her lips lingered on his, wanting desperately to stay in the moment forever.

"I'm so happy to see you, babe." Chad smiled as he put her feet back on the ground.

"I'm happy to see you too, sweetheart. I just wish—"

"Let's not talk about all of that just yet. Please, Reese. Please just enjoy this moment with me."

Reese smiled in agreement, "Okay."

Chad grabbed her bag and tossed it in the trunk of his Dodge Charger, moving swiftly to open the car door; Chad motioned Reese to get in. She sat in the passenger seat and decided to text her mom before she forgot and before Maggie could worry something bad happened on the way to Washington.

REESE: Hey, Mom, just wanted to let you know that I made it here, safe and sound. Chad came to get me and we are heading to his house. I love you.8:49PM

Maggie replied right away.

MAGGIE: Glad you made it safe, Sis! Please keep us in the loop of what's goin' on.8:50PM

REESE: I will, Mom. Xoxo.8:51PM

Reese enjoyed the ride to Chad's house, doing their best to talk about everything except for the case. Reese told Chad about how much Taylor's grown and how much her little personality is developing since they last saw each other. They held hands and shared the occasional loving gaze. For the first time since all of this began, Reese felt safe.

When they arrived, Chad carried her bag inside, and in the spirit of enjoying the moment, he took her to bed. He kissed every inch of her body before making love. It wasn't rough and it wasn't forced, it was incredibly sensual and romantic. Afterward, they lay naked in each other's arms, continuing to bask in the moment. Reese didn't want the happiness to end but, she couldn't get rid of the nagging guilt and fear she felt.

"Chad," she spoke softly.

"...I know we need to talk about this." He sighed.

"I just need to know what's going on." Pain lingered on her face.

"Let's get dress and talk on the couch."

"Okay," she agreed.

They both took their time putting on their clothes. Reese wasn't sure she wanted to know the full extent of the situation any more than Chad seemed to want to tell her.

"I'm sorry," Reese apologized behind him as they came down the hall.

"Why are you apologizing?" He turned to face her.

"I'm sorry for putting you in this position."

"You didn't do anything wrong Reese," he lightly caressed her shoulders.

"This whole thing just puts you in a bad spot." She dropped her head. "I can tell you're reluctant to tell me about everything."

"You're right, I don't want to tell you everything but, that has nothing to do with me blaming you or thinking you have anything to do with that psychopath. It's because I don't want to burden you and hurt you more than you've already been hurt." He placed his hands on each side of her face and gently drew her closer. "None of this is your fault, babe. Alex did this, not you."

"But, had I known," Reese paused, usually this was the point where anyone she was talking to would stop her from saying anything further and tell her it's not her fault and to let it go but, Chad didn't jump in. "Had I seen the signs, then maybe I could've stopped him. Or at least, maybe those poor girls would still be alive today." Tears spilled over, Chad still didn't stop her. "It's just, those girls are dead, Chad, they're dead! And it's the biological father of my child who did it! How could I not see it?" Chad wrapped his arms around her holding her tight. "I just don't understand."

"I know... shoot, Ree, I don't understand. What I do know is you're blaming yourself for this, and I get why but, I need you to listen to me very carefully." He stepped back and looked into her eyes. "When you go on scene of a fatal car accident, do you blame yourself for not being able to stop it?"

"What?" Reese felt confused, *what does that have to do with any of this?*

"Do you?"

"Well no, of course not. I can't control people."

"Exactly, now say it again."

"I can't control people."

"How can you expect yourself to be able to stop an accident when you don't even know they're in danger?"

"I don't know but, that's not the same—"

"Yes it is," he cut her off. "It's exactly the same thing. You're not responsible for this. None of us knew what he was capable of—it wasn't just you. We all knew he was a piece of shit, especially now, knowing all of the things he did to you but, I never thought this would be him. I never thought that it would be his face I saw on the videos, and I never thought he would end up being the Auburn Schoolgirl Killer."

"You watched the videos?"

"Yea," for the first time, Chad broke eye contact with Reese. "They are awful, Reese. They're beyond awful. I don't even know a word that could describe it." His voice trembled. "Detective Stone and I have had to comb through them a few times when Alex tried to say it wasn't him on the videos, that it was his brother."

"Lance? There is no way Lance would do that."

"I know, because we interviewed him, just like we are going to interview you."

"Wait... Wait, what?"

"Come, let's sit down."

251

Chad gently grabbed Reese's hand leading her to the couch.

"Do you want me to finish explaining about Lance? Or do you want me to explain your stuff first?"

"My stuff, please, I need to know." Reese clasped her hands together so tight her knuckles turned white.

He placed his hand on top of hers, "So, as I'm sure you've seen, Vanessa Alvarez was a part of it too."

"I briefly saw that."

"Now she's claiming that the woman on the videos is you, and not her."

"What!" Reese shouted.

"Hold on, let me finish," Chad calmly said, and Reese loudly huffed in defiance. "She claims you're the reason Alex started all of this in the first place," Reese's eyes widened in horror. "She states you taught him."

"Chad... Oh my God," Reese exhaled as her voice shook with fear. "Taylor, they're gonna take Taylor."

"No they aren't. Breathe, babe, just breathe." Suddenly the room had no oxygen left. "Reese, listen to me because I want to make sure you hear me correctly." She looked Chad in the eyes. "No one believes her story."

"Well, maybe Stone does? She was short with me about the whole thing, and threatened to haul me in."

"In the same way she threatened to haul Lance in." Chad scratched his head, "Well, until she found out he is the reason we have the videos."

"What? I mean, how?"

"What he told us was Harper came home from a sleep over at Alex's house and told Lance she felt very uncomfortable around Alex. She said he was looking at her in a way that

252

creeped her out, and he kept making comments about how her body was changing and she was almost just the right age."

Reese felt her heart sink, "He didn't–"

"No, he didn't. Lance said he was pissed off and wanted to talk to Alex, so he went over to his house but, he wasn't home. Lance called him and found out him and Vanessa were on shift together. The house was empty, so Lance decided to use his key and let himself in to take a look around. He said after you left, Alex, became dark and withdrawn." Guilt once again knocked at the back of her heart. "He wrapped himself up in Vanessa, although he controlled her the same way he did you." The flash of her past made Reese cringe, "He said he knew there was something off, and then when Harper came home and told him what he said, he had to investigate things himself. He happened to look on Alex's desktop and saw files with names of girls on them. He opened one of the file videos and immediately recognized one of the teen girls from the news. He found a flash drive in the desk drawer and saved the videos onto the drive and sent it to Stone as an anonymous tip. No one knows that though, Reese, and I can get in a lot of freaking trouble telling you."

"I won't say a word, I promise." She put her hands up in surrender of her promise.

"So when Vanessa started throwing your name around Stone got angry. She told me herself that she knows they are both grasping at straws. The crappy part is you both have brown hair and her light brown skin on the video could be white or Hispanic, you can't definitively tell."

"But, she's a lot shorter than I am."

"I know that, and Stone knows that too." Chad reassured her.

"I hope so. I am barely holding it together but, if they think I'm actually a part of this and they take Taylor away..." unable to finish her statement she put her head in her hands.

Chad wrapped his arms around her and held her while she wept. Despite, her feeling guilt and sadness for what was to come, she spent the rest of the night wrapped up in his arms feeling safe. She remained safe from Alex, safe from the accusations that awaited her tomorrow, and safe from judgment. Chad let her be vulnerable without making her feel bad for it. He let her get out her fears and her guilt and helped her to realize that blaming herself was not the answer. Of course, the guilt still lingered in the back of her heart but, it was manageable there and Reese had no intentions of letting it rule her again.

Once Reese was finally asleep that night, she struggled with nightmare after nightmare. She was stuck in a cold dark interrogation room with no windows. The only lighting provided was by a flickering florescent light that hung from the ceiling. Reese sat, handcuffed to a chair pulled up to a table, and she stared at the two empty seats sitting across from her.

The loud screech of the metal door opening startled her. When detective Stone walked in the room, Reese began her plea.

"Please, you have to believe me! It wasn't me! I didn't hurt those girls!"

Natalie said nothing as she looked down at Reese with disgust.

"Save your tears for the jury, Reese." A voice from behind Natalie scoffed.

When Natalie fanned out to the side she was able to see it was Chad standing behind her. Reese's mouth fell open and her eyes became enlarged with shock. She spent what felt like hours being berated by Natalie and Chad.

She continued to dream Natalie used Alex to torture her into talking. She shoved his ample body into the room and slammed the metal door shut, locking her inside. Alex was enraged and looked as he had before in her nightmares; larger than life and his eyes glowed green. Reese could see the large veins down his arms pulsate and bulge out even more when he clinched his fists. She sat, handcuffed to a chair, defenseless and alone. She desperately tried to scream for Chad even though nothing came out of her mouth. She began whimpering as he slammed his fists into her face and body, over and over again. Blood covered the floor around her as she tried so hard to cry for help. It felt as if her mouth was glued shut. It wasn't until he choked her so hard she couldn't breathe that she sat upright, gasping for air.

Beads of sweat trickled down her face and chest, her lungs burned from breathing so hard. As much as Reese believed Chad about her not having to worry about it all, she couldn't help the fear that gripped her sub-consciousness. She still feared Alex, no matter how much she didn't want it to be true, her nightmares only proved it.

She gave up on sleep and decided to make some coffee. She threw on one of Chad's sweatshirts to keep her warm; she loved how comfy it was, the best part, it smelled just like him. Even just the smell of him helped to calm her nerves as she held the sweatshirt up to her face and inhaled deeply. *Mmm,* she thought with a smile on her face, forcing down the memories of the nightmares that haunted her sleep.

Reese lightly drummed her fingers on the counter as the coffee maker took its time brewing her cup.

"Not awake yet, are ya?" She whispered to the machine.

"He doesn't wake up until at least five," Chad mumbled.

Reese whipped around startled, "Good gravy, Chad, you scared the shit outta me!" She exclaimed.

"I'm sorry, babe," he rubbed his tired eyes and scratched his messy hair. "Why on earth are you up?"

"I couldn't sleep."

"Babe, I told you not to worry."

"It's like you don't even know me at all!" Reese smirked trying to make a joke.

"You're right, I should've known better," he smiled. "Can you make me a cup?"

"Hon, you don't have to stay up with me, it's okay."

"Reese, you're not alone in this, and I think maybe right now you need to be reminded of that."

"How do you do that?"

"Do what?"

"Know exactly what to say and exactly what I need." She answered as she stirred the creamer into her coffee.

"Because I know you," he softly spun her around to face him. "I know you better than you think I do, Ree. I love you, and I will always be there for you and Taylor. I would never let you walk into a trap, or hurt you in any way. You don't have to do any of this alone, not anymore."

He kissed her deeply holding her face in his hands.

Her lips softly caressed his, "Thank you," she smiled. "I love you so much, Chad. What would I do without you?"

"You're a strong woman, Reese, I have no doubt you could survive anything, no matter what this crazy life throws your way. I've stood in awe as you have handled yourself with so much dignity."

Reese huffed, "Dignity?"

"Yes. Most people would've lost their cool by now, thrown in the towel, or maybe even ran and hid under a rock. But, not you, you've chosen to handle it all the best you can and you keep putting one foot in front of the other."

"I don't feel like I have an ounce of dignity left. Everyone stares at me, all the time. They judge me with every step that I take. I'm barely holding it together, Chad."

"They're staring at you, waiting for you to break. Are you really gonna give the world the satisfaction of giving them what they want?"

Reese put her coffee mug down on the counter and stood up straight. She held her head high for the first time in weeks. Chad was right. She knew she would never give them the pleasure of watching her crumble. Alex couldn't break her back then, and he certainly won't break her now.

"Absolutely not!" she proclaimed.

Chapter 24

REESE AND CHAD walked hand in hand into the Auburn Police station. The building had a sleek design of metal and glass. Reese couldn't help but admire the big glass doors. It seemed so light and airy—inviting even—although, Reese still held a slight fear there was a windowless interrogation room waiting for her.

Chad pulled open the door and she walked through it easily enough.

"Reese? Is that you?" a woman exclaimed.

Reese turned around to see Jess standing there. She had cut her beautifully long hair short and was currently rocking a sassy bob that suited her stunning face.

"Jess? Oh my gosh!" Reese released her death grip on Chad's hand and ran over, wrapping her arms tightly around Jess. "What on earth are you doing here?"

"I did my interview yesterday, and Chad sent Kyra and me a text seeing if we could be here for you today." Reese turned back and lovingly smiled at Chad. "He's a keeper, Reese."

"He certainly is," she smiled. "Thank you for coming today," she turned back to Jess. "Where's Kyra?"

"She's in with Detective Stone right now. She changed her time so she could do her interview and then be here for you."

"You guys are seriously the best!" Reese wrapped her arms around Jess again.

"We love you, girl. No way we'd let you go through this alone." Jess squeezed her tightly.

Reese let go and took a step back when her phone went off in her pocket.

EMILY: Hey! Remember to breathe. Everything will be OK.8:54AM

"Who's that?" Jess asked.

"It's from Emily, one of my partners back home."

"That's sweet. See, you're not alone, Reese."

The girls went and sat down in the lobby while Chad let the front desk know they were there. It wasn't more than a few minutes when Kyra came out of the glass door separating the lobby and the waiting room.

"Kyra!" Reese shrieked popping up from her seat. She quickly made her way over and threw her arms around Kyra. They stood wrapped in their embrace for several seconds, neither one saying a word.

"I've missed you so much!" Reese said breaking the silence.

"I've missed you too, Reese!"

"Thank you for bein' here, I had such a hard time sleeping last night."

"Nightmares?"

"Yea, how'd you know?"

"You're my best friend. I know how you work."

"Good point," Reese laughed.

The glass door swung open wide and a woman was standing in the doorway, holding open the door. She was tall with slightly wide hips that filled out the skinny jeans she wore. She had tactical boots on laced up over her jeans, and a teal green V-neck t-shirt. Her naturally wavy hair flowed down each side of her face. One side was tucked tightly behind one of her ears.

"Reese Landon?" Her voice rang loudly through the waiting room.

Natalie Stone wasn't drop dead gorgeous but, she was pretty, with big hazel eyes and high cheek bones. Reese could see the years of stress and experience around her eyes along with the dark circles put under them by the sleepless nights Alex had undoubtedly given her too..

"Yes, I'm here," her voice trembled.

Chad walked closely behind her.

"Chad, you know you can't be in there."

"I know, but—"

"No," Natalie cut him off. "Captain Ward and I will be conducting the interview. You can't be anywhere near this one."

Reese turned around and faced Chad.

"It's okay, babe, I got this." She kissed him lightly and walked through the open door.

Once the door swiftly closed behind Reese she followed closely behind Detective Stone. Natalie didn't hesitate for one second.

"Follow me."

She led Reese through the maze of desks in an open floor of detectives. There was a second level up a few stairs where there were more desks and offices encased by glass. *Maybe those are for the higher ups.* She examined the cubes. Her suspicions were confirmed when she recognized Captain Ward stand up out of his under-sized chair. His eyes looked black as well. *Alex has wreaked havoc on all of them,* Reese sympathetically thought.

When Captain Ward caught up with them he said, "You must be Reese Landon."

"Yes, sir, I am. I recognize you from the news, Captain Ward. It's nice to meet you."

Although Reese wasn't thrilled about the way she was meeting Chad's new boss, she was genuine in her words. She continued to walk behind Detective Stone, ignoring the pounding of her heart. Reese knew she had done nothing wrong, she just hoped Detective Stone believed her when she urges her innocence.

"Right this way," Natalie gestured Reese through a door she held open that lead to another cubical.

Reese noticed when she entered the room that it obviously wasn't an interrogation room. The lack of a two-way mirror was the first clue and there was a couch and two chairs thoughtfully placed around a round coffee table. This cubical had solid walls that Reese figured was for privacy but, there was one window that showed the green lawn out of the front of the building and the parking lot. The one window in the room was tinted but, it brought in just enough natural light from outside they almost didn't need the light on in the room.

Natalie motioned Reese to the sofa, "Can I get you anything to drink? We have coffee, water, or soda." Her tone was much softer now.

"Um, water would be good."

Reese felt worried this was some sort of a good cop, bad cop situation. Maybe they were trying to trap her into lowering her guard so she might say something they can deem as suspicious and warrant further investigation.

Detective Stone came back with a bottle of water and handed it to Reese.

"Thank you."

"No problem," she smiled.

Detective Stone sat in the chair closest to Reese and reached into the bag that leaned up against her chair, pulling out her tape recorder, a notepad, and a pen. She sat the tape recorder down on the coffee table, and pushed record.

Natalie looked up as she leaned back into her chair, "This interview will be recorded." Reese wasn't sure what to say, so she nodded her head, "Miss. Landon?"

"Yes?"

"I need you to verbally acknowledge you're aware and understand this interview is being recorded."

"Oh, of course, yes I understand you're recording this interview."

Natalie leaned forward, placing her mouth closer to the recorder.

"This is Detective Natalie Stone with Captain Bart Ward, and we are conducting the interview with Reese Landon." She leaned back into the chair and scribbled something onto her notepad before making eye contact with Reese. "It has come to our attention you may personally know our suspect, Alex Cunningham." She paused and scrutinized Reese's face. "Do you know him?"

"Yes I do, well I haven't spoken to him in several years, but—Um, I mean, yes, I know him." Reese could feel the words getting stuck in her throat.

"What is your relationship to him?"

"We don't have a—We aren't in a—" Reese drew in a deep breath and took a moment to compose her thoughts. "We had a romantic relationship for a few years, but that ended."

"What do you mean by a few years—Two, three, or five? Can you be more specific?"

"Um," Reese paused jolting her eyes upward and to the right as she tried to recall the time frame. Reese could hear Captain Ward in the background of her thoughts clear his throat as the seconds slowly passed. "Two-and-a-half years," Reese finally said. "But, it ended around, well, two-and-a-half years ago ironically."

"Okay," Natalie continued to write in her notepad. The sound of her pen scratching at the paper filled the room. "When was the last time you spoke with Mr. Cunningham?"

"Two-and-a-half years ago when I broke things off with him."

Natalie nodded her head without looking up from her notebook she said, "Were you aware of what he was doing?"

There was a silence that fell through the room and the pain of that question became noticeable on Reese's face. *Even they think I knew.* Her head and shoulders dropped as she exhaled.

"No, I had no idea."

"Can you describe your relationship with Mr. Cunningham?"

"What do you mean? I already told you he was my boyfriend."

"I mean, how was your relationship? Where you happy? Was he controlling?"

"To put it lightly, yes."

"Can you elaborate?" Natalie asked without looking up from whatever she was writing.

"Well, I don't typically like to talk about it, but yes I can. Alex was the greatest boyfriend, and then a light switch flipped within him and then he wasn't." Reese stared off at the thought of a past she didn't want to think about anymore. "He became intolerant of my relationships with my co-workers and male friends."

"Just with the men?"

"Yes, well, he wasn't a fan of my Partner, Kyra Vaughn, either but, that was just the beginning." Reese shuffled the full bottle of water back and forth in her hands. "Well, when I didn't follow his rules he would get really mad."

"What do you mean by mad?"

Reese realized she had never expressed specifically the things Alex had done to her. Sure, she told her mom and Chad he was abusive and physically hurt her but, she had never elaborated, and she didn't want to give specifics. She didn't want to talk about any of this. She wanted to go home.

With a deep breath she said, "Well, he would grab my face really hard with his hand, like this;" Reese held out her hand in front of her and cupped it around as if she was grabbing a face. "He also choked me and left marks most times. Um, he slapped and punched me more times than I honestly care to recall. He had pushed me down the back steps off our patio. I ended up dislocating my shoulder, sprained both of my ankles, and probably broke a few ribs. He threw me into the wall and the door to the bathroom. He drug me down the hallway by my hair." Reese abruptly stopped when she heard Natalie scoff. "Did I say something wrong?"

Natalie startled from her own thoughts, "No, no, you are doing great. I just don't understand why you didn't report him?"

Reese stopped fidgeting with the bottle and looked at Natalie.

"Have you ever been with a controlling and manipulative man before, Detective Stone?"

"No, I would nev—"

"Before you finish that statement, you should know I used to say the same thing. I used to look at battered women like they were weak and too stupid to leave. It wasn't until I became one that I truly understood. It isn't about how weak they are. It's about how much their significant other has broken them down. I mean, it can be anyone—men and women alike can find themselves stuck in an abusive relationship. It takes one person to fracture who you are and then chip away at what's left, all before you even realize what's happening. They subtly and delicately make small and insignificant comments about you or the way you do things and without even realizing you begin to make the changes they are telling you to make. You think you're being a good girlfriend and compromising, trying to meet in the middle with this person you love. Next, you feel like all of the problems in your relationship are your fault because you aren't giving enough." Reese leaned forward. "And next thing you know you're telling yourself if you just followed the rules he wouldn't hit you. If you were a better girlfriend, your scalp wouldn't burn and your hair would still be on your head and not balled up in the trash. He hits you because you deserve it and you just need to be better so he doesn't get mad. So, you shut everyone out, you push them all away for your safety and well-being. You become so turned around you don't know which way is up and you're left fighting for air to just breathe." Reese placed her hand on her chest. "I was a strong-willed and independent woman, but I was ignorant. I thought no man would ever be able to manipulate me like Alex did. I was wrong. I had no idea how flawlessly he would be able to execute it."

Natalie sat across from Reese, her jaw slightly hung open. Even Captain Ward had a look of shock on his face. Maybe Reese should've felt a tinge of regret for standing on her soap box in the middle of an interview with the police, but she didn't. There was nothing meek or timid about the things Reese had been through. She certainly wasn't going to try and shrink it down for anyone. Especially, to someone she felt was judging her.

"Well," Natalie cleared her throat. "I see your point, Miss Landon, my apologies."

"Forgiven."

"It's my understanding you have a child," Natalie continued.

"My child is none of your business."

Reese instinctively became even more defensive than before. She didn't uproot her entire life to protect Taylor just to have them obliterate it.

"Excuse me?"

"I thought we were here to talk about Alex, Detective Stone, you can ask me anything you want about him but, I will not answer any questions about my child."

"Fair enough," she paused to scribble down something on her notepad. "Were you aware there've been accusations made against you during our investigation?"

"Accusations? About what?"

Reese knew she had to play the part, Natalie couldn't know Chad told her last night.

"Well, Miss Alvarez is saying it isn't her in the videos we've received, it was you."

"Wait, wait..." Reese slightly put her hand out in front of her, "What?"

266

"Is it you on the video tapes molesting and torturing those young girls, Miss Landon?"

"Of course not!" Reese sat up straight. "Do I need a lawyer for this interview?"

"Do you want a lawyer?" Natalie stared at Reese, again visibly analyzing her body language.

"Well, these are some pretty big accusations, Detective Stone!"

Natalie reached over and shut off the recorder.

"Look," she sat back and looked at Captain Ward. When he gave her the nod of approval, she continued, "We know Alvarez is full of shit, Miss Landon but, we have to ask you these questions. There's a significant height difference and several features are distinctively different between you two. If she pushes the issue, we can have an analysis done to survey height, weight, eye shape, mouth shape, etcetera. If we don't talk to you and ask you these questions, the defense will tear apart our case in court."

Natalie went to turn back on the recorder; Reese stopped her, "Wait."

"Is there something you'd like to tell us?"

"Yes, it's about my daughter."

"Okay," Natalie readjusted her posture.

"I'm assuming if it comes to it, I'll have to testify?"

"Yes."

"I will tell you now I will not answer any questions pertaining to my child, even on the stand."

"Can I ask why you're so protective?"

"Well, first of all the accusation is I hurt young girls, and I have a little girl. Second of all, I will not discuss my child in front of Alex." Natalie looked at Reese, still clearly confused. "I moved thousands of miles away and left the birth certificate blank for a reason, Detective Stone."

Reese raised her eyebrows and nodded her head as if to signal what she meant. She couldn't bring herself to say the words out loud.

"I understand, Miss Landon, however, I cannot control the defense."

"I understand."

Natalie clicked the record button back on.

"So, Miss Landon, is that you in the videos with Alex?"

"Absolutely not!"

"Had Alex ever suggested doing these types of things with you before?"

"No," Reese sternly answered.

"Have you ever participated in elude acts with a minor before?"

"No!" Reese could feel her defenses building back up. "I would never do that to a child!"

"I believe you," she reassured Reese. "We go to trial in a few days. We need you to stay in town because you're on the witness list to be called to the stand."

"Um, what about my job?"

"We already called them and explained everything. Your boss understood and stated it would be fine."

"Oh, um okay then."

"Great, thank you so much Miss Landon for coming in today." Natalie clicked off her recorder, stood up, and put her hand out to shake Reese's hand. "We'll be in touch."

Reese stood and placed her hand in Natalie's, "Okay."

She felt dazed as she watched the two of them swirl out of the room. Reese just stood there at the realization she would have to face Alex in court. After everything, that was the absolute last thing she wanted but, most of all, she feared he would make his lawyer ask her questions about Taylor because she was under oath and had to tell the truth or risk being charged with perjury.

"Miss Landon?" Natalie poked her head back into the room where the door was now propped open and Reese was expected to leave. "I'll take you back to Chad."

"Oh, sorry," she became painfully aware that she was apologizing for no plausible reason, again.

Natalie lead her back through the sea of desks, and although Reese's body had left the room, her mind remained in the same exact spot as she pictured having to come face to face with the only person that has ever made her tremble with fear.

Once they got back to Chad's house, Reese couldn't shake the question of what happened to the girls. She felt an overwhelming and unexplainable need to know what those innocent girls went through.

"Babe, can I ask you something?"

"Sure," Chad nonchalantly said.

"How bad did Alex hurt those girls?"

Reese's entire body sunk low as Chad looked up at her with disbelief.

"Trust me, Reese," his tone changed as he obviously relived the details of the case. "You don't want to know."

"Yes I do," she said struggling with her inner guilt. "I need to know."

Chad shot up off the couch, visibly uncomfortable. He paced back and forth in front of her rubbing his hand on the back of his neck. After several grunts and huff's he finally stopped dead in his tracks.

"I don't want to be the one to tell you. I don't want to be the one responsible for breaking your heart even more."

Reese slowly stood up and wrapped her arms around his neck, pulling him close and holding him tight.

"My heart is already shattered. Please, I need to know."

Chad released her body with a drawn out exhale and walked off down the hall. Reese stood there unsure what to do. She couldn't explain the relentless need she had to know exactly what Alex had done. Maybe she thought it would help her process, maybe she needed to know exactly what Alex was capable of before she testified against him at the trial. Whatever the reason, Reese knew she wouldn't be able to let it go, but worried maybe she shouldn't have pushed Chad. She knew it was unfair to ask him but, she didn't trust anyone else to tell her the ugly truth.

Chad dragged his heels across the carpet as he came back down the hall but, now he was carrying a folder in his hands. The somber look on his face broke Reese's heart. *Should I be asking him to do this?*

"Babe, you don't—" she started.

"Yes I do. If you're going to hear the details, you should hear them from me." He sat down next to her. "Before I give you this, I want you to understand something. These pictures are the most horrifying thing that I've ever seen, and even Captain Ward said they are the worst he has seen too. Several analysts were unable to complete their tasks due to how graphic these are." Reese's heart sunk into her stomach. "Are you sure this is what you want?" Chad asked, subtly asking her to reconsider.

"I'm sure. I don't expect you to understand why I need to know, hell, I don't even fully understand why but, I know I need to know."

"I know you well enough to know that when you say this is something you need, you don't say it lightly." He handed her the file. "Would you like me to stay?"

Reese grabbed the file and considered what she wanted. She knew this wasn't going to be easy, and having Chad with her might be the best thing. On the other hand, this was something she needed and there was no reason to put him through that again.

"I'm okay, you can go."

Chad didn't say anything more. He got up, kissed her on the forehead, and with his hands shoved deep in his pockets he walked down the hallway.

Reese swallowed back her fear and took a long drawn out breath before opening the file. It was filled with countless pictures. Reese gasped at the sheer volume. She flipped through several blurry pictures that look as if they tried to create still frames from the video. She flipped to the next picture that was clearer, and found a hot pink post-it stuck to it that said "Penelope Stevenson". Her young face twisted in agony and fear. Reese felt a prick of pain behind her eyes. Terror filled Penelope's face as her mouth screamed in obvious pain. Alex had her bent over, his fingers dug into her shoulder, and his expression was wild with pleasure.

Reese's stomach turned.

She flipped quickly to the next picture and saw a girl much younger than Penelope. Her picture also had a post-it, hers was orange, and it was marked "Claire Clemmons". Her hair looked as if it was once French braided, in the picture there were several strands of hair that fell around her scared face. Reese could only see the girls profile in the picture but, it was enough to know that she was petrified. Her eyes wide and panic-stricken and Reese noticed it was because Alex's fist was ready to connect with her face.

Reese's mind flashed back to her own memories. It was the same face he made when he used to hit her. His features scrunched together allowing his teeth to be fully exposed. She remembered the spit that flew from his mouth and onto her face. Her breath hiccupped. Her eyes darted back to Claire, and delicately ran her fingers over her face.

"I'm so sorry," she whispered with tears making their slow decent down her face.

The next picture revealed a yellow post-it marked, "Sara Higgins". Just by the picture Reese could tell she was much tougher than the other girls. Maybe it was the attitude that came with the red hair but, she was clearly trying to fight back. Freckles sat on the bridge of her nose scrunched up with defiance dripping down her face like sweat. Her teeth were exposed and she was smashing them together hard enough that they could've broke. Alex wrapped his giant hands around her slender and fair-skinned neck so hard his fingers drowned in her skin. His face looked like a body-builder who had maxed out on weight as he tried to pull the dumbbell up. Alex was clearly using all of his strength to hurt this girl and yet, there was a twinkle in his eye that was noticeable in the fuzzy picture.

The twinkle in his eye didn't surprise her. It was the absence of life in the next photo that broke her heart. Sara had no more fight left. Her eyes had gone dark, her mouth hung open, while her head lifelessly hung back. The girl who put up a fight ceased to exist at some point between these two photos. More tears found their way to the surface and slid down Reese's face and neck.

Reese frantically sifted through the pictures that sprawled across her lap for another picture of Sara. She needed to find one of her with the will to live still in her eyes. She needed to see that fight. Instead she found Sara's lifeless body sprawled out as Alex defiled her one last time. Her neck turned a deep red and purple and her fiery hair flowed down from the top her head toward the ground as if she was hanging upside down.

"Shit," Reese breathed through the tears. "Shit, shit, shit."

The tears kept coming as she quickly moved through picture after picture, girl after girl, and torture after torture.

The next thing Reese knew, she felt the warmth of Chad's arms around her.

"I'm sorry, baby, I'm sorry," he whispered as he held her.

"How—How could he—" her breath was erratic with heartache.

"I don't know, babe. I just don't know."

Reese pulled herself away from him and took several deep breaths in hopes to center her emotions. She wiped her cheeks and neck while she sniffled to keep the snot from escaping her nostrils.

"How long did he have these poor girls?"

"From what we can gather, he kept them captive anywhere between a few days, to possibly a week."

"Those poor babies," she turned to Chad. "They're just babies."

"I know," he rubbed her back. "This isn't your fault, Reese. Please tell me that you know that."

"I do, that doesn't make me feel any better."

"I know what you mean. I had to watch the videos over and over. I'll never be able to get the sounds of their blood curdling screams out of my head."

"Oh honey," Reese turned to him with woeful eyes and placed her hand on his.

"Even now I still wake up in the middle of the night drenched in sweat because I hear them. I hear them begging him to stop, I hear them screaming in pain, I hear them begging God to take them." Chad put his head into his hands. "I just don't understand how a human being can do that to a child."

"I don't understand it either."

Chad ran his hands down his face as he lifted his head.

"Natalie suggested I go see the shrink."

"That might not be a bad idea. When I was fixing myself and I went to therapy, it really helped. Honestly, it was the best decision I've ever made."

"You guys are probably right but, I just want this whole thing behind me."

"Take it from the girl, who spent a year trying to fix the damage this monster did, you need help to repair and work through this. I know you want it to be over. I wanted it to be over too, and I still do, but the reality was that until I dealt with it in a healthy way I was going to be stuck exactly where I was."

"True."

"Maybe give the shrink a call and maybe go see them before the trial starts."

"Okay."

"I know I'll be calling my therapist when I get home." Reese lightly touched her lips to his. "I love you, Chad Platt, and we are going to get through this."

"I love you too," he gave her a second peck on the lips.

Chapter 25

"THIS IS AMY Cho, coming to you live from outside the Auburn Courthouse. Today's trial begins for alleged Auburn Schoolgirl Killer, Alex Cunningham and his accomplice Vanessa Alvarez. They are both standing trial today for the brutal rape and murders of several young girls in the Auburn area." Reese could hear the newscaster as she walked passed the large marble pillars that held up the old brick building. "Both have pled 'not guilty' and plan to go forward with a full trial. Multiple witnesses are on stand-by and plan to be called to the stand over the next few days. The list includes family, co-workers, and Alex Cunningham's ex-girlfriend."

Reese's heart fell into her stomach, "I can't do this," she whispered to Chad.

"Yes you can, babe." Chad reassured her squeezing her hand in his.

"We have one of the victim's mother's here with us today, Prudence Stevenson." The news caster turned toward the victim's mother, a short frail looking woman who had clearly spent the night crying, "Is there anything you would like to say?" Amy Cho continued.

"My daughter was such a wonderful and happy young girl with so much promise. She had her whole life ahead of her, and those monsters took her away from me, and I can never get her back." Her words pushed through her heartbreak.

Reese recalled the pictures of Penelope and the agony on her face, she felt tears well up behind her eyelids, guilt crept in slowly, and Reese was beginning to lose her breath. Chad, sensing Reese's oncoming break down, put his arm around her shoulder and pulled her into him. They walked further away from the row of newscasters standing in front of the Courthouse.

The weight of Chad's arm around her shoulders gave a sense of comfort. It made her feel protected. He was her safe space in this world and she felt so thankful for him.

When they came through the heavy glass doors they were greeted by a long line waiting to go through the metal detectors. Reese went through the standard motions of removing her earrings and her necklace. She placed her purse in the bucket and walked through the threshold of the machine before putting her body in a starfish shape to be scanned by a metal detector wand. She collected her belongings and put her jewelry back in place. She remained quiet, feeling weak and timid.

The thoughts in her mind tormented her. *They're going to tear you to shreds, Reese. You can't beat me, you never could. You thought I would never find out about Taylor? You thought that you could run from me, you can't. Not even your prince charming can protect you from what's coming... he can't protect you from me.*

"Come on, babe," Chad broke through her thoughts. She looked up only to realize they were on the elevator and Chad was holding the doors open at the floor they were to get off on. Confusion swarmed her face before she took her first step towards him. "Are you okay?"

"Yes– well, no not really but, I'll be fine."

He motioned her to sit on a bench outside of the courtroom.

"What's freaking you out the most?" Chad placed his hands gently on hers once they sat down.

"Taylor. What if they ask about Taylor?"

"You have the right to plead the fifth."

"What?" Reese felt like she was standing in a fog her mind couldn't navigate through.

"The fifth?" now even Chad seemed confused. "You know, the Fifth Amendment? It protects you from self-incrimination?" Reese still seemed clueless. "They can't force you to answer questions about Taylor."

"Oh, right, the fifth! I don't know what's wrong with my brain." *I do, it's because you're stupid and incompetent.* Reese shook her head trying to get Alex out of her thoughts. *It's going to take more than that to get rid of me, you stupid bitch.*

Reese just wanted to curl up into a fetal position and cry but, she knew she owed those girls at least her statement. If they had to endure the torture that Alex brought upon them, then she could certainly stop freaking out long enough and do this for them. *I need to do this for Taylor too... hell, for myself as well. You can do this, Reese, you have to.*

Reese heard the distinct cracking of the judge's gavel being slammed onto a sound block even from outside the courtroom. The trial had begun and Reese's stomach was in knots. Chad stayed on the bench with Reese since she wasn't allowed to be in the courtroom until after she had given her testimony. She sat outside of the door with sweaty palms and a racing heart.

She had been so nervous since Detective Stone had told her she would be called in to testify. After they'd left the police station when her interview was over, she couldn't bring herself to eat more than a few bites here and there. The sound of Alex's voice in her head grew louder and she shrunk to becoming more like the woman she was when she was with him. There was a constant tug-of-war happening in her head. She was battling Alex even though he was long gone from her life.

When she would Face Time with Taylor every night, Reese was forced to put on a happy face. It was like she was living a secret life; a secret life of pain and destruction under the surface.

The only person who seemed to take notice was Chad. He was the one who coaxed the truth out of her. He was the one who held her while she cried and shook with fear. He was the one who spoke louder than Alex did in her head to remind her of her own strength. Chad was her rock, her solid foundation, and she knew there was no way she would ever survive this life without him.

The whoosh of the double doors to the courtroom startled Reese but, she welcomed the rush of cool air into the stuffy hallway. Detective Stone came walking out obviously perplexed about something. Her high waist pant suit made her legs look a mile long as she walked toward them.

"You're not gonna believe this!" She announced, tucking a piece of hair behind her ear.

"What?" Chad asked.

"They changed their plea!"

"What does that mean?" Reese choked back the hope in her voice.

"They just plead guilty to all counts against them!"

"Are you serious?" Chad huffed with a laugh of disbelief.

"I'm dead serious!" Natalie smiled.

Chad hopped up out of his seat and hugged Natalie. Reese saw them out of the corner of her eye celebrating their victory. She knew how hard they had worked on building the case against them both. She also knew she should be celebrating the fact she didn't have to testify or even look Alex in the eye but, for some reason she was drowning in disbelief and felt a shroud of sadness knowing she wouldn't be able to look him in the face. The feeling didn't make sense at first. Then she felt a surge of anger, Alex took away her opportunity to overcome her fears. Just like that, she was supposed to walk away and never look back? Not a chance.

Reese allowed that anger to grow and bubble up over the surface. *Alex has taken so much from you. Don't you dare let him take this too.* She stood up and her eyes zeroed in on the large wooden door. *On the other side of that door is your biggest fear, Reese. Are you going to let it control you? Or are you going to go in there and face it?* Before she knew what she was doing her feet were moving and she heaved open that big heavy door.

The cool air rushed across her face and the entire courtroom turned around to see who was hastily entering the courtroom, but Reese could only see one person. When Alex turned around, they locked eyes.

"Miss, can you please quietly take a seat?" The judge said in the background of her heartbeat.

Reese let the door close behind her when she took a step inside. She kept her eyes locked with Alex as she walked in his direction. His fiercely green eyes tracked hers, like a mountain lion tracking its prey. Reese refused to be the first to look away. The anger she felt brewed so hot in the pit of her stomach she hadn't realized how tight she was clinching her fists. Her breath was steady yet sharp, and she continued to look straight into the eyes of the man who tried to destroy her. He tried to take everything from her, and this was her way of giving him the middle finger, her way of overcoming him and proving she was, in fact, strong enough.

Alex let out a long winded breath and mouthed the words "I'm sorry" to her. Reese knew he wasn't the kind of man to just apologize. He never saw his own transgressions he only exploited everyone else's. Reese just shook her head and rolled her eyes at the pathetic attempt of an apology. One sharp crack of the gavel broke the stare down between the two of them.

Alex turned around.

"Sentencing will be held here in two weeks, court dismissed." The judge announced followed by a final crack of the gavel.

Alex stood up and turned towards Reese, "I'm sorry to put you through any of this. I love you." His face twisted with agony.

Reese stood up, the fear she felt earlier was long gone now. It was replaced with hatred. She didn't want to hear his empty words. They meant nothing to her now.

"You're not sorry, Alex, you're only sorry that you got caught. Burn in Hell, you piece of shit!" She forced the words quietly through clinched teeth.

And just as if a light switch flipped, the agony was gone and replaced by a devilish grin. Reese knew she was right, but to watch him switch gears so flawlessly caused her lips to part with dismay.

"You know me so well, sweetheart."

"Fuck you," Reese turned on her heel and walked back to the door.

Her nerves had resurfaced but, she had done it, she faced the devil himself and survived. Maybe Chad was right, maybe she was stronger than she realized. She walked a little taller out of the courtroom that day, and with her head held high she walked into Chad's arms. She melted into his chest and held on with everything she had.

It wasn't until she pulled away from him that she realized she was crying. His chest was wet from the tears that effortlessly flowed from her eyes.

"Are you okay?" Chad asked, "Why in the hell did you go in there?"

When Reese looked up she saw the horrified look on Chad and Natalie's faces.

"I had to," she drew a long breath in. "I had to face my fear and look him in the eye. I had to show him that he didn't break me."

Chad wrapped his arms around her, "I love you."

"I love you too," she whispered.

Natalie's face caught her eye, she looked proud, which was odd because Reese didn't even know her beyond the interview.

"You've got balls of steel, Miss Landon," Natalie said when Chad let Reese go. She stuck out her hand toward Reese, "It really was a pleasure meeting you."

"I'm more of a hugger," Reese smiled wrapping her arms around Natalie. "Thank you for working so hard to put him away. You have no idea what that means to me." Reese whispered in her ear.

"You're welcome, Miss Landon."

Reese let Natalie go, "Reese, please call me Reese." She smiled again.

"You're welcome, Reese," Natalie laughed. "You take care of him," she pointed at Chad. "You two are made for each other. Now that this whole mess is over, you both can get on with the rest of your lives." She looked at Chad the way a proud Mother looks at her honor roll student. "Chad, you've become quite a detective."

"Does this mean I'm officially a part of the 'D Squad'?" he joked.

Reese looked at Chad with wide eyes filled with amusement.

"Asshole," Natalie sneered before walking away.

"What was that about?" Reese chuckled.

"I'll tell you in the car," Chad snickered.

He wrapped his arm around her waist this time as they walked out of the courtroom, arm in arm, victorious. They had beat Alex at his own game.

Chapter 26

REESE CALLED MAGGIE when they left the courthouse to tell her the news. Of course, Maggie already knew thanks to Amy Cho at NCN reporting live. Maggie gushed about how happy she was now this whole mess was finally over. Reese was happy to have the fear of the trial behind her—even though she knew the mess Alex had left would never fully be behind her. One day she would have to tell her daughter, and pick up the pieces of Taylor's heart and help her glue them back together again. She pushed those thoughts out of her mind, for today, they celebrate.

"Taylor's fine here, go ahead and stay a few days and spend some time with Chad." Maggie insisted.

"Are you sure, Mom?"

"Yes, I'm sure," Maggie said without hesitation.

"Okay, thank you," Reese smiled.

When she hung up the phone she looked at Chad and grinned from ear to ear. She couldn't remember the last time they had more than a day or two together. They had already spent more time together than what they usually get and the dread of leaving was ever-present. She didn't want to leave his arms. They were both excited their goodbyes were postponed for a few more days.

They spent every waking second together over the next couple of days. The first day was spent in bed, but neither of them slept. They ate every meal with their fingers woven together, and more times than not, they gladly paused their meal to make love.

On their last day together, Chad had convinced Reese that they needed to put clothes on and go outside. He planned the whole day for the two of them. First they drove into Ruston and rode the ferry over to Vashon Island. Reese was in awe of the breath taking views, the boat ramp, and the magnificent houses on the water but, nothing compared to standing on the beach with the sand between her toes. The water was calm and there was a light breeze. Chad stood behind Reese with his arms around her waist as they stood there silent taking in the fresh air.

The hills surrounding them were emerald with large trees shooting up from the earth trying to touch the heavens. They saw a beautiful mansion that was built up just off the beach.

"Rough life," Reese joked.

"No kidding. Could you just imagine waking up to this view every day?" Chad moved around the side of Reese and gestured to the never ending water line.

"As long as I woke up next to you I'd be happy." Reese smiled.

They got back into Chad's car and drove north across the island with the windows down. Reese let her hand move through the wind up and down like a roller coaster. She missed the freshness of the air in Washington. Sitting next to Chad, Reese realized she had actually relaxed. Every time before the trial, Reese was unable to relax when she flew to see Chad, especially when she brought Taylor with her. Her nerves would crumble any confidence she had when they would simply go to the store out of fear of running into Alex. But, the last few days her fears seemed to melt away. She knew no matter where they went she would never run into Alex again. He couldn't control her life anymore, and more importantly, he could never come after Taylor.

Maybe she could consider moving back, she could actually live in the same city as her boyfriend, and maybe work on a happily ever after. *Is that what Detective Stone meant when she said we could get on with our lives?* Reese wondered.

"I can see those wheels turning, "Chad smiled at her. "What are you thinking about?"

Reese tucked her hair behind her ear as she turned to face Chad.

"I was just thinking about how my fear of Alex seems to be melting away. I know I won't run into him on accident, or have to run calls with him. He is no longer controlling the nerves in the pit of my stomach when I'm here."

"I was hoping you would start to feel that way."

He grabbed her hand and weaved their fingers together.

"I was also thinkin' maybe I could live here again..." She sheepishly smiled at him, unsure of what his reaction would be.

His lips parted with shock before quickly spreading wide across his face.

"Are you serious?"

"Yes, babe, I'm very serious."

Chad kissed her hand and then held it to his chest, as if Reese had just given him the greatest news of his life.

They boarded the ferry on the north end of the island and hitched a ride into Seattle. They stood out on the deck of the boat laughing as they mimicked the scene in Titanic, standing on the railing with their arms spread wide.

Reese sang out off-key, "Near, far, wherever you are."

"I love you, babe, but you might not want to quit your day job."

They laughed uncontrollably before Reese turned around and kissed him. The rest of the world faded away as one kiss turned into several minutes of sweet kissing with long and loving looks into each other's eyes.

When they left the ferry boat Chad drove them to Lincoln Park where they enjoyed a picnic for lunch. When Chad grabbed the blanket and ice chest from the trunk Reese was surprised.

"When on earth did you have time to pull all of this together?" She rejoiced, pleased with the surprise.

"I had plenty of time while you were sleeping, of course, lazy bones!" Chad joked.

"It's perfect! I love you so much," she kissed him on the cheek.

"I love you too, babe."

They drank the champagne Chad had brought while enjoying the finger sandwiches he made. He had also prepared a salad with strawberries and goat cheese, and for dessert he brought her favorite, strawberry cheesecake.

"This is beyond incredible," Reese gushed.

"You're beyond incredible," Chad smiled.

Reese felt like she was sailing on cloud nine, she figured he would plan a great last day together, but this was the most incredible day.

The more time Reese spent in Chad's arms, the more she wished she didn't have to leave tomorrow. Rather than dwell on the inevitable she decided to enjoy the short time she had left with the love of her life.

Reese tenderly marveled at Chad, thinking about how much she had fallen in love with him. His smile, his charm, his humor, his lips but, most of all she had fallen for the way he made her feel. He made her feel worthy even when she was broken. She always thought that people who said they needed someone were crazy, and she rolled her eyes at the thought of finding a soulmate but, Chad had successfully changed her mind.

She had put herself back together. Although Chad helped boost her confidence and supported her throughout the process, she held the glue and pieced her soul back together on her own.

Her heart ached for him soon after, and she realized he was the only man she ever wanted to laugh with. He had become her best friend before they gave it another shot. Reese felt the need to tell him about her day. She felt the need to include him in her and Taylor's nightly routine. And, he fit into their lives like he had been there all along. Sure, he wasn't Taylor's biological father but, he was her daddy. No one would ever replace him in their hearts and in their lives.

Chad was going to be her forever. She had decided that a while ago. Now that Alex was incarcerated, the decision carried the weight of reality. To Reese's surprise, the thought didn't scare her. Instead, it brought a jolt of excitement to her heart.

"You ready to head out?" Chad asked packing the ice chest. "We got to get movin' if we are going to get through the rest of the plans we have today.

"There's more?" she gasped.

"Oh yea," he smiled.

When he stood up, he reached his hand down for hers pulling her to her feet. He drew her in close and brushed the hair from her face with his hand. Her whole body flapped with butterflies as if they were fluttering through her veins. She had known lust with Alex but, she had never known love like this before. He softly kissed her several times on her lips.

Once they were in the car, Chad weaved his way through the bustling city of Seattle. Traffic was surprisingly light for the city and they were able to leisurely make their way through. They continued to drive with the windows down and enjoy the slightly chilled air, on such a beautiful day. The sky was blue and vibrant with bold puffy white clouds that looked like Christmas ornaments, perfectly placed on a tree.

When Chad parked the car, Reese could see a giant sign that read, Public Market Center, in big bold red letters.

"Pike Place Market," Reese exclaimed, "I love this place!"

"I know you do." Chad said with a twinkle in his eye. "I thought we could go and get coffee to warm us up at the very first Starbucks that was ever opened."

"Oh my gosh, how did I not know the first Starbucks was here?"

"We didn't get to it last time we came up here, because someone was fascinated with the fish market."

"That was incredible! I'd never seen anything like that before. The chanting and the singing they did when they tossed the fish from person to person, it was amazing!"

"It was pretty cool but, I think watching your reaction was the best part. You were like a kid in a candy store," he smirked.

"I felt like one too," she beamed.

They walked hand in hand down the lively street. There were people from all walks of life hustling down the street, and others were stopping for Instagram worthy photo's to be taken. The sea of people parted around them without missing a beat.

She could hear the faint sound of a solo trumpet playing in the distance. The sweet melody of the song, "When the Saints Go Marching In" got louder with each step. Reese hummed along with each note and dropped a five dollar bill in his trumpet case as they walked by.

Reese window shopped at the countless souvenir shops they passed, and of course she found a few items she couldn't live without. Chad didn't pout or groan. He told her to go ahead, and he waited for her outside. When she came out with a pack of bubble gum in her hands they each put a piece in their mouth and headed to the stairwell that led to the gum wall. They each took their gum out of their mouth, gave each other a peck on the lips, and placed their pieces of gum right next to each other on the wall.

After coming back up the stairs they headed to where the very first Starbucks opened. They finally approached the building and found a young man who couldn't be more than twenty years old playing his guitar and singing. His raspy voice sounded more like BB King rather than a young fair skinned man with boyish features. Reese tugged at Chad's arm and they stood and listened to him finish his song. Reese pulled another five dollar bill out and tossed it into the bucket the kid had next to him.

When they finally arrived at the building the line exceeded the door.

"I guess everyone else had the same idea," Reese laughed.

"I figured it would be busy, it's practically a national monument." Chad laughed.

Once they breached the doorway, they could see a large gold pole that stood at the edge of the counter. As they got closer they could see that it displayed the words, FIRST STARBUCKS STORE. It took several minutes to get through the line before they could order their drinks, and several more to wait for them to be made. Reese had decided to order the kid outside a grande coffee in hopes it would help warm him up. She was happily holding onto his coffee as it warmed her ice cold fingers. She stood in awe as they watched the overwhelmed baristas pump out drink after drink.

After getting their drinks, they weaved their way out of the coffee shop and Reese made a B-line for the young man they saw earlier. She walked up alongside him, and as to not interrupt his song, she simply raised the cup in his direction to catch his attention, and set it at his feet. He incorporated "Thank You" into the song and tipped his head to her.

They walked back to the car and Chad was off heading for another destination.

"Where are we going now?"

"To a place with the best view in all of Seattle," Chad snickered.

"The Space Needle!" Reese screamed.

"Yes, ma'am."

"You're the best!"

"I know," he sarcastically said.

Once they made it to the top of the Space Needle, Reese looked out across the vast scenery—they had arrived at the perfect time. The sun had begun its decent and the sky lit up with orange, pink, and purple. Yellow reflected off the glass of the buildings surrounding them bringing her love for this view even higher on her list.

"Do you remember the first time we came here?" Chad asked her wrapping his arms around her from behind.

"I do," she smiled still looking at the horizon. "We came with Jess and Nate before we were dating."

"That's right."

"Did I ever tell you that trip was the first time I knew I loved you?"

"You did," he squeezed her tight. "Did I ever tell you my epiphany that day?"

"No, you never did."

Reese turned her body around to face him.

"I was standing here, right here in this very spot actually, that I knew."

"You knew what?"

"I knew that one day I would marry you."

Chad slowly descended to one knee pulling out a tiny black box from his jacket pocket.

"What are you doing?" Reese choked back her tears.

"Reese Elizabeth Landon, I never thought a love like this was possible but, you came into my life and you changed everything. You are my best friend and I couldn't imagine living this life without you by my side forever. I want to grow old with you, Reese Landon. Will you do me the honor of making me the happiest man on earth? Will you marry me?"

Tears freely flowed from her eyes, the world around them had stopped, and impatiently waited motionless for her answer.

"YES! OH MY GOD, YES!" Reese yelled as loud as she could.

She sat down on his knee kissing him deeply as the crowd around them cheered loudly. Reese hadn't even noticed the ring, all she saw was Chad. He could've proposed with a piece of string and she still would've said yes. All she wanted was him. She wanted to choose him every day for the rest of her life.

Chapter 27

EVER SINCE REESE was a little girl she had imagined falling in love the way most little girls did except, what Reese wanted always seemed to differ just a little from the others. Her friends all wanted their Prince Charming to come and rescue them in the same way their favorite princesses were rescued. Reese still wanted her Prince but, she didn't want to be rescued. She wanted him to be her best friend in the whole wide world. She wanted someone who was going to love her, even in her most unlovable moments. She wanted a partner in this crazy life and more importantly, she wanted someone who made her better, and someone who pushed her harder. That is exactly what Chad did for her, he was her best friend, and he lifted her up when she needed it. He was her partner no matter how hard things were. And he always pushed her to be the best she could be.

It seemed surreal, like the feeling was sure to fade away. They weaved their way through the roads home, Reese realized, this feeling she had is the same one she had that day at the Fill the Boot. It was the same butterflies flitting around in the pit of her stomach—the feeling had only grown and become more predominate. She had loved Chad long before she was capable of realizing it, and now he was going to be her happily ever after. He was going to be next to her with grey hair, holding her hand as they reminisced about the life they built together.

Reese felt so happy, she could explode.

"You totally surprised me, babe! I seriously had no idea you were going to do this!" Reese gushed.

"Can I tell you a secret?"

"Of course!"

"I didn't know I was going to do it either."

Reese tilted her head in confusion, "What do you mean?"

"Well, I brought the ring with me just in case the right opportunity presented itself."

"Can I ask you how long you've had the ring?"

"Ever since I made detective..."

"Seriously?" Reese was shocked it had been that long.

"I've known for a while I wanted to do this life with you, Ree, I just needed the right opportunity. One worthy of you and what you mean to me." Chad paused with anguish on his face. "But then I got the call about a young girl who was murdered and everything kinda fell apart from there." Reese gently placed her hand on his. "Once I knew it was Alex," he exhaled sharply. "I was so worried you would hate me forever."

"I could never–"

"The thought of possibly loosing you because of Alex was infuriating. I hoped you would understand, and I'm so lucky you did. Not all women would've."

"A year ago I don't know that I would've, but because we took a step back, and I put myself back together, and you showed me I could trust you, I feel like that is the biggest reason why I was able to. Had I not fixed the brokenness within me, had you only told me to trust you and not shown me I could, things would be much different right now. We stepped back, we built our relationship, we built our friendship, and most importantly, we built our trust in each other. I knew something was off, and when I saw the NCN broadcast I never once blamed you. I trusted you didn't tell me for a very good reason." She ran her hand through his hair and across the back of his neck. "I trust you one hundred percent, babe. And guess what?"

"What?" he smiled.

"You're never going to lose me. I'll always be here, right by your side, lifting you up."

"I love you so much, Reese."

"I love you too, Chad," she leaned over and kissed his cheek as he drove. "Now, I wanna finish hearing about what made you decide to pop the question tonight."

"I don't know. I planned to maybe surprise you in Texas in a few weeks, and toyed around with ideas but, today was just perfect. I thought to myself, why am I going to try and recreate what we already have today? And when we made it to the top of the Space Needle, and we were standing in the same spot as when I realized that I wanted to spend forever with you, it was like a sign. I looked out and saw this magnificent sunset and remembered how much you love sunsets. There was no way I could bring this kind of magic another day. I knew this was the moment I had been waiting for. So, I did." His entire face lit up with a grin.

"It was perfect," she squeezed his hand before looking at her ring. "How did you know?"

"Know what?"

"What kind of ring I wanted."

"I asked Jess and Kyra, I figured they were my best bet."

"Those little brats!" Reese laughed. "Kyra asked me some random question about the size of my finger and said it had something to do with the gifts Jess wanted to give her bridesmaids when her and Nate got married one day. I knew she was full of it!"

They both laughed.

When they pulled up at Chad's house Reese asked, "Are we gonna live here?"

"Well, this is a good house but, there isn't much of a back yard for Tay." Chad pulled his car into the garage. "I talked to a realtor and had an estimate done on the house. We could get pretty good money for this place and then have plenty to put down on a bigger house with a backyard for the kids to play."

"Kids?"

"Well, yea. Taylor is going to need a brother and a sister to play with."

"If we had a son, what would you want to name him?"

"I like the name Elliot, after my Grandpa Calvin Elliot."

"That's your Dad's father, right? Wait, is that where your middle name came from?"

"Yea," Chad's head sunk low. "He was killed when my mom was pregnant with me. He's the reason I became a cop." He looked back up to meet Reese's sympathetic gaze. "I grew up hearing so many stories about him. My dad would tell me about all of the bad guys that he had put away, and how he was the top homicide detective in Auburn, until he was killed in cold blood. He was left to die in an ally, alone, and unable to call for help. He was dead within minutes. He bled out from a gunshot wound to the chest, center mass."

"Did they ever catch the guy that shot him?"

"Yea, his partner caught the guy a few days later. He never made it to the station."

"Oh," Reese said, shocked.

"Yea, the rules were different back then."

They finally exited the car and headed inside the house.

"What about if it's a girl?" Reese attempted to lighten the mood.

"I don't know," Chad's mood remained somber.

"Hey," she gently moved him around to face her. "I'm really sorry about your grandpa, love."

"I'm sorry, babe, today is a happy day. I don't know why that story always hits me, even when I tell it."

"Well, you didn't get to meet your hero. I get it."

"God, I love you."

Chad grabbed her around her waist and kissed her passionately. Their lips mashed together and their tongues became tangled. It wasn't long before their naked bodies intricately moved against each other as Reese felt her body tingle with pleasure. In the past they had connected physically on such a deep level but, this was more than that. It was as if their minds, bodies, and souls had connected at the same time. The rest of the world no longer existed. They were together now and they will be forever.

The next morning when they woke up, they decided it was time to let the rest of the world in on their little secret. They started with their parents, and then their friends. Once the people they loved knew, they made it official by posting it to all of their social media accounts.

Reese had no idea Chad had actually paid a woman twenty dollars to capture the proposal on his phone. They chose the best picture from the bunch, one of them kissing with Seattle and its breathtaking sunset in the background, and of course, the ring. It was exactly what Reese had wanted for as long as she could remember. A slender diamond band with a large princess cut diamond in the middle. It sparkled even in the dimmest of light, and it looked as if it belonged on Reese's finger her entire life.

The social media world blew up with hundreds of comments from people telling them "congratulations," the most important comment came when Reese's phone rang.

"Chief Gibbs?" Reese answered.

"How'smy favorite paramedic doing?"

"I'm doing really great!"

"I heard. Audrey told me about your engagement, and so I wanted to call and tell you both congratulations."

"Thank you so much, Chief. How's your wife doing?"

"She's doing great, just running the kids all around. Hey listen, there's one more thing I want to talk to you about."

"Okay."

"Are you planning on moving back to Auburn?"

"That is indeed the plan as far as I know."

"In that case, I want you to know that I'm officially giving you an open invitation to return to station twenty-three any time you're ready." Reese was at a loss for words. "I've filled your spot with temporary medics but, I haven't been able to find one that fits just right. I—We—We would all love it if you would come back."

"Chief, I don't know what to say!" She cleared her throat. "I—uh—I would love to come back but, I don't know when I will be able to. We haven't discussed any of that yet."

"I understand, that's why it's an open invitation, I wanted to let you know all of this before you got too far into your plans. We miss you, Reese."

"I miss all y'all too!"

After catching up for a few more minutes, they hung up the phone and Reese ran down the hall to tell Chad the good news. And after a short discussion, Reese called back Chief Gibbs and told him she would be happy to return to Station 23. She asked if he would be willing to give her six weeks to give her notice at MedStar, and to move everything back to Auburn, which he greatly obliged.

Chapter 28

THE NEXT MORNING, her kiss lingered on Chad's lips before parting ways at the gate, leaving Reese to reluctantly board the plane back home to Texas, alone. During her flight she used her ear phones to tune out the poor toddler who had been crying like crazy since they'd taken off. *Thank God this isn't a long flight.* The cry of the little boy made her miss Taylor even more but, she couldn't help but be excited that soon she wouldn't be torn between two states anymore.

A flash of pain entered her heart when she realized she would have to leave her parents and Uncle T behind. *How in the hell am I going to tell them? I mean, they've gotta already expect it, right? They know Chad and I are engaged now.* She looked down at the sparkles from her ring, loving how it twinkled. *They'll understand, I hope.*

Reese's body jolted when the wheels of the plane touched ground in Texas, pulling her attention up from the bride's magazine she was indulging in. It had only taken them a few minutes to reach their gate and they were directed to gather their things and exit the plane. Reese pulled down her carry-on with ease and flung her purse over her shoulder. She looked like an experienced traveler. Well, she kind of was experienced at this. She had flown back and forth so many times she didn't feel nervous doing it anymore. It had become a part of her routine.

She would work a few months and fly out to see Chad. She would come home, work another month or two and he would come to see her and Taylor. Back and forth, hoping between states had become her life—splitting in two, thousands of miles away from the other. It felt weird to know the next time her and Taylor head to Auburn, it'll be for good.

Reese found her car, tossed her carry-on in the back, and headed for home. *Well, I guess it's not my home anymore.*

She drove in silence most of the way to her parents' house. She was so far inside her own thoughts between the wedding, returning to AFD, and having to leave Denton, she didn't notice the radio wasn't on. She was a cocktail of emotions swirling between utter bliss and devastation. She wished she could scoop everyone up from Denton and take them to Auburn with her, in the same way she felt just a few short years ago about her crew from 23. Her forever would be in Auburn but, she had to come to terms with the fact that her heart would always be torn between two states. She knew someday she would have to make her peace with it, but that day would not be today.

Dust kicked up behind her as she came down the long driveway. She gazed at the large farmhouse and already felt the pain of missing it. The house already seemed different to her somehow, something had changed. It stood the same way it had for decades but, the feeling in her heart had changed. She felt grateful for this safe-haven. This little farmhouse protected her and her daughter when they needed it most. But, now they didn't need to be protected anymore. Alex would never be able to get to them, he would never be able to take Taylor away, and he couldn't hurt anyone ever again. The darkness that lingered in the back of Reese's mind was finally gone, and she felt free. Free to show off her daughter and not hide her under a rock. Free to move back to Auburn and put down roots with the man she loves. Free to crawl out from under the lies she told to protect them from Alex. Freedom had never felt so good.

"Mama!" Taylor shrieked jumping off the last step of the porch. "Mama! Mama!"

Reese's face lit up as she got out of her car.

"Hi, baby girl, Mama missed you so much!"

Reese scooped Taylor into her arms and swung her around in a circle before bringing her into her body and holding her tight. Although Reese enjoyed her time with Chad when it was just the two of them, nothing in the world compared to how it felt coming home to her daughter. Being the parent of a toddler was not an easy job, Taylor was not always the perfect child; she often threw tantrums and it made Reese want to pull her hair out pretty much every day but, the love Reese felt for Taylor far surpassed anything else she's ever had. They were bonded as Mother and daughter and nothing, not even Alex, could take that from them.

Taylor helped Reese bring in her things by carrying Reese's phone up the stairs where Maggie was waiting for them.

"Hi, Mom," Reese wrapped her arms around Maggie as she reached the top step.

"Hi, sissy, we missed you!" Maggie let go of Reese. "Now let me see that ring!"

Maggie grabbed Reese's hand and gazed at the ring while shifting her finger side to side. She marveled in the glittery sparkle of the flawless rock.

"It's beautiful! He did good!"

"Yes he did," Reese smiled.

"Well, come inside and tell me all the details!"

Maggie grabbed the small suitcase at Reese's feet and quickly took it inside. Reese made her way to the living room couch where Maggie had made them each a cup of coffee. They both sat on the couch sipping away at their drinks and Reese told her all about their trip into Seattle.

As she filled Maggie in on all of the magical details of the day leading up to her engagement, she thought about how far their relationship had come. Reese had always been close with her parents, but this was different. Maggie had moved out of the "mom role" and into being not only her friend but, one of her best friends. Maggie stood by her at her darkest moments and never made Reese feel terrible about it but, she also bluntly told Reese the truth. Even when she didn't want to hear it or how much it hurt. More importantly, she helped bring Reese back to church and into a better relationship with God. Helping her realize blaming Him for her life was like blaming the rain for getting you wet.

Maggie looked at Reese with sparkles in her eyes listening to the story of Chad's proposal. She seemed wrapped up in wonderment of Reese's story.

"Look, Mom, there's something we need to talk about."

"I already know what it is, and I want you to know, although we will miss you, we support you moving back to Auburn."

"How did you know?"

"Chad called Daddy a while back to ask for your hand."

"He did?"

Reese felt shocked he didn't tell her, but proud he asked her father. Having Rusty's blessing was important to Reese.

Sure, it was a tad old-fashioned but, it was something she needed.

"Yes he did. He had Face Timed us before he officially made detective. You were at work so he knew he would be able to call without you knowing. He asked both of us for our blessing and without hesitation we gave it." Maggie took a quick sip of her coffee. "Now we didn't know when, how or where he was going to pop the question. But, we knew when the time was right we would get that wonderful phone call from you. We also knew the time you had left here in Denton would be limited, and that's okay. Yes, Daddy and I will miss you. Uncle T and Robert will miss you. Even Penny and Emily will miss you but, we all know Chad is the one for you. After everything you've been through, you deserve to be happy."

"Thank you, Mom."

That night, Reese typed out her resignation letter for MedStar with the intent to turn it in the next day when she came back on shift. She sat staring at the printer as it made her resignation permanently on paper and thought about all of the people she would miss at MedStar. Emily, of course, was at the top of her list. She had helped Reese find her inner passion for being a paramedic again and reminded her she was deserving of Chad's love. Of course, there was Cal too, who treated her like a friend and not a criminal when Alex was arrested. Reese would even miss seeing Opie. Jerry and James, although they were her supervisor and her boss, they didn't have to show her compassion but, they did anyway. She knew the friends she had made at MedStar would remain lifelong friendships despite the distance between them.

The next morning she walked into James' office and closed the door behind her.

"Miss Landon, welcome back."

"Thank you, sir. Can I talk to you for a minute?"

"Of course, have a seat."

"I came in a little early for my shift today to give us some time before I log on. I wanted to turn in my resignation."

James' eyes grew wide, "What?"

"I know it seems a little out of the blue but, my boyfriend proposed to me while I was away, and we have decided to live in Auburn. I'm genuinely appreciative of the opportunity y'all gave me here and I will forever cherish the friends and the memories I've made here but, it's time for me to move back to Auburn."

"I know we will all certainly miss you around here, Reese but, I definitely understand why. Congratulations on your engagement."

"Thank you so much, sir."

Reese stood up and put out her hand to shake his but, James stood and came around the front of his desk and wrapped his arms around her.

"You're welcome."

Chapter 29

"YOU'RE LEAVING?" Cal's voice cut through the halls of the emergency room. "I can't believe you're just going to leave!"

Reese hugged him, "I'll miss you too, Cal."

"I just don't understand why? Is it because of the way everyone reacted when Alex got arrested?"

"No, not at all, Cal! Chad and I are engaged. I thought you would've seen it on Facebook."

"Oh, uh-well, congrats then," he mumbled before walking away.

Reese stood there staring at the back of Cal's messy head confused about why he was acting this way. They had become friends but, they weren't inseparable. *Is he mad I didn't call him like I did Emily?* She headed out after Cal.

"Hey," she called out. "What was that all about?"

"It's nothing."

"It's obviously something, Cal, now spill it."

"I don't know, I guess it's just you didn't think to call me and tell me Chad proposed."

"Oh," Reese's shoulders sunk. "I'm sorry, Cal, you're right, I should've called. I honestly thought..." her voice trailed off.

"You thought what?"

"I didn't think you'd care."

"You're my friend, Reese, of course I care."

"You're right. I screwed up, and I'm so sorry. What can I do to make it up to you?"

"I don't know... I'm just being dumb I guess."

Reese grabbed out her phone and scrolled through her contacts to find Cal's name. She pushed his number and held the phone to her ear. When Cal looked down at his phone he looked at her with a raised eyebrow.

"Aren't you gonna answer it?" Reese asked.

"You're right here."

"Yea but, you should answer anyway."

"Ugh, fine," he touched the screen and held the phone to his ear. "Hello?" he sarcastically played along.

"Cal, oh my goodness you're never going to guess, I'm so glad you picked up!" Her voice echoed through the phone. "I have some incredible news!"

"Oh yea, what's that?" Cal said sarcastically.

"Chad and I are getting married!" Reese yelled. "I know I should've called you sooner than now, and I'm really sorry for that. But, I'm hoping you can find it in your heart to be happy for me anyway. Because I love you like a brother, and I would be devastated if you didn't come to the wedding just because I screwed up."

A faint smile danced on his face, "Well, Landon, I wouldn't miss it for the world."

"Oh good!" she cleared her throat. "There's one more thing. I'm gonna be movin' back to Auburn." There was silence between them. "I know how much that sucks but, that's where we've decided to lay down our roots and build our family. I put in my two weeks' notice with James yesterday, and I have six shifts left here at MedStar. I actually got my old job back at station twenty-three and I start next month. I know leaving everyone here isn't going to be easy but, it's something I have to do." She huffed a heavy sigh, "I'm gonna miss you when I leave, Cal."

"I'm gonna miss you too, Landon."

"I gotta go, there's this goofy guy with crazy messy hair just staring at me and I have to go and kick his ass. Talk to you later?"

Cal laughed and hung up his phone.

"Thank you."

"I'm sorry I didn't do it sooner."

Reese wrapped her arms around his husky body hugging him tightly.

The next two weeks rapidly flew by. She worked all of her final shifts with Emily at her request and they flipped through countless wedding magazines and googled venues. Reese and Chad spoke every day and tried to narrow down a time frame of a wedding date. They both knew they didn't want to drag out the planning of it because they didn't want to have to wait an entire year to become husband and wife. They both had finally come to an agreement of an October wedding. The weather in Washington would be cool but not quite freezing yet, and their chance of terrible weather was slim.

"I'm thinking mid to late of October for our wedding day but, Chad thinks we should do the first weekend or even the last weekend in September." Reese told Emily.

"Well, he has a point, weather-wise, the closer to summer the better, especially since you want an outside ceremony."

"I know, I know."

"Then why are you fighting him on this?"

"I don't know," Reese laughed, realizing she was being ridiculous about the whole thing.

The truth was she didn't care what day they got married. She didn't care if the weather was perfect or if it was pouring down rain, she was going to marry the man of her dreams no matter what obstacles got in her way. So later that night, she called Chad.

"Hello?"

"Hey, babe, listen, I'm sorry about being dumb about our wedding date."

"You don't have to apologize, Ree, its okay to be passionate about when we get married."

"I know but, the truth is, you're right. I know like all the movies and TV shows always show the husband and wife battling for power by never admitting the other is right. But, I don't want to live like that. You're right. We have a better chance for good weather end of September or early October."

"Well, I've been thinking about the last weekend in September. That Saturday falls on the twenty-seventh, which was my Grandpa Calvin's birthday. I thought it would be a nice way of him being a part of our wedding."

"Oh, babe, I love that. The twenty-seventh it is!"

Once their date was set they decided to wait until Reese and Taylor got settled back into Auburn before making any more major decisions. Of course, that didn't stop Reese from googling venues and photographers every chance she had. She wanted a rustic venue to fit her southern roots, hoping Chad would be okay with it.

Before she knew it, it was her second to last day at MedStar. Her life had significantly expanded since the first time she left Auburn. There was no way she could fit all of her things, let alone Taylor's things, in a tiny U-Haul. Fortunately, this time Chad was flying in to drive the big truck while Reese and Taylor followed behind him in her car.

Reese felt ready to move on with her life. She refused to allow any form of fear to control her life anymore and vowed to never let it swallow her whole again.

She tossed her last pair of Converse into the box marked "shoes" and headed off down the hall to get her uniform from the dryer. She had washed all of the uniform shirts MedStar had given her so she could turn them all in at the end of her shift. She folded each one of them methodically paying attention to the crease lines of each fold, before gently placing them in a paper bag from the grocery store. There it was, the last two and a half years of her life stacked nicely in a grocery size paper bag.

The next morning, the sound of the rooster woke her at the crack of dawn. Reese had several hours before she had to be out the door for work. There was no sense in going back to bed since Jimmy Hendrix, the rooster Reese named for her mom a few months after moving back home, wasn't going to shut up now that he was awake. Every few minutes he croaked out his announcement of dawn and unfortunately he had chosen to do it right in front of Reese's window.

"Ugh," Reese sighed, throwing the covers off and quietly stomping her feet to the kitchen for coffee.

"Hey Reesey Piecey, what'cha doin' up so early?"

"Jimmy Hendrix is workin' his way towards my dinner plate," she grumbled, shuffling past Rusty and to the coffee pot.

"I see," Rusty laughed under his breath. "So, today's your last day at work, huh?"

"Yea, I'm excited to move on but, I'm sad I have to leave. I never thought I'd find another EMS family like the one I had in Auburn but, I did." She took a quick sip of her hot coffee. "I wish I could take them all with me, you know?"

"I think I do. I felt that way about Clyde and Gary, my old ranch hands. They ended up leavin' town and movin' up north to Oklahoma and got a job at one of the ranches up there. Those guys were a part of our family there for a while. You had moved to Washington, Sophie had gotten married to Paul. It was just your mom and I. Clyde and Gary became our friends. We had family dinners with them after work most nights because they didn't have much to go home to. When they left I was heartbroken, but I felt happy they moved on to a bigger ranch with better pay."

"Awe, Dad, I had no idea you had gotten so close to those guys." She gently rubbed her hand on his shoulder. "They were really nice guys."

"Yea they were... my point is I understand how you feel leaving. I know it's bittersweet for you but, everything will be okay. It's just like when you got here and you weren't sure if all of this was going to work out and, in time, it did. It'll smooth itself out again." He closed the lid on his coffee thermos. "Life always has a way of working out the kinks if you give it enough time and space to do so."

"Thanks, Daddy," Reese smiled as Rusty kissed her forehead.

And with the screech of the screen door, Rusty was off to work and Reese was off to get ready for her last day at MedStar.

Chapter 30

THE MORNING WENT as it always did before work. Reese showered, did her hair, put on her uniform, and got Taylor up and dressed. Maggie met the two of them in the kitchen to take over breakfast duty with Taylor, Reese kissed her little love good-bye, and headed out for her last day of work in Denton.

On her way to work she felt bad for the excitement pumping through her veins. It had built up and took over her lingering sadness. This was one more step closer to forever with Chad and there was no hiding the joy that realization brought her.

She envisioned their life together. Going on adventures as a family, she thought of how amazing it would be to have him by her side as she brought more of their children into this world. She would never have to do anything alone again. Most women would take the time to fantasize about their wedding day but, for Reese their wedding was only the beginning of their life. She not only wanted a wedding, she wanted a marriage with the man she loved. So, she fantasized about the type of marriage she hoped they would have. Family dinners, picnic's in the park as their kids played on the playground. The occasional date nights where they hired the teenage girl down the street to keep their kids alive for just a few hours, so they could keep that spark in their relationship. It was the perfect image of a well-balanced marriage with her once in a lifetime love.

"What's that smirk on your face all about?" Emily asked. "Thinkin' about the wedding night?" She winked.

"Ha ha, no, I was actually thinking about our life."

"You really do love him, don't you?"

"I really do. I know it won't always be sunshine and rainbows, I know marriage is a constant balancing act of compromise and hard work but, I couldn't imagine doing it with anyone else."

"Awe," Emily sighed. "I'm so excited for you but, damn it if I ain't gonna miss the shit outta you!" She threw her arms around Reese.

"I'm gonna miss you too, Em."

The girls logged on for their last shift together and headed out into the city.

The streets of Denton seemed so far away as Reese continued to fantasize about her life with Chad and Taylor in Auburn. She thought about how great it would be to go back home to Station 23 and how wonderful it would be to ride with Kyra again. She looked to her left and her eyes scanned Emily and the sadness rolled back in. *Bittersweet indeed,* Reese thought recalling the conversation with Rusty that morning.

"I hate this," Reese mumbled under her breath.

"You hate what?" Emily asked.

"I hate the fact I have to leave people I love behind, again."

"I know. I'm not a huge fan of it either but, I'm definitely a fan of you being happy. Chad has a good job in Auburn and your old job fell back into your lap. If that ain't a sign, I don't know what is."

"I know, you're right but, it doesn't mean I have to like it."

Dispatch broke through their conversation, "Medic seventy-one, priority one at the intersection of King and Maple. Priority one for a traffic accident, unknown injuries."

Reese picked up the mic, "Medic seventy-one copy, show us responding."

When they arrived on scene, there was a car smashed on all sides. The windows were blown out except for the shattered windshield that hung together by a prayer. All four doors were smashed inward from rolling several times and the front end was smashed nearly into the dashboard. They could see the airbags that had deployed all the way from the ambulance; the car was stopped by a tree. Reese prepared herself to find someone dead, if not multiple people. She wasn't able to distinguish the make or model of the car which was something she rarely saw with car accidents.

Both girls grabbed gloves and hopped out of the ambulance.

"I'll check in the car, you go talk to the people standing over there." Reese pointed to the small crowd gathering a few feet from the car.

Emily nodded her head in agreement and headed off in the direction of the bystanders.

Reese walked alongside the driver side of the totaled vehicle, her eyes scanning for a body—she saw no one in the car. Confused, she moved her face closer to where the window would've been and cupped her hands around her eyes to shield the glare of the sun. Still, no one was in the car. Turning around she scanned the area around the vehicle and in the tree line, looking for anyone who may have been thrown from the car. She crouched down looking under the car. Nope, not there either. *What the hell?*

She finally stood up and noticed Emily waving her over to the crowd. Reese headed over to Emily and moved away from the group of people.

"There's no one in the car. I even looked in the tree line and around the car, but no one's here. Maybe they took leg-bail?"

"No they didn't, they're standing right over there." Emily pointed at the crowd. "The car belongs to the two teenagers."

"Wait," Reese turned back to look at the remains of the car behind her, examining the excessive amounts of damage in disbelief. "Those two were in there?"

"Yup..."

"And they got out of the car on their own?"

"Yup, he said they crawled through the window."

"And they're fine?"

"Yea... They both have minor scratches."

"Seriously?"

"Seriously."

Reese followed Emily over to the two kids to see for herself.

"Hey," Reese started, "You two were in this car?"

"Yes, ma'am," the young man's voice trembled.

"Which one of you was driving the car?"

"I was," his voice continued to jump.

"Do you remember what happened?"

"I looked down to change the radio station and when I looked back up I was off the road. I—I must've over corrected." He ran his dirty hands down his sweat soaked face. "I just remember feeling like we were tumbling." His voice cracked. "It

317

felt like it was in slow motion. It happened so fast." He shook his head. "I know that doesn't make sense."

"It makes perfect sense," Reese put her hand on his shoulder and looked them both in the eyes. The young girl who was the passenger stood next to the driver, sobbing. "You both are extremely lucky, take a look at your car. I've seen people not walk away from less."

The young man's brown eyes grew wide with fear, "My parents are going to kill me!"

"Hey, what's your name?" Reese asked softly.

"Bobby."

"Look, Bobby, I'm a mom and I know if my daughter got into an accident I would be thankful she was alive—and in your case—walked away without a scratch! If there's one thing I've learned, its cars can be replaced, and people can't. Yea, your parents might be upset about the car but, they'll also be grateful you're both alive." Bobby exhaled sharply and nodded his head. "What's your name?" Reese asked the girl who wiped her jet black hair from her face.

"Nikko."

"I like that name—Nikko—are you two friends?"

"Bobby's my boyfriend," Nikko wiped the tears that remained from her eyes.

"How old are you guys?"

"I'm nineteen," Bobby said, "And she's eighteen."

"Okay, you both are adults but, I still think we need to call your parents. These officers are going to have some questions for you guys and it might be nice to have someone here when they do."

"Okay," Bobby pulled out his phone and made a phone call... "Dad?"

While he spoke to his father, Reese walked over to the officers.

"Hey, sounds like he over-corrected. They're both really lucky."

"You can say that again," the officer said from behind his clipboard.

"They are both adults, barely, so he called his dad."

"Sounds good, are they going to the hospital with you guys?"

"I don't think so. They both have minor scrapes and bruises but, I'll let you know for sure when I know."

"Sounds good, thanks," he didn't look up from his clipboard this time.

Reese headed back over to Bobby and Nikko.

"Did you get a hold of anyone?"

"Yea, my dad is coming," Bobby said.

"Good. Do you guys want us to take you to the ER?"

"I think I'm okay," Bobby turned to Nikko. "What about you?"

"Yea, I'm okay."

"Are either of you hurting anywhere?" They both looked at each other, back at Reese, and shook their heads no. "Well, I hate to be the bearer of bad news but, you will hurt in places you didn't know you could hurt by tomorrow. Ibuprofen and Tylenol are going to be your best friends for the next couple of days. We are gonna take off, unless you'd like us to stay and wait until your dad gets here."

"My house is only a few miles from here. He should be here soon but, thank you."

"Alright, you both take it easy the next couple of days, and if you change your mind or pain develops; don't hesitate to go to the doctor or call nine-one-one, okay?"

"Okay, thanks."

"Thank you so much," Nikko said.

Reese headed back to the rig and found Emily putting the gurney back into the ambulance.

"I take it we're canceling?"

"Yes, ma'am, non-injury, I still can't believe it." Reese pulled her phone out and snapped a quick picture of the demolished car. "If this ain't a sign from God, when it's not your time to die, then I don't know what is." She told the officer, "We're outta here, neither of them wanted to go."

"Okay, sounds good," he gave her a thumbs up.

"Send me that picture!" Emily said.

"Already did!" They got in the front and Reese grabbed the mic, "Medic seventy-one, show us canceled, non-injury."

"Copy medic seventy-one canceled non-injury, stand-by for post."

The rest of the day they continued to cancel on an array of calls from tummy aches to the elderly just needing help up off the floor. All in all, it was a pretty easy and quiet day.

"Medic seventy-one, priority one, cardiac arrest at two-forty-five N Qualls for a forty-two year old, CPR is in progress."

Emily grabbed the mic, "Medic seventy-one copy's, show us responding."

Luckily they were just a few blocks away. It felt like mere seconds had passed when they turned the corner to the address and saw the fire department had already arrived on scene. *Something's not right,* Reese thought to herself as she saw three guys from the engine crouched down on the sidewalk outside of a rundown home. *Forty-two year old's aren't typically small enough to be huddled together like that for a cardiac arrest.* Reese grabbed her gloves and hopped out trying to put the pieces together hoping she was wrong.

"Reese," the seasoned officer called her name as he hastily walked toward her. "It's a child."

There it was, the worst statement any paramedic could hear. The words echoed in her mind but, there wasn't time for panic. Reese refused to let the fact it was a child sink in her mind and wreak havoc.

"Okay, we'll be right there," she calmly said.

"What did he say?" Emily asked.

"We need to go, now."

Emily didn't say another word, she just pulled the gurney out and they quickly walked over to the huddled group of firefighters. Reese didn't stop to breathe, let alone allow the little girls lifeless face to sway her train of thought. She couldn't allow her emotions to take over her thoughts, and like so many times before, she remained calm.

"What do we know?" She asked.

"Not much, I'm not sure the mom speaks English," Mac huffed pumping the small child's chest one-handed.

"Monitor's on," Emily announced.

Everyone stopped and stared at the screen of the monitor. There was a flat line running across the screen.

"Asystole, keep going," Reese called out.

Everyone returned to their jobs. Reese stretched out the Broselow-tape she had removed from the bag. She placed it out next to the little girl's body, ignoring the ringlet curls that fell around her motionless face. Reese felt thankful to whoever came up with the Broselow—it made her job much easier with a chart that breaks up into sections. It gets stretched out, starting at the victim's head, next to the child and whichever box their heel lands in, it gives instruction on what to do. Letting Reese know the size tube to use for intubation and it also provided all of the drug dosages Reese would possibly need.

Reese noticed a small blue bag flying through the air toward her.

"Thanks," Reese called out as the intubation kit landed next to her.

She unzipped the bag and pulled all of the equipment she'd need. Seconds later she was set up and ready to go.

"Okay, everyone hold," she directed them.

The cement was warm on her body when she laid face down on the ground. Sweeping the ringlet curls away from the little girls face she noticed her lips were blue. She placed the blade down her throat trying to visualize the chords but, there was something mushy and white in the way.

"What the hell?" Reese said under her breath.

She advanced deeper into her throat, past her vocal chords, only to find even more white mush.

She asked loud enough for the mother to hear, "Was she eating?"

The officer who stood next to the mother relayed the question, "Was she eating?"

The woman looked lost and she faintly lifted her shoulders up.

"Comida?" Reese insisted in Spanish.

The officer continued as her echo, "Comida?"

"Si," the woman finally spoke. "Ella tenia pan."

"El Pan?" Reese asked.

"Si, yes."

"What is it?" Emily asked.

Reese dug out the forceps, "I think there's bread stuck in her throat."

Reese tried a few times to get out the white mush but, all it did was fall apart every time she grabbed it. *What do I do?* Reese felt lost. She knew what was wrong but, she didn't know how to get the bread out.

"Shit," she mumbled at her last failed attempt. "Screw it."

Reese grabbed the tube she had already prepped and decided to intubate her. She thought if she could simply push through the bread or even push the bread into the lung they could at least get oxygen flowing and worry about the bread later. She watched the tube pass the tiny vocal chords and slide through the white mush, and when they tried bagging her, there was movement in her chest.

Reese grabbed her stethoscope from around her neck and checked placement. She first listened over the stomach for any gurgling noises indicating the tube was in the stomach and not the lungs but, there were no sounds. Next over the left lung, good air exchange, then the right, it was gargling but, there was exchange. Reese exhaled a sigh of relief and quickly taped the tube in place.

"Start compressions," she called out. "Let's get her on the gurney. I'll worry about an IV in the rig."

"You got it, boss," Mac called out.

They carefully moved her over to the gurney and continued CPR.

Reese jumped in last and Emily closed the doors behind her.

"I think she's trying to breathe on her own!" The pudgy guy who's name Reese could never remember said.

"Everyone stop."

They all looked at the little girl waiting for any sign of life. Reese felt the underside of her upper arm for a pulse.

"I feel a pulse!" she announced. "It's not super strong but, it's there!"

Just then the girl took in two quick gasps but, it wasn't enough to be helpful to her.

"Sweet! Keep bagging her!"

During the fast-paced ride to the emergency room, Reese was able to obtain an IV and give the sweet little patient who was fighting to live some fluid. *Come on, sweet pea, keep fighting.*

When they transferred her over to the bed in the emergency room, everyone was eagerly waiting their arrival. Reese loudly and directly spoke to the room filled with doctors, nurses, and ER technicians. She found herself next to Dr. Jackson when she began speaking more to him than anyone else. She explained they left the tube in place out of fear of closing off her airway with the chunk of bread that was stuck even though she was taking more breaths on her own now.

Dr. Jackson sternly shouted out orders but, he didn't shout in a frantic way, it was more matter-of-fact. He calmly listened to Reese. He reassured her leaving the tube was most definitely the right call.

When the tube met resistance and they were unable to get her oxygen anymore, Dr. Jackson made the call to pull the tube.

He positioned his slender body at the little girls head and quickly removed the tape that held the tube in place. He grabbed the tiny tube between his thumb and first finger and pulled. The tube slid out of her mouth and on the end of the tube was the biggest chunk of bread Reese ever thought possible.

The soggy white piece of bread was easily the size of an apricot pit. The entire room gasped with utter disbelief that this tiny little girl could get that big piece of bread down her throat.

"Hi there, sweetheart," Dr. Jackson spoke in a voice meant for two-year-old's and when Reese looked up she understood why. The little girl had opened her eyes and was rapidly blinking them. Reese felt the all too familiar pang in her eyes but, she shoved her emotions aside, unwilling to turn her emotions back on yet.

"Is she awake?" Mac asked from over Reese's shoulder.

"She is!" Reese beamed from ear to ear.

"Landon," Dr. Jackson called for her attention and she turned around to see a smile dash across his face. "You saved this little girls life today."

"No, I didn't. You pulled out the piece of bread."

"Yes but, your quick thinking saved her life. This win is yours."

He clapped his hands together, and one after another, person after person, joined in.

"Woo, way to go, Reese!" Sara, one of the nurses, shouted.

Another person whistled and that pain behind Reese's eyes spilled over and down her cheeks. No one had ever celebrated her like this before.

"I was just doin' my job, y'all, stop it."

Reese got a few hugs and pats on the back from various people, including Mac and Dr. Jackson. She'd be lying if she said she didn't walk out of the room a little taller that day, and even taller after the mother thanked her incessantly in Spanish.

"Not a bad way to end your last shift!" Emily hugged her tightly.

"It was kind of the perfect ending."

They cleaned everything up, and remained out of service as they went back to headquarters to log off. There Reese was met by a group of her co-workers for a small little farewell party in her honor.

The sun was setting on another chapter in Reese's life but, it was ready to rise again for a new day.

Chapter 31

"CALL ME WHEN you stop for the night and let us know how it's goin'." Maggie pleaded with her arms firmly around Reese.

"I will, Mama, I promise."

Maggie let go of Reese and latched on to Taylor, delaying their departure a little longer.

"Drive safe out there, Reesey Piecey," Rusty kissed her on the cheek.

"We will, Daddy."

Rusty shook Chad's hand and tipped his hat. He backed up over to Maggie and peeled Taylor from her arms, he kissed his grand-daughter on each cheek and handed her back to Reese.

"We love you both! We'll see you soon!" Maggie called after them.

It was a much longer drive from Texas back to Auburn, they stopped frequently at parks and fast food places with playgrounds so Taylor could burn off some energy. All in all, Reese and Chad couldn't complain too much though, Taylor did quite well in the car. Before leaving, Reese made sure to have an activity back pack ready, full of coloring books and small toys. She even broke down and bought a portable DVD player for her to watch.

It seemed as if the days melted together between moving, unloading the U-Haul, and unpacking their things. Of course there were a few disagreements and even one major fight about whose dishes to keep but, once they both realized how ridiculous the whole argument was they decided to just keep both sets. They experienced the standard aches and pains of learning to adjust when living with another person but, they both compromised and found happy mediums for just about everything.

Reese was setting out the last of her decorations and boxing up some of Chad's things to donate. It was hard to believe an entire month had passed already. It felt like just yesterday Chief Gibbs had called her offering her, her old job back. It seemed surreal that in just four days she would be heading back to station 23.

The front door abruptly opened, "Babe?" Chad called.

"In the bedroom," Reese answered.

She could hear his quick paced footsteps come down the hall.

"I have good news," he grinned.

"What kind of good news?" she asked as Chad kissed Taylor on the forehead while she played with her Barbie's on the floor.

"My mom offered to watch Taylor for us so we don't have to pay for childcare."

"Really?" she beamed, "That's amazing!"

The truth was Reese hadn't even thought about child care. She was so used to Maggie being there for her. The thought of Maggie not watching Taylor felt like a knife wrenched in her gut. Reese hadn't stopped long enough to let herself come to terms with the fact, the comfort of her parents was no longer going to be at her beckon call. Her parents and her favorite uncle were thousands of miles away now... and so were Emily, Penny and Cal.

Her heart ached underneath the happy façade. Of course she was thankful for Chad's mother, Linda, and all she was willing to sacrifice for them but, Reese missed her own mother.

"I gotta be honest, I hadn't even thought about child care." Chad looked at her with wide eyes. "I know that sounds stupid and careless and probably irresponsible but, I am just so used to my mom." Her voice got caught in her throat.

"I didn't think about how hard this must be on you."

Reese looked up at him with watery eyes, "I hadn't realized it either. I miss them, you know?" She sucked in a large amount of air. "I'm so excited to be here with you and to start our life together, but..."

"It's okay to be excited and happy here and to miss everyone you've had to leave behind."

He hugged her tightly and kissed her forehead.

"Thank you, I needed that."

"I love you, Ree."

"I love you too, Mr. Platt."

"I cannot wait for you to become Mrs. Platt."

He kissed her neck while his hands explored her back. Reese felt caught up in the tingles he sent through her body. She gripped his shirt and almost let herself get lost in him, until she heard the clicking of Barbie's who had gone shopping.

Reese released her grip on Chad and stepped away from him.

"I think that's gonna hafta wait until later," she huffed, catching her breath.

"Good idea," he held his hand to his face and laughed out a long sigh.

The next four days were spent adjusting and readjusting decorations and where her clothes went in the closet. She had spent an entire day just organizing her clothes and shoes, all in which were organized by color and size. Her OCD always seemed to flourish when she felt as though things were going to get out of her control. Even the cabinet under the kitchen sink had been organized multiple different ways until it was just right.

It seemed as if the days just mashed together. It hardly felt time for her first shift back with AFD.

"I figured I would drop Tay off with my mom on my way to the station today, that way you don't have to worry about doing that." Chad offered.

"Thank you," she puffed her cheeks out as she slowly exhaled.

"Today will go great, babe."

She turned to face Chad, once again thankful to have such an amazing man in her life.

"I didn't expect to be this nervous."

"Those nerves will go away once you get there and see everyone, you'll see," he kissed her cheek. "Come on Tay-Tay, let's go to Gama's!" he called out.

"Gama! Gama! Gama!" her little voice shouted running into their room.

"You're gonna do great today, Ree," he kissed her again, on the lips this time. "I love you."

"I love you more," she softly smiled.

A smile parted her lips stepping out of the front door when she saw the sun beaming its beautiful golden rays over the mountain range. Texas would always be where she was from and a piece of her heart would reside there forever but, this was where she belonged. She hadn't paused since arriving in Auburn to appreciate its overwhelming beauty. The air was fresh, crisp, and smelled of the beautiful trees that surrounded the city.

She got into her car with her coffee cup in hand and started her drive to work. The nerves turned in her stomach as she got closer to the station that she used to call her home. The knots in her grew tenfold rounding the corner catching the first glimpse of the red brick building. Her heart picked up its speed and her hands slightly trembled. She couldn't tell if it was all nerves or if it was excitement that brought on a rush of adrenaline. It looked like there was something hung across the front of the building. When she pulled into the parking lot in front of the station she saw a white banner hung on the bay door in the middle: WELCOME HOME, REESE. The ball in her stomach quickly faded and her eyes danced with delight.

There was no one outside as she breached the doors of the bay. It was as if she'd never left. She admired the big beautiful white and red ambulance in the bay, running her finger tips down the length of it as she methodically walked by.

"Hey, girl," she whispered. "I've missed you."

Her head swiveled, looking for any signs of life around the station but, she remained unsuccessful. She opened the industrial looking door leading into the hallway of the station. Still no one was there. She took her time, reacquainting herself with station 23. She gazed up at the framed newspaper clippings of various Auburn Fire Department personnel, stopping at the article of Chief Gibbs and the little boy. There were also several pictures that had been taken at training's and sporadic calls over the years. Some were faded in black and white with young and tired men in old uniforms. The engines were still impressive back then, in their own way—the open cab where the crew sat, rain or shine, on the way to every call. One had various firefighters placed around and on the engine, posed for a picture. Reese looked at the faces of the young men and wondered where they all were now. Some might still be alive but, some had more than likely passed on from this world, leaving their legacy in these pictures on the walls of the station they once resided.

"Now there's a face I'm happy to see," Chief Gibbs startled Reese.

She gasped, "Oh my gosh, Chief, you scared me," a faint laugh huffed in her chest. "Good morning," she awkwardly stuck her hand out toward him.

"Oh, no, a handshake isn't going to cut it." He reached out and firmly wrapped his arms around her. "It's so good to have you back."

The hug was out of character for Mark at work, Reese knew he typically maintained a professional demeanor and only broke that code a handful of times; lucky for her, this morning was one of those times. She had to bend slightly at the knees to hug him but, she didn't mind one bit.

"It's good to be back, Chief." They let each other go. "Where is everyone?"

"I have no idea." he tilted his mug toward her, "Coffee?"

She raised her coffee in return, "I could use a warm up."

They walked side by side down the hall. When she came through the doorway and into the common room her eyes widen.

"Welcome back!" They all shouted in unison.

"What?" Reese laughed.

Her hand covered her mouth in surprise and tears pricked the back of her eyes. She couldn't believe they would do this. Her eyes scanned the breakfast that filled the counter in the kitchen. The biggest stack of waffles she'd ever seen piled high next to a bowl of scrambled eggs and sausage. They had even put out cans of whipped cream because, what were waffles without whipped cream? They were simply pointless in Reese's opinion and the entire crew knew that.

"You guys, I can't believe you did all of this!"

She was met by a cascade of hugs and loving words welcoming her back to station 23.

"I've been so excited for this day!" shrieked Jess, breaking through the sea of people. "We're all seriously so happy you're back. This house hasn't been the same without you."

"Thank you! My world hasn't been the same without all of you! I mean, this... this is incredible! Y'all didn't have to do all of this!"

"Of course we did," Stump came up behind Jess and gave Reese a solid hug. "This place lost something the day you left. The liveliness had faded because the heart of this station had left. We all understand why you had to leave but, it didn't mean we were thrilled to see you go."

"I wasn't thrilled either. I'm so happy to be back!"

They all made their breakfast plates and the "EMS call-gods" allowed them the pleasure of getting reacquainted over waffles piled high with whipped cream. They told stories of the different medics that came in and out of the house. Come to find out, the medic Kyra had a crush on ended up having some rather odd fetishes.

"He wanted me to roll play with him as a baby and have me be his mom! We're talkin' he's a grown-ass man swaddled in a cloth diaper with a pacifier in his mouth!"

"I think the real question here, Kyra, is how authentic was he willing to be?" Reese asked.

"What do you mean?"

"I mean, were you gonna hafta change his diaper?"

"Hell if I know, I split before I found out!"

They all boasted out with laughter.

"Then there was the 'can you dig it?' guy." Kyra continued, rolling out her on going nightmare. "He was the worst! Ugh! He would make guns out of his fingers like this," Kyra demonstrated placing her thumb straight up in the air and her pointer finger out in front of her. "Can you dig it? Pew, pew, ugh... a nightmare!"

"Oh that's bad," Reese laughed, "So, so bad!"

The loud speaker rang out interrupting their laughter.

"Medic twenty-three, emergency traffic; fall victim at twenty-three forty-six West Cobble Street."

Kyra and Reese looked at each other, "Millie."

The girls got up, leaving their empty plates and warm coffee behind, and rushed out to Millie's house. Reese hoped Millie was alright, she couldn't help but be a little excited to see her favorite patient again after being away for so long. She hadn't been able to find anyone like Millie in Texas. Probably because there is just no one else like Millie, she's truly a one in a million.

Reese allowed her mind to wander, fantasizing about how in fifty years she and Chad would have memories like Millie and her late husband William did. Maybe she and Chad will share dancing in the kitchen, or maybe they would cook meals together. She could picture them chopping, stirring, and tasting together around a kitchen filled with music and glasses of wine. Taylor would be off playing somewhere while they built the fondest of memories together. Of course she knew reality would be much less attractive. Taylor would probably be screaming over something trivial and the spaghetti sauce would come from a jar doctored up with some ground beef and maybe a few veggies Reese could sneak in. There wouldn't be movie glamour but, maybe a few more memories of laughing, like the failed attempt at fried chicken that ended up burnt on the outside and still raw in the middle. There most definitely will be a few silly arguments that place bumps in their relationship at the time but, would create laughter down the road. A lifetime of memories, glamorous or not, is all she wanted with Chad, and she relished in the thought of being Millie's age reminiscing with "her Chad" and knowing darn well Chad would be the one telling her to use her walker, and Reese would be too stubborn to listen.

"Oh, Millie," Reese said as they walked into her house and found her lying face down on the floor.

"It's not as bad as it looks, sweetheart." Millie's words were muffled with her face smashed in the floor.

"What happened?" Reese asked.

"Well, I lost my balance, and down I went."

"Are you hurting anywhere?"

"No, no, I'm not hurting anywhere, I just can't get up." Millie laughed into the tan carpet.

"Okay, let's get you up off the ground."

Reese and Kyra worked together to roll Millie over and onto her back.

"Reese, is that you?"

"Yes, ma'am, it's me alright." Reese smiled. "Let's get you up off the ground and then we'll catch up."

"That's probably a good idea."

The girls sat Millie upright and directed her to bend her legs before pulling her to her feet and helping her into a chair.

"Oh thank you girls so much." Millie said gratefully, "You two, oh I cannot tell you how good it is to see you two back together again. You girls make quite the team!"

"Thank you, Millie."

"Oh Reese, when did you come back?"

"Today is actually my first shift back! I moved back to town about a month ago."

"What is that on your finger?" Millie asked grabbing her hand and yanking it toward her.

Reese smiled, "I'm engaged to the most amazing man."

"I want to hear all about him!"

"Let's make sure you're okay and then I'll tell you everything, deal?"

"Deal," Millie agreed.

Reese did a quick assessment of Millie and found no injuries in the process. She and Kyra sat down on the couch next to Millie's chair and Reese took several minutes to fill her in on a condensed version of the last few years. She boasted about Taylor and fought the sting of tears when she talked about what Alex had done. Her face lit up with love and excitement as she spoke about Chad and told her of how he proposed and how living together has been. She gushed about what an amazing father he is and how she finally feels like the luckiest woman in the world.

Millie said, "I always knew you would find someone that would love you for exactly who you are, Reese. You are a precious gift to this world, my dear, and I just know that God has big plans for you."

"How do you know that?"

"Because He told me, honey," she gently placed her cold and frail hand on Reese's. "The moment I met you I knew you were pure of heart and as I got to know you more and more, God revealed to me just how special you are. He told me you were going to feel incredibly lost and tragedy would cast down upon you in your life. Although He doesn't intentionally cause terrible things to happen to us. He does, however, use that pain to bring forth something positive. He has a plan, Reese, and even in the darkest of times you can always lean on Him for comfort and peace." Millie paused, "Can I ask you a question?"

"Of course you can."

"Why are you holding God at arm's length?"

Reese felt the breath leave her body but, her voice stood silent. She had dealt with a lot of her anger towards Alex and most days now, she didn't even think about him. For the most part, she had let her past go. She had forgiven him over and over and over again. Some days she forgave him every hour, and on the worst days, with every breath. She had to repeat her forgiveness until it became real. She even took the advice of her therapist and forgave herself, even though that was a little more difficult than she thought it would be.

Her therapist pointed out, she had yet to take responsibility for the role she played in the abuse she endured. Reese immediately put up her defense and got viciously angry.

He explained, "Reese you allowing the relationship to continue and your choices to forgive Alex over and over again for his transgressions but, you're unwilling to forgive yourself for yours."

That was the day things finally changed for Reese. She finally began to heal, which led her to this life she now has. It led her back to Chad, where she belongs. But, in all of her forgiveness, she had yet to take responsibility for her anger

337

toward God. Millie was right—she was holding Him at arm's length but, the why was something she couldn't put into words. Maybe she hadn't taken full responsibility like she thought she had. Maybe she wasn't ready to lean on Him yet—her stubbornness always did seem to get the best of her.

"I honestly don't know."

"Of course you do, Reese but, you don't have to tell me. That part is between you and God. I'm only here to remind you that He loves you more than you could even fathom. He wants you to have peace, real and genuine peace within your soul. He has a plan for you. You just have to be brave enough to let Him lead."

"Millie, I..." Reese's voice trailed off, unsure what to say.

"I'm so glad you're back, Reese, and that you're happy. I look at the two of you like my granddaughters and I care about you girls so much."

"We care about you too, Millie." Kyra chimed in as Reese was still at a loss for words. "We had better get going. Our dispatchers have already status checked us."

"Okay," Millie smiled. "Thank you for rescuing me again."

"It's our pleasure," Reese finally spoke.

"Remember, Reese, sometimes the darkest environments create the most beautiful flowers. The lotus flower for example, it can only grow in the mud which is dark and dirty and most certainly not an easy place to be. It fights it way through the thick and heavy mud but, something strange happens when it breeches the surface. It doesn't bloom all at once. It slowly blooms pedal by pedal until the last pedal drops, revealing its magnificent beauty. You're a lotus flower, Reese. You've been born in the dark and the heavy but, you are so close to breaching the surface. Just remember, it always gets so much harder before you see the light."

"I will, thank you, Millie."

"You're very welcome, my dear. Now go out there and help someone else."

Chapter 32

REESE OFTEN THOUGHT of what Millie had told her over the next several weeks. She continued to work with her old therapist over the phone as she searched for a new one in Auburn. She knew there was, in fact, more darkness for her to push her way through. She wanted to reach the surface and bloom into the person she was meant to be. She couldn't shake the gut-wrenching feeling that this wasn't the darkness Millie spoke of. *Just remember, it always gets much harder before you see the light.* Reese had left most of her hard times in the past but, she couldn't shake the feeling something bigger just might be coming for her.

"Reese?" Chad broke through her thoughts. "What do you think?"

Reese steadily scanned her surroundings. The white fencing surrounding the venue was beautiful and brought the feeling of Texas to Washington. Horses ran in the fields on each side of the long dirt driveway, with an abundance of green grass everywhere. In the slight breeze, the air smelled fresh with a hint of sweetness from the hay. There was even a beautiful structure made of reclaimed barn wood at the end of the cement pathway for the isle.

"This place is beyond perfect!"

"I think so too!" Chad happily agreed.

Reese turned to the owner of the venue, "What happens if it rains?"

"Well, if it's raining or if there is a forecast of rain, we can move the ceremony in the barn where we do the reception. We can set the tables up and make an isle for you, and still have room for dancing."

"Okay, decorations, are there any restrictions?"

"Not at all, we provide a lot here at Dove Hallow Ranch. We have a large selection of linen's in an array of colors and patterns. We also carry a large amount of rustic themed decorations and center pieces."

"Wait, does it cost extra to use your stuff?" Chad asked.

"Not at all," the owner laughed. "Everyone always asks that."

"That's just an unbelievable deal!"

"We've been pricing everything, and my better half and I have been kind of freaking out." Reese said.

"Weddings can very quickly turn into fifty thousand dollars of debt. I just believe every couple deserves to not stress about all of the little things adding up to large piles of debt." She led Reese and Chad through the pastures. "I've been doing this for a long time now and I've accumulated quite a large amount of stuff. I considered charging extra to use it but, I thought to myself, I don't need more money so there's no reason to exploit young couples for my gain."

"Wow," the words slipped from Chad's lips.

"I think you just sold him," Reese forced out a faint laugh. "Honey, what do you think?"

"I think—" he sighed. "It's perfect."

"I agree." Reese smiled.

They walked back to the office and gave the thousand dollar deposit needed to hold their date.

Everything was finally coming together. Reese had found the perfect dress and even the perfect footwear. The bridesmaid's dresses were in their final alterations as they counted down the last ten days before the wedding.

"Hey babe, you boys are at the final tuxedo fitting, right?" Reese got right to why she was calling, *no time for hello, just straight to business,* she thought.

"Yes, my love, we're all here. Vince said it shouldn't take long. Most of our tuxes fit well."

"Awesome! We're almost done here at the bridal shop for our final fitting. Y'all wanna do a late lunch?"

"Yeah, that sounds good, I'm starving!"

"Okay, I'll let you know when we're done. I love you."

"I love you too."

"Ditching us for your man already?" Kyra's voice trailed out from her changing stall.

"Typical," Jess huffed before they both burst out with laughter.

"Now ladies, don't give her a hard time, she chose Chad over all of us long before now!" Emily came out of the changing stall.

They all laughed hysterically. Reese was thrilled Emily fit right in with her close circle of friends. In fact, Emily and Kyra had become quite close and were doing more things together aside from wedding stuff with Reese. Despite the age difference, both Kyra and Emily got along. Partially, because they loved Reese, but also because they were both single and able to hit the town and scout out the local bachelor's.

"I was actually thinking all of us but, whatever, brats!" Reese laughed.

"That would be fun, I'm in!" Jess announced walking out wearing her bridesmaids dress.

"Me too!" said Kyra.

"Yeah, I'm down." Emily agreed.

"Oh my God, you guys look perfect!" Reese gasped, as the girls came out of their fitting rooms and stood side by side modeling their attire.

They stood there in their midnight blue dresses and Reese gazed at how the A-line chiffon skirts flowed down around their knees. Their multi-layers and different lengths fit beautifully with the dark brown cowgirl boots Reese had bought them all. The thick straps and V neck flattered all of their different body types.

"That color looks amazing on all of you!" Reese shrieked, "Eek! And it's gonna look so good with the sunflower bouquets!"

"The only thing I want to know is why on earth didn't you tell me how comfortable these boots are?" Kyra moved her foot all around as if she was trying to find an uncomfortable position in them.

"I have been telling you that for years," Reese laughed.

"Your turn, Reese," Jess said. "Come on girls, let's change out of these and let the bride try on her dress."

The three girls changed and Reese was pleased to know her dress fit perfectly, unfortunately, it also meant she couldn't afford to gain even five pounds before her wedding. *Ten days, I can manage to not gain anything for ten days,* she nervously told herself.

It felt as if the day's swirled together going at warp speed, it was now only three days before the wedding.

Reese was relieved, according to her weather app on her phone, rain wasn't in the forecast. Not that rain would ruin the day but, the day after final dress fittings there was a huge storm that flooded the roads, the last thing she wanted was stranded guests. Thankfully, it hadn't rained since. All of the water had soaked into the ground or made its way to the storm drains, and the wedding was in the clear.

Reese could hear heavy steps running toward her door and her lips parted into a smile.

"BACHLORETTE TIME!" Kyra, Jess, and Emily yelled in unison, bursting through the front door.

"Let's go, hooker!" Emily joked.

"Come on!" Kyra pleaded loudly.

"They may have pre-gamed a little bit," Jess laughed. "We really should get going though."

"I'm all yours, just be gentle with me."

"No way! Go hard or go home!" Emily yelled. "Woooo!"

Once Reese was in the car they made her put on a blindfold.

"Seriously?"

"Yup, put it on," Jess ordered.

They drove for what felt like forever, all Reese could see was blackness and all she could hear was Emily and Kyra singing loudly off key to Katy Perry and Taylor Swift. Reese didn't feel the car come to a stop very often so she wondered if they were taking her out of the city.

When they finally did stop, the blindfold came off and her eyes adjusted, she could see the city lights of Seattle come into focus.

"We decided you couldn't miss the view coming into the city," Jess explained. "We have a whole night planned, so I hope you're ready!"

Emily and Kyra started hollering in the back seat before chanting, "Bride to be, Bride to be, Bride to be!"

Reese allowed the excitement of the car to steal her level head and with a celebratory scream she joined into the chanting.

Once they parked, Jess pulled out a duffle bag from the trunk of the car. She grabbed out a headband veil and a sash that said "Bride" on it. She also had beaded necklaces with little wedding rings all over it. The girls all wore brightly colored pink feathered boas around their necks and silver plastic tiaras. Next, Jess handed out the main necklace, one with a shot glass attached to it.

"All shots tonight will be taken out of these glasses!" She ordered.

"Yeah!" they all cheered.

Reese could feel her excitement building. She had convinced herself earlier she just wanted a quiet evening with her girls; she didn't think she could get this excited about club hoping in Seattle. But, there she was, walking arm in arm with her girls like they were on the catwalk in New York City.

The first club they went to looked, smelled, and felt like the clubs Reese had tried out in her twenties—dark, there was an aroma of liquor and vomit, and a little dirty...okay, a lot dirty. The girls were determined to be the life of a very dull party and decided to enjoy a few shots and dance. They all four consumed enough shots to be tipsy and danced their cares away under the colored lights.

"You ready?" Jess yelled to Reese over the music.

"I'm ready if you are."

Jess led them out of the bar, and although the street outside was quiet the girls still yelled when they spoke to each other and giggling with excitement.

"Where to next, ladies?" Kyra asked.

"This next club I'm excited about, it's called, 'The Shaft'."

"What kind of name is that?" Reese laughed.

"It's a gay bar but, I've done a lot of research and it says that bachelorettes should, hands down, visit this bar for their party!" Jess looked at the skeptical faces staring at her and added, "If it sucks we can leave, promise."

"I'm down, let's do this!" Reese yelled, pumping her fist into the night sky.

When they walked into The Shaft, their eyes danced with delight. It was incredibly chic with large couches wrapped around tables and a wide open dance floor. There were men who wore baby oil in place of their shirts and several others whose boas matched theirs. There were men in fedoras and men with jeans so tight you could see everything—nothing was left to the imagination. Reese felt her mouth drop open, she had never seen anything like this before, and it was incredible.

"Ladies," a deep voice said. "Looks like you girls are celebrating tonight." Reese turned around to see a man, whose make-up was a million times better than any of theirs on their best day, wearing a tight black sequin vest as a shirt, and tight light blue ripped jeans. His skin was like milk chocolate and his eyes were shockingly blue, like the ocean. "You must be the bride to be!"

"That would be me." Reese sheepishly admitted.

"We've got a live one, boys!" he shouted over the music. "Come with me darlin', we'll happily give you a night you won't forget." Grabbed her hand he led Reese into the crowd. "Now tell me, what does your man do?"

"He's a cop, well a detective."

"Oh honey, nicely done." his mouth shot toward the ceiling. "She's bagged herself a cop, boys!" He yelled and the crowd cheered around her. "When's the big day?"

"Saturday," Reese said as an oiled up man placed his boa around her neck.

"Oh honey, that's so soon. Just by lookin' at you he is one lucky man. I may bat for the other team but, honey, you're gorgeous."

"Oh, thank you," Reese smiled embarrassed by being put on the spot.

"Here is our bridal table," he gestured with his arm to a beautiful golden couch big enough to seat ten or more.

"Oh wow," Reese muttered. "This is too much. I mean, there's only four of us."

"Nonsense, it won't be just four of you for long. Now sit, the first round of drinks are on me." He smiled, winked his eye, and sent air kisses with his deep red glittered lips.

"This place is amazing." Emily exclaimed gawking at the table.

The tables had flecks of gold embedded into the glass top and long flowing cream colored cloths with gold shimmer hanging from the ceiling in multiple places. The music was perfect for dancing and the men were eager to meet them all. In the time it took for their drinks to arrive, they had filled the booth with multiple men. Some wore elaborate clothes but, many of them were in jeans and tight t-shirts. They spoke to the girls as if they had all been best friends since the second grade.

The first round of drinks came, and then another, and then another. Drink after drink and dance after dance, Reese was pulled in every direction and at one point, placed in a chair, and had the most awkward lap dance of her life. There isn't a feeling that quite describes being a straight woman and liking a lap dance given by an oiled up gay man in jeans that may as well have been tights. But, Reese had the time of her life.

They remained at The Shaft for the rest of the night, and at two in the morning Reese vaguely remembered pouring herself into an Uber with the girls. It was an incredible night, one she hoped to remember for years to come but, for now, she let the alcohol envelope her and blissfully take her over.

Chapter 33

THE DAYS LEADING up to the wedding both Chad and Reese nursed their lingering hangovers while finishing up the last minute details. Chad's groomsmen had quite the night planned for him on the same night Reese went out. The guys headed out to watch the local band, Epic Riot, at the local dive bar which led to a few clubs with the band and then convincing the owner of the batting cages to stay open while they drank and hit balls until almost three in the morning.

Reese woke up on the day of her wedding with butterflies in her stomach. *Today is the first day of forever with Chad.* As much as she tried to push down the smile plastered on her face she couldn't, she was soon going to marry her best friend and her soulmate.

She peeled back the sheer drapes hanging in front of the window at Jess' house and peered out at the vibrant blue sky filled with white puffy clouds. Not a raindrop in the air or in the forecast, and Reese smiled once more.

There was a faint knock at the door before it slowly opened.

"Good morning," Jess said in a voice far too chipper for seven in the morning.

"Hey, good morning."

"I have coffee for the beautiful bride."

Jess handed Reese a steaming cup, smelling of salted caramel.

"Mmm, thank you, and thank you for letting us use your house for 'bride central' until we head over to the ranch."

"Of course, you know I'd do anything for you."

"I appreciate it. The boys have taken over my house and it has become 'groom central' until they leave for the ranch too. I really wanted to hold the tradition of not seeing each other until the wedding ceremony."

"I totally get it, and you know my door is always open."

Reese smiled taking a sip of her coffee.

Jess continued, "So, we have about an hour until the girl doing our hair is going to be here. You will go first so your hair is done and you can get ready for make-up. I would imagine it wouldn't take long since you're wearing your hair down, right?"

"Yes, ma'am, I'm just hoping she can achieve beachy waves because I can never get them right."

"Julie is amazing! You're going to love her!"

"I have no doubt," Reese smiled enjoying another sip of coffee. "I think I'm gonna go out back and sit on your back deck on your beautiful new patio furniture. Wanna come?"

"Sure, I have a light breakfast for us too. I can bring it outside."

"You've just thought of everything haven't you?"

"It's our job to make sure that you are relaxed and happy."

"Speaking of 'our', where's Kyra and Emily?"

"We are right here," Emily announced as her and Kyra walked into the room.

Reese pulled all three of them into a giant hug. "I'm just so happy I have you three standing with me today. Thank you guys for always being there no matter what, I love each of you like sisters."

"We love you too."

"I'm sorry I'm late!" A voice yelled from the other side of the house. "Ree Ree? Where is everyone?"

Reese recognized that voice immediately, "Soph, we're comin'."

They all scurried down the hall to find Sophie and Piper standing in the living room in what looked like their pajamas.

"Oh my God, Piper, look at how big you've gotten!" Reese exclaimed picking her niece up and swinging her around in a circle. "I've missed you so much!" she showered Piper with kisses all over her face.

"Auntie Ree," Piper giggled, "Stop!"

The room was filled with the innocent laughter of a little girl who was more loved than she knew. Her light brown hair fell down around her round face with natural curls.

"Where's Tay-Rae?" Sophie asked.

"She's with Mama. They should be here soon."

"Tay Tay!" Piper exclaimed as the door opened and Taylor and Maggie walked through it.

"Pipa," Taylor shrieked.

The little girls ran toward each other giggling and hugging.

"Okay ladies," Jess announced. "Now that everyone is here I'm going to run down the itinerary real quick. First, my friend Julie is coming to do hair and make-up. Reese is getting done first, obviously. Julie said each bridesmaid shouldn't take more than twenty to thirty minutes max. We don't have endless amounts of time so everyone needs to be ready to go when it's their turn. Once hair and make-up is done, we'll have about forty-five minutes to get our butts to the ranch. They have a bride's suite and a groom's suite for all of us to get dressed in. The boys should be ready first so they will take pictures first but, we need to get ready quickly so we can be ready when it's our turn to take pictures. Once pictures are done, we come back to our suite to toast our beloved Reese, and then we have ourselves a wedding."

Kyra and Emily began cheering and the rest of the women joined in.

"But, first, breakfast," Jess motioned her arm to her dining room table that was filled with various foods: donuts, fruit, hard boiled eggs, and even bacon. "If nothing here suits your fancy than I do have cereal in the pantry.

"This is wonderful," Reese said as she shoved a maple bar donut into her mouth. "So good, thank you guys," her voice was muffle by the chomping of food.

Julie arrived shortly after they finished eating, and her bubbly personality was infectious. She brought vibrant life to a part of the day Reese was worried would be stressful. She helped Reese feel at ease and beautiful. The two of them talked non-stop while Julie did her hair and make-up and a new friendship began to unfold.

She turned Reese around on the stool to face the mirror when she was done and Reese saw herself in the mirror, she almost didn't recognize herself. Her hair flowed down around her perfectly contoured face with flawless loose curls. Her lips were outlined and filled in with crimson red to make them look full and luscious. Julie had successfully turned this casual girl into a bride. This was exactly how Reese had envisioned herself on her wedding day; beautiful, happy, and excited for what the future may hold.

All of the girls enjoyed their time getting ready. Reese was worried she was going to be so stressed out she wouldn't be able to enjoy this day but, her girls made it effortless. Reese had no stress on her radar for miles and miles. Today was a celebration and thanks to everyone surrounding her, it was going to be nothing short of incredible.

Piper and Taylor were the last to get their hair done. Taylor's once straight and fine hair had transformed into ringlet curls that came down to just above her shoulders. The blonde hair seemed to make her crystal blue eyes pop even more than normal today.

"Okay, ladies," Jess announced. "We are actually running early, so we have an hour to get over to the ranch. And since some of you have asked already, Julie will be coming with us to the ranch to touch up our make-up if needed."

They all piled into their cars as the fanciest women in yoga pants ever seen—it's not every day women with full hair and make-up hang out in their pajamas. Maggie took Sophie and the girls in her car, Kyra and Emily went in Kyra's car, and Reese rode with Jess and Julie in Jess's car.

"I still can't believe Chad and I are getting married today." Reese confessed.

"I know how you feel," Julie chimed in. "On my wedding day everything felt so surreal, I couldn't wrap my head around it until I walked down the aisle, and I saw him standing there. It all hit me, he was the only one I wanted forever, and everything seemed to snap into reality."

"Wow," Reese breathed the words.

Reese was never much for the sappy love stories, she tended to be more cynical than that but, today as she thought about all she and Chad had overcome, she felt as if they were meant to be and she couldn't shake the word soulmate. It was like there was something driving them together, pushing them toward each other. And he turned out to be everything she needed in her life. He had become her everything. The more time that passed, the less she cared if they were sappy. He had always been there to catch her, even when she pushed him away, he didn't budge.

When they started down the long dirt drive to the ranch, Reese felt a sense of peace. There was no need for nerves. She had zero doubts about marrying Chad, for she knew this was exactly where she was meant to be. The long white fence that flowed down each side of the road accentuated the ranch. There were green rolling hills as far as the eye could see, and beautiful horses casually grazed in the fields, reminding Reese so much of Texas. The feel in the air was as if both of her homes had come together as one.

The sweet smell of hay hit her nostrils as she got out of the car. All of the girls pulled their dresses out of the cars and walked to their bridal suite with full arms. There were totes filled with make-up for touch ups, boxes with boots in them, boxes with bouquets, dresses zipped up in bags, and even mouthwash for right before they head off down the aisle.

It wasn't long before the bridal suite exploded to life. The make-up was unloaded and lined up for easy access. Curling irons were plugged in for last minute fixes, multiple pairs of boots graced the floor, and robes were tossed in all directions. Everyone was dressed except Reese.

"Are you ready, sis?" Maggie softly asked with the wedding gown in her hands.

"Yes," Reese smiled.

The white gown was the most beautiful gown Reese had ever seen. She knew from the moment she tried it on that it was "the dress". There was no doubt in her mind, and she felt that way just as much today, as she did the day she first put it on. Maggie and Jess helped Reese step into the gown and they each pulled it up around her.

The top of the dress hugged her body tightly, and the sweetheart neck line accentuated her bust. The fabric gave the illusion of wrapping around her body and tucked into the neckline, like a towel. It was fitted all the way down to the top of her hips, where there were flowers made out of fabric woven in between the jeweled detail on the left hip. The skirt of the dress flowed down in a subtle tiered A line all the way to the floor. Although it went against tradition, she didn't want a veil to block the dress, so she opted not to wear one.

Maggie laced up the corset back as Reese stood admiring her transformation.

"Reese, you look absolutely beautiful!" Kyra shriek walking back into the room.

"Thank you."

Reese hadn't realized how satisfying it would be to feel exactly like a Disney princess. In fact, her story was nothing short of unbelievable but, regardless she had overcome and persevered in her life. She defeated the evil that stood in her way and found her prince charming. The only difference was she didn't need Chad to rescue her, she just needed him to love her, and that's exactly what he did.

Finally the pictures were all taken, and the guests had finally arrived. Reese could hear the crowd of people get louder as more people showed up. It was almost time for the wedding to start when she heard a loud booming voice announce, "Please take your seats. The wedding will begin shortly." It was the undeniable voice of their Auburn pastor and friend, Richard.

Richard Morton was the most incredible Pastor Reese had ever had. He spoke to his congregation as if he was having a conversation with each person individually. He spoke about his hardships and of the many things he had to overcome in his very imperfect life. Reese loved the fact Richard was a man who she could relate to on many levels. He was an imperfect child of God and he had no problem admitting it. To Reese, that spoke volumes about the kind of man he was. She was so happy he agreed to officiate their wedding even though they had just begun coming to the church regularly when she moved back. When Richard agreed, they took marriage classes with him and his beautiful wife, Marie. They learned so much from the two of them that Chad and Reese had already started building a firm foundation for their marriage to rest on.

The door squeaked open, pulling Reese from her thoughts as she stood in front of the mirror.

"Reesey Piecey, you look absolutely breath-taking, my love."

"Thank you, Daddy."

"Well, it's about that time, are you ready?"

Reese could feel her body shake with fear, "Maybe I shouldn't have invited two-hundred and fourty-eight people. I mean, all of those eyes on me. What if I fall?"

Rusty gently took her right arm and wrapped it around his. "I won't let you fall," he softly smiled.

"Thank you, Daddy," Reese fought the sting behind her eyes.

She picked up her bouquet of white peonies, sunflowers, and violet iris', and looked down at the lace wrapped around the bouquet. She smiled at the picture of Gran that hung from it. Reese also wore Gran's sapphire bracelet on her wrist. She fit all of the requirements, something old was the lace wrapped around her bouquet that came from Gran's wedding dress. Something new was her wedding dress, the something borrowed was the small keychain size picture of Gran that belonged to Maggie, and the something blue was the flawless sapphire that sparkled on her wrist.

"I wish she was here," Reese whispered.

"She would be proud of you, kiddo," Rusty smiled.

Reese stood out of sight watching her bridesmaid's walk arm in arm with the groomsmen down the aisle. Their bright yellow of their sunflower bouquets looked vivid next to the deep blue of their dresses. Taylor and Piper soon followed, walking down the aisle in off white lace dresses with ruffled skirts and jean jackets. They too wore brown cowgirl boots on their feet. Julie happened to have headbands that match their dresses—they looked adorable coming down the aisle. Reese could see them giggling as they threw handfuls of rose pedals into the air. Lastly, it was the ring bearer's turn. He's Chad's ex-partner's son and was deemed Chad's Godson when he was born. He wore a charcoal tux minus the jacket, just like the groomsmen. He too had a sunflower boutonniere with lace incorporated. He held up his sign, turned to look back at Reese, and smiled before heading off down the aisle. Reese giggled as she watched the expressions and laughter come from the audience as they read his sign. DON'T WORRY LADIES, I'M STILL SINGLE.

The solitaire standing doors that stood at the entrance of the isle were closed, it was time. Reese took a shaky breath in. Rusty kissed her on the forehead.

"You look perfect. Just like a princess in those fairy tales you used to love." Rusty boasted. "Are you ready?"

Reese smiled, "I'm ready."

They stood behind the closed doors and the woman who rented them the ranch did a quick lap around Reese, fixing her dress. The acoustic version of, I'll Be, by Edwin McCain was the song she wanted to walk down the aisle to. Shortly after they had moved in together, Reese was cooking dinner with music in the background and when this song came on, Chad took her hand and they slow danced in the kitchen. That was when she knew she'd found the song she'd been looking for. The guitar intro strummed through the speakers, Maggie stood, and the rest of the guests followed suit. Reese felt butterfly's in her stomach. With a deep breath, the doors opened.

Reese glanced across the crowd locking eyes with Chad. This was always her favorite part at weddings. She loved to see the groom's reaction to the love of his life walking down the aisle but, today, this reaction was for her. She could see the tears gather in his eyes as his hand came up to cover his mouth. She breathed a laugh through her smile and a few tears broke through and down her cheeks. Her heart fluttered with excitement walking closer to her future with the only man she ever truly loved. The toes of her white glitter Converse shoes poked through the bottom of her dress as she walked closer to her love. The rest of the world faded into the background, there could've been a million people there in the crowd but, she only noticed Chad.

When they reached the end of the isle Richard asked, "Who brings this woman to be united in marriage?"

"Her mother and I do," Rusty called out before turning to face Chad. "Today, I give you one of the most precious things God has blessed my life with, her." He turned and smiled at Reese before he continued with Chad. "Thank you for making this so easy for her mother and me. We see how happy you've made her, and that warms our hearts. Take good care of her, son but, most importantly, remember there are no refunds, exchanges, or returns!" There was a roar of laughter that came from behind them. He then turned to Reese. "Your Mama and I are so proud of you and we love you so much." He kissed her on the cheek, turned and shook Chad's hand, and placed Reese's hand in Chad's.

As they walked up to the gazebo where Richard stood, Rusty joined Maggie in the empty chair next to her and Reese handed Jess her bouquet. All eyes were on Reese and Chad but, their eyes were only on each other.

"You may be seated," Richard began. "Good afternoon, we are gathered here today to celebrate one of life's most precious moments as we witness the joining of two hearts. We are also here to celebrate the power of love and what it has brought to their lives. For those of you who don't know me, my name is Richard Morton. I'm the Pastor at The Auburn Community Church, and I met Chad and Reese about six months ago. They walked into my church on a Sunday morning with smiles on their faces, and when I spoke to them after the service was over, I found out they were recently engaged. They introduced me to Taylor, and Chad introduced her as 'my daughter'. It wasn't until two months later when I learned, biologically, he was not her father. I was shocked—I had watched this man with his daughter and with his fiancé and there was no hesitation of love there. When he told me the story of Reese and Taylor and how their lives came to be one, I have to be honest, I shed several tears. I've watch the two of them grow as partners and as parents in the short time that I've known them. The love they share is not only strong, it is infectious.

They bring happiness with them wherever they go. During the six week marriage counseling course I had them take with my beautiful wife and me, they excelled. They came into a deeper understanding of what marriage is and what they want it to be. Marriage is not simply a happily ever after, a constant ride into the sunset. Marriage is sacrifice, its compromise, most importantly its love above all else. It's about loving your spouse even when you're not sure you like them because you've had to pick up their dirty clothes for the millionth time, or because they leave dirty dishes in the sink. Those of you, who know them well, know exactly which one is guilty of what." Laughter rumbled through each person. "Anyone who has spent more than five minutes with these two knows they are meant to be together. They balance each other and they complement each other like chips and salsa, which is the best combination of anything that ever existed." Another roar of laughter followed. "Love—there are so many things I could say about love. They say love is patient and kind but, love truly is the experience of writing your own story. It's about what works for the two of you, and what is going to keep your love alive year after year. Now before we go any further, if there is someone who objects to this couple being united in marriage, I'm going to kindly ask you to stay silent because you're wrong." Laughter again filled the air. "They've written their own vows, so Chad, let's start with you."

Chad smiled, squeezed Reese's hand tight, and began. "Reese, I knew from the moment I met you, you were an extraordinary woman. We were on scene of a call and I looked over to find you barking orders to several rookie cops, and it was the funniest thing I'd ever seen. I don't know if I ever told you this but, I began to fall in love with you right then and there. As our friendship grew, especially over the last year before we started dating, I no longer could see my life with anyone else but you. You make me a better man and a better father, you have loved me even when I wasn't very lovable, and you have continued to amaze me over and over again. My love for you grows stronger every day, and I vow I will never stop loving you. It's you and me, forever, and always. I love you." The best man handed him the ring and he slipped the diamond wedding band onto her finger.

Reese wiped the tears that silently fell from her eyes.

"Reese," Richard announced.

"Chad, when I started to write my vows I felt so incredibly overwhelmed. I feel like I could stand up here for hours talking about what you've done for, not only my life but, Taylor's life as well. You took the broken pieces of my heart and loved me as if I was brand new. You were willing to be my friend when that's all I could handle, and you never hesitated in loving me. Thank you for standing by me in spite of the damage I had and showing me my true worth. This path I've walked hasn't been easy," Reese voice trembled. "But, I am thankful for that path because it led me to you. I will never stop loving you, and I will never stop chasing after you—today, tomorrow, forever—my partner, my best friend, my equal. I love you." Jess handed Reese the ring and when Reese turned around, she peered at Chad behind watery eyes to see a tear fall down his cheek before slipping his wedding band on his finger.

"I'm told Chad has prepared a surprise," Richard placed his hand on Chad's shoulder. "Go ahead."

Chad let go of Reese's hands and walked over to where Maggie sat with Taylor on her lap. He reached his hand out and when Taylor slipped her hand into his, he led her back to where Reese stood. Tears spilt over and down Reese's cheeks when she realized what he was doing.

Chad got down on one knee, "Taylor, on this day when I marry your mommy I also marry you. I promise to love you forever and always. I promise to be silly with you, and to have dance party's in the living room with you whenever you want to. I promise to always protect you. I promise I will never turn my back on you, and lastly I promise I will strive to always be what you need me to be. I love you, my sweet Tay-Rae."

Reese wiped the tears from her face and leaned down and kissed Taylor on the cheek. Taylor turned and clung to Chad, "I love you, Daddy."

"I love you too, princess."

Chad put Taylor down and walked her back over to Maggie, kissed her on the forehead, and returned to Reese.

"Chad, do you take, Reese to be your lawfully wedded wife?"

"I do."

"And Reese, do you take Chad to be your lawfully wedded husband?

"I do."

"By the power invested in me, by the state of Washington, it is my honor to pronounce you husband and wife! You may kiss the bride!"

Chad grabbed Reese and their lips locked. A jolt of electricity shot through her body and ignited an even bigger flame for Chad as their lips lingered amidst the cheers. Chad suddenly wrapped his arms around her and dipped her across his body and kissed her again.

"Ladies and Gentleman, it is my pleasure to introduce for the very first time, Mr. and Mrs. Platt!"

The crowd cheered even louder this time. Taylor joined them and they walked down the aisle as a family. Reese kissed her husband with an overwhelming joy.

One day, Reese will wish that her naïve sense of happiness had lasted longer. In fact, she just might forget that happiness exists at all.